through teachers' eyes

Millie Blaisdell
East H.S.

through teachers' eyes

**portraits of writing
teachers at work**

SONDRA PERL
NANCY WILSON

With a Foreword by James Moffett

Heinemann • Portsmouth, New Hampshire

Heinemann Educational Books, Inc.
70 Court Street   Portsmouth, NH   03801
Offices and agents throughout the world

10 9 8 7 6 5 4 3 2

Library of Congress Cataloging in Publication Data
Perl, Sondra.
   Through teachers' eyes.

   1. English language—Composition and exercises—Case
studies.   I. Wilson, Nancy, 1940–   II. Title.
LB1576.P54 1986   808'.042   85-30242
ISBN 0-435-08248-5

DESIGNED BY MARIA SZMAUZ.
PHOTO ON BACK COVER BY ARTHUR EGENDORF.
PHOTOS OF THE TEACHERS BY AUDRE ALLISON, SUNIL BADAL, ROSS BURKHARDT, AND DAVID GAMBERG.
PRINTED IN THE UNITED STATES OF AMERICA.

To all the teachers
in all the classrooms
whose stories have yet to be told

Contents

Foreword

These six portraits play variations on the theme of what happens when a teacher who has gone through a National Writing Project summer institute implements a process approach to teaching writing. Since the school district these teachers work in supports their efforts extraordinarily well, the orchestrations of this theme do not feature the conflicts, so common elsewhere, between innovative teachers and a recalcitrant system but center instead on the dynamics of the classroom itself, on the interactions between teacher and students, and among different sides of the teacher.

The theme modulates into subthemes according to the particular circumstances of each of the six teachers. What happens when a teacher accustomed to ninth graders and to centering classwork around writing is suddenly faced with eleventh graders worrying about being able to analyze literature and pass SATs and Regents Exams? What happens when a teacher who has always avoided writing launches first graders into authorhood, replete with conferences and revision, before they have learned to spell or read? Or when an eighth-grade English and social studies teacher used to running classes by delivering polished performances invites self-expression and tries to get out of the way of his students' creativity? Or when a social studies teacher given to psychological analysis and committed more to students' personal growth than to an academic subject deals with his twelfth graders' senioritis by having them write far more than they had expected? When a science-trained teacher using writing as only one way to engage students in inquiry learns that his fourth and fifth graders prefer making up stories to writing about personal experience and that his directing of them toward realism may conflict with his own goal of empowering free expression? When a teacher gifted in relating to students during the difficult transition to adolescence tries to emphasize process journals with a group soured by the apparently similar approach of last year's teacher? Every teacher operates within some particular personal framework and local circumstances against which his or her efforts at implementing need to be viewed. Readers of these portraits should find it very useful to place themselves among these six teachers and see how those most like or unlike themselves fare.

What ethnographic research does that experimental research does not do is preserve the web of factors and circumstances that make up the complicated process of language learning. Writing is thinking. For an activity so interwoven with the whole of one's mental and social life, ethnography seems especially appropriate. Where an author's material comes from, who or what the author is writing for, what inhibitions he or she is running up against, how subjects are inwardly verbalized and outwardly vocalized, how trials bring on revisions— a myriad of factors go into writing that only an ongoing, flexible, and pluralistic sort of research can do justice to.

Because Perl and Wilson are also teachers, they can register what is going on with more sensitivity and perception than someone who has not experienced what a teacher and a class may be going through, especially in an activity as intricate as writing. The authors also know the thin spots, the cave-ins, and the ego involvements of teaching, but when they bring these out, they do so with all the sympathy of one who identifies with the teacher's predicaments and frailties. Sometimes the authors identify with the students and join in classroom activities. Not so much at risk as the teacher, they take advantage of this rare role as both insider and outsider to see with the understanding of a kindred professional or more detached alter ego, inclined neither to criticize with the maddening insensitivity of those who don't understand what it's like nor to romanticize like a foreigner.

Perl and Wilson have brought to the complexity of their subject not only their observational logs and periodic summaries but also the teachers' journals, the students' writing, and sometimes the students' journals. Issues are often illumined by a rich intersecting of points of view that also tends to cancel partialities. To this dialectic is added generous quotation of dialog from conferences, from peer writing-group conversation, from classroom discussions, and from after-hours exchanges.

The results of this research seem to me remarkably evocative, judicious, and useful. Assuming the value of the process approach to teaching writing, the researchers set down the ins and outs, the twists and turns of this approach so as to understand better what it entails, what can go wrong, and what makes it work. Both they and the teachers experience surprises and challenge things they took for granted. *Through Teachers' Eyes* is an honest inquiry. It raises questions about what a process approach to writing actually is, whether it always succeeds, and whether teachers are attracted to it for personal reasons they will have to come to grips with. Does good teaching depend more on the person than the process? Staff development is self-development. But is the self-scrutinizing that teachers may regard as essential for their growth always appropriate for learning to write, especially for *youngsters* learning to write?

These portraits will make excellent conversation pieces for inservice sessions. They are accounts not only of particular teachers but of certain students, certain classroom circumstances, and certain junctures in relationships or learning dynamics, presented for us to carry forward in our thoughts and discussions. To a degree, these are case studies like those used in business, medical, and law schools to develop professional understanding about how to handle real situations. Getting down to the cases in this book should help teachers enormously to make the most of the current movement to honor writing and teach it realistically.

JAMES MOFFETT

Preface

Through *Teachers' Eyes* is a study of writing teachers and how they see themselves. It is a study of what matters to them, what touches them, what challenges and excites them. In it we take you inside the classroom and show you daily life, not prettied up or made tidy for outsiders but opened up and made visible for other teachers to look at and understand. We show teachers with their doubts and fears, their questions and dilemmas as they try to make writing—its discovery and its power—available to students. In *Through Teachers' Eyes* we show teaching as teachers see it.

Our title, however, refers not only to the teachers we describe. It refers to us as well. Teachers ourselves, we took four years off from our own teaching lives to observe the lives of other teachers. We spent several years in their classrooms and several more coming to understand them. We lived day to day behind the scenes, watching and documenting as the teachers made decisions, made mistakes, experimented, and tried again. We watched and documented as lessons were enacted, connections formed, consequences dealt with.

As we watched, we worked to understand what we were seeing. We wrote, made charts, categorized, and organized. We talked, told stories, refined, and reflected. Eventually, we discovered the themes that informed and the patterns that gave shape to these teachers' teaching. *Through Teachers' Eyes*, then, also presents teachers through our eyes, as we came to see them after several years of study.

While we now share a common view of the teachers and their teaching, we did not begin this work with the same history or knowledge. Sondra had been working in the school district teaching summer institutes since 1979; Nancy first visited in 1981. Sondra knew all of the teachers who volunteered to participate in the study, some of them quite well; Nancy met them for the first time when she entered their classrooms. Sondra conceived the research project, wrote the proposal, ran the study group, and directed the investigation. Nancy asked questions, immersed herself in the work, and slowly came to find her own footing.

As the years passed, however, and as analysis and reflection took the place of observation, our working relationship changed. Just as in the early years we formed partnerships with the teachers, so in subsequent years we formed a partnership with each other. First, reading each other's drafts, we began to offer each other insights as each saw something the other hadn't. Soon we were suggesting approaches to each other, each coming up with suggestions for the other's work. Later we began to plan chapters together, and one of us would do the drafting. Eventually we wrote together, each of us offering a line, a phrase, a paragraph. We knew our working relationship had evolved into a true partnership when, in rereading certain lines or phrases, neither one of us could remember who had written what.

Each of us, of course, drafted the chapters on the teachers she had studied. Yet even here each came to know the other's data and the other's style so well that each was able to revise and edit the other's chapters as if she had written them herself.

The first and last chapters, too, passed back and forth between us. Chapter 1 grew slowly, with both of us contributing to it, until Nancy gathered together the parts we wanted to keep and rewrote them into the chapter as it now stands. Chapter 8, on the other hand, remained unwritten until the end, when Sondra took on the task of sifting through all our years of work together, our hours of talking and writing, and put into words what we both believe to be true about teachers and their teaching.

And so, for much of what we write, we use the pronoun "we." In describing events that took place before Nancy's arrival, however, we switch to the third person, using Sondra's full name to refer to the work she did before 1981; occasionally, where a "we" would be inaccurate or misleading, we use "Sondra" or "Nancy" for the sake of clarity. In the chapters on the six teachers, each of us has written from her own perspective, as "I": the "I" in the chapters on Diane Burkhardt, Ross Burkhardt, and Reba Pekala, therefore, is Sondra; in the chapters on Audre Allison, Len Schutzman, and Bill Silver, it is Nancy.

The order of the chapters on the teachers follows not grade level or chronology but rather our intuitive sense of how these chapters fit together. It offers contrasts, balances, and echoes rather than a logical sequence. Nor have we attempted to make these chapters uniform—in tone, in focus, or even in length. Each follows, we hope, an internal logic—but the logic in each case is different. The chapters on Audre and Diane are the longest, but while the chapter on Audre deals with a number of different aspects of Audre's teaching, the chapter on Diane explores one single issue in depth. In the chapter on Reba, we look closely at two first graders; in the chapter on Len, at four twelfth graders in a single writing group. The chapter on Ross follows a sequence of events; the chapter on Bill is organized around a theme. And, in the various chapters, our involvement as researchers varies too. In some chapters, the researcher remains more or less in the background; in others, she plays a more central role.

The events we describe all took place in the classrooms we observed. For the sake of readability, however, we have chosen for the most part not to interrupt our narrative with explanations of exactly when things happened. In order to capture the flow of classroom life, we have sometimes written as if two classes were one: as if, for instance, students from Diane's English A and English B sat side by side, or students from Audre's periods 1, 3, and 5 classes met together. But although we have used our judgment in combining classes, we have not invented what occurred. The students and teachers we describe spoke and wrote the words you will read. Even their spelling and punctuation are authentic.

The teachers' names are authentic, too. Collaborators with us from the start, the teachers read their chapters as we produced them, responded to our various drafts, and worked with us to help make the chapters we wrote accurate reflections of them and their teaching. We are pleased that they have chosen to appear under their own names.

In most cases, we have also used the real (first) names of students. In instances where we judged that students' anonymity needed to be preserved, however, we created pseudonyms. And, in classes where there were just too many Matts and Sues, we found ourselves, for the sake of clarity, forced to invent substitutes.

Through Teachers' Eyes is, in the end, about vision—how teachers see their students, how they act toward them, how they help them become writers. It is our hope that the stories we tell will enable other teachers to see themselves and their own teaching more clearly.

Acknowledgments

The Writing Project institutes in Shoreham-Wading River and the classroom research that grew out of them did not happen overnight. Many colleagues and friends contributed, some over and over again, to the process of building the writing community we describe in this book.

The New York City Writing Project is itself the result of many people's efforts. By conceiving and developing the National Writing Project, Jim Gray, with Mary K. Healy, gave us our parent organization. Without their support and the model of teacher training they offered, the New York City Writing Project would never have existed. John Brereton, in his year as co-director of the Project, was an invaluable teacher and friend. Richard Sterling was and continues to be a source of the Project's strength. His energy and imagination helped to build the Project in New York and to start another in Shoreham-Wading River. His commitment to literacy in the broadest sense continues to inspire an ever-expanding network of teachers.

The Writing Project in Shoreham-Wading River owes its start to Mark Goldberg, who first invited Sondra and Richard to work with the district's teachers. Over the years, Mark has been a friend to the Shoreham Project in every way, attending summer institutes, reading, writing, and learning along with us. From the start, Richard Doremus, Superintendent of Schools, has offered not only his own support and keen interest in writing but also the support of his administration and the school board.

In the summers of 1979–81, many people brought their individual stamps to bear on the teacher training led by Sondra and Richard in the Shoreham-Wading River district. In 1979, James Moffett spent a week writing and teaching in the summer institute; in 1980, Lucy Calkins visited for several days to work with the Shoreham-Wading River teachers. Between 1979 and 1981, Lil Brannon, Nancy Martin, Gordon Pradl, Lee Odell, and Joe Trimmer each spent a day in a summer institute, bringing their own expertise to the questions raised by teachers.

In 1981, with funds from the National Institute of Education, we began the research project described here. Our work during the school year brought other colleagues to Shoreham-Wading River and the district to the attention of many others. Before we began conducting our research, we spent hours talking with Claire Woods, probing her understanding of what it meant to do ethnographic research in schools. Once the project was underway, we made constant phone calls to and asked hundreds of questions of Perry Gilmore and David Smith who, in addition to offering us guidance and support by phone, traveled many miles, through sleet and rain, snow and sun, to work with us as we worked in classrooms. In later years, Pat D'Arcy, Peter Medway, and Susan Sowers visited the district at our invitation and shed new light on what was becoming all too familiar to us.

Several colleagues read our drafts in progress. Donald Graves spent a morning examining our data, listening to our stories and inspiring us with his own. Nancy Martin made a long wait in a hotel lobby pass quickly as she read through and exclaimed over our fieldnotes and classroom write-ups. Dick Larson stood over our shoulders at Lehman College, watching and encouraging as the drafts piled up. Late at night, we'd turn to him for help in settling editorial disputes. Carla Asher and Gordon Pradl read our first manuscript. Carla's reading was rigorous: chapter by chapter, her questions forced us to clarify our thinking and helped us bring our portraits to life. Gordon read impressionistically, for themes and patterns. His questions helped us define our own.

Others, too, were crucial to the development of this work. In 1982, funding for the research described here was almost withdrawn. In Washington, D.C., in the offices of the National Institute of Education, Marcia Farr and later Steve Cahir championed this project, making sure its potential was recognized by those whose task it was to cut the Institute's research budget. Without their wisdom and savvy, there might never have been an NIE grant, a project entitled "How Teachers Teach the Writing Process," or a Shoreham-Wading River study group.

So, too, there might never have been a book written without the generosity of the John Simon Guggenheim Memorial Foundation. The Foundation made it possible for Sondra to spend an extra year studying and writing about the data we had collected on the NIE project.

The work originally funded by NIE, the job of collecting data in ten classrooms, began in 1981. At that time, James Carter took a leave from his regular teaching job to join us as a researcher. For two years, his voice joined ours as we read our fieldnotes aloud, his drafts piled up alongside ours, and his jokes kept us laughing long after midnight.

Ten Shoreham-Wading River teachers also joined us in our effort to understand teaching. Six appear in this book. Three others, Phyllis Glassman, Jack Schwartz, and Marcia Sitver, worked with us during the first year of our study. Their teaching, their journals, and their comments in our study group added breadth to our view of classrooms. A fourth teacher, Anita Graves, was especially generous throughout the project. A member of the study group for the entire three years, she wrote with us, shared her students with us, and enlivened our meetings with her humor. She and her fourth-grade students will be the subject of James Carter's dissertation.

Many students contributed to the project in ways we could never have anticipated. Sue Scheld read the high school chapters from the first draft on and sent pages of insightful and always encouraging response. Teresa Hannan, Theresa Kallmeyer, and Alexandra Kroeger read chapters as they were nearing completion and gave valuable suggestions. Margaret Coughlin, David Ecklund, Teresa Hannan, Alexandra Kroeger, and Sue Scheld spoke along with us at conferences, joined us in leading workshops, and showed us again and again why this work mattered.

Even when we were in Long Island, our own writing community, the New York City Writing Project, served as home base. It was here—to the Project—that we returned again and again for colleagueship and support. Over the years, dozens of Project members inquired about our progress; those who knew us best cheered us on, laughed at our bulging file cabinets, and knew not to interrupt us when our door was closed. Three teacher-consultants, Maurice T. Bolmer, Lillian Rossi-Maida, and Elaine Spielberg, read chapters. And Ellen Hegarty, the Project's secretary, always responded graciously to our requests for help. As deadlines neared, we knew we could count on her for last-minute typing, organizing of chapters, mailing, photocopying, encouragement, patience, and good humor.

As the book took shape, others were equally helpful. Philippa Stratton, our editor at Heinemann, showed interest in this project from its earliest stages. Over the years, she has continued to encourage us. Barney Karpfinger, our agent, was equally excited by the promise he saw. Glenda Bissex, as a reader for Heinemann, helped us find our focus. Donna Bouvier, who saw the book through production, gave it the kind of care we wanted it to have. And typists Tim Oliver and Judy Schnitzer were two of our earliest and most appreciative readers.

Our friends stood by, too, always encouraging if not always pleased by the amount of time we spent in Shoreham. Louise DeSalvo, by introducing us to one another, sowed the seeds of our partnership. Judy Malamut read chapters and sent words of encouragement. Elizabeth Fox-Genovese read the whole manuscript and asked penetrating questions. Elaine Avidon was a companion to us and to this project from the day we started. As colleague and friend, she shared with us both the professional and personal sides of our lives and brought to our inquiry an interest born out of her own commitment to teaching.

Our families have also contributed to our work. Helene and William Arnstein have shared with Nancy their lifelong love of language and learning. Ruth and Milt Fox, Sheri Migdol, and Richard and Robert Perl have responded with deep respect and boundless enthusiasm to whatever Sondra has chosen to pursue.

Finally, our husbands, Arthur Egendorf and Peter Wilson, supported this project from the first. By serving often as mother as well as father to three growing children, Peter made it possible for Nancy to live part-time in Shoreham. As the years went on, he read drafts, discussed students and teachers with us, and came to know the world of Shoreham-Wading River almost as well as we did. Arthur was a behind-the-scenes partner in this work from the beginning. When our funding was threatened, he lobbied for the project; when we were tired of traveling and writing, he offered us encouragement; when we couldn't see our way out, he listened and reminded us that not knowing is the first step to insight. Having his own vision of what is possible in teaching, he challenged us, at each stage of the work, to deepen ours.

Robert, Sasha, and Elizabeth Wilson have grown up with this project. Since it began, they have learned to cook, travel independently, and live with grace and good humor with their mother's work. Sara Perl Egendorf, born during our third year of work, has grown into a toddler accustomed to finding her mother in front of a computer screen.

We thank all the people who have contributed to this book. More than anyone else, we thank the six teachers who opened their classrooms so we could study and, through studying, learn.

through teachers' eyes

Introduction

Chapter 1

Teachers Learning

In the Shoreham-Wading River Central School District, writing is as popular as baseball—and as widely practiced. A first grader greets a visitor: "Can I read you my first published book?" Three second graders surprise their teacher with journals they've been keeping at home. A fourth grader, her writing interrupted by a fire drill, takes her notebook outdoors and goes on writing, sitting cross-legged under a tree until the drill is over. Two eighth graders ask their teacher to join them over spring vacation in an informal writing group. An eleventh-grade boy writes poems on scraps of paper and stuffs them into the back pocket of his jeans; another sends poems to his girlfriend as gifts. Two juniors get together on a Saturday night, stock up on potato chips, and write. A senior is disappointed in love and starts a novel.

Students in Shoreham-Wading River pick up their pens on trains and ferry boats, on the beach and in the woods, at school board meetings. They write when school is in session—and on evenings, weekends, and school vacations. They keep personal journals, volleyball journals, softball journals, reading logs, science logs; they write letters, song lyrics, editorials, stories, poems. Some write mainly in school or for school assignments, others mainly out of school, for themselves or their friends. Many do both. When something happens in Shoreham-Wading River, chances are that someone will be writing about it.

So many writers, in one small school district. How did it happen? Where did it begin?

3

A Classroom in the Middle School

The story as we know it began with the school district's interest in writing. In 1979, Richard Doremus, Superintendent of Schools, and Mark Goldberg, the district's administrator for language arts, invited Sondra Perl and Richard Sterling, the directors of the New York City Writing Project, to lead the first of four Writing Project summer institutes in Shoreham-Wading River.[1] From that time on, Shoreham-Wading River administrators welcomed the Writing Project into their schools, Shoreham-Wading River teachers gave up parts of their summer vacations to enroll in New York City Writing Project institutes, and the Shoreham-Wading River school board supported its teachers' growing commitment to Writing Project work.

We know, of course, that there were writers in Shoreham before 1979. In Shoreham-Wading River, as in any school district, there had always been sixth graders who like to write stories, high school students who kept diaries, and a handful of innovative teachers who experimented with new approaches to teaching writing. But, until 1979, these students and these teachers, like those in countless other districts, worked in isolation, cut off from developments in composition research and unaware, except in rare cases, of what their colleagues in other classrooms were doing. The first of the summer institutes marked the end of this professional isolation and the beginning of a new community: a network of teachers, writers, and researchers who gathered together to share and expand their knowledge of the teaching of writing. For us, then, the story of the first summer institute is a beginning, the beginning of a new community. Like most of the stories we will tell, it takes place in a classroom.

On a Monday in July 1979, Sondra, Richard, twenty-two teachers, and three administrators met, for the first time, in a large airy room in the district's middle school. "S-WR's version of the BAWP [Bay Area Writing Project] got under way this morning at 9:00," wrote Diane Burkhardt, in her role as "historian" for the course, "with coffee and Dunkin' Donuts and 25 people in varying stages of writing readiness." Some of the teachers knew one another; others, teaching in different schools, had never met. Sondra and Richard were strangers to nearly everyone. Only Jack Schwartz, a second-grade teacher who had taken the New York City Writing Project institute at Lehman College the summer before, knew what to expect. While the others were still chatting, Jack was opening his journal.

"We don't like to talk a lot about writing without actually doing it," said Sondra, fifteen minutes into the first session. She suggested a topic: What is most difficult for me to teach when I teach writing? "Let's write for about fifteen

---

[1] The New York City Writing Project is the New York City branch of the National Writing Project, which began, in 1973, as the Bay Area Writing Project. Housed at Herbert H. Lehman College of the City University of New York, the New York City Writing Project has been operating since 1978.

minutes," she said and picked up her pen. After some nervous chatter, the teachers settled down. Conversations subsided; heads bent over papers.

Fifteen minutes later, Sondra asked the participants to pause, to think about and then write about what had happened to them while they were writing. "What was it like to write what you just wrote?" she asked. "What observations can you now make about the process you just went through? Open your notebooks and jot down whatever you can remember about your writing process from the time I gave you the topic until the time you finished. We'll take about five minutes to do this."

When everyone had finished both a piece of exploratory writing and a note on the process of writing it, Sondra asked members of the group to take turns reading what they had written to the rest of the class. "Anxiety increased for the reading part," Diane reported, noting "shaky voices, hastily lit cigarettes, leg-jigglings, toe-tappings, hesitant disclaimers. ..." Sondra sympathized. "I always find reading in front of a large group scary," she said. And first a few, then many, took courage and read.

Audre Allison, a high school teacher, said her students usually liked to write first drafts but didn't like to revise them. "How can you get them to care about exploring possibilities?" she wanted to know, "to see all the different things you can do with language ... to recognize the power of it?"

Diane, a middle school teacher, wrote that most of her students, though they participated in writing groups, were not as involved in helping each other as she wanted them to be. "Their responses are often perfunctory. ... In my mind I often blame the students, but in my gut I feel I haven't taught them well enough. ... There must be something I could do better."

Bill Silver, an elementary school teacher, wondered if his students really believed that they could make their own decisions about their writing. "I tell kids over and over again, to convince them—to convince myself—that their writing is theirs, that my job is to help them, not to make decisions for them ... but I have difficulties with the 'consultant' role. ... How can I give feedback that will help them without getting them to write for me?"

Reflecting on their writing processes, the teachers' comments were equally varied. Bill reported that, when he let himself write without thinking too much about it, the words that came out were "less coherent" but "had more feeling." Audre said she had "worked to find the groove, the track; to get in it, or on it, and to cruise—as if moving from a cobblestoned road in a wooden-wheeled wagon—onto the monorail." She added, "This is what I'm always after, I guess." And Diane, after reading both her piece and her process note, stepped back to comment on the process of writing about the writing process: "Should I be *thinking* so much? Is this really honest?"

As the teachers read, taking turns around the circle, Sondra and Richard responded to each by repeating back, in a questioning tone, the gist of what they thought the writer had said. "So your main concern is that your students don't seem to care about their writing?" or "You're wondering if this approach can work with ten-year-olds?" After the first few had read, they encouraged the teachers, too, to learn and practice the technique students call "sayback": responding to writing by reflecting or mirroring a writer's meaning.

By the time Sondra read her own piece, there were practiced responders in the room. By lunchtime, everyone had had a chance to write, to read, and to respond to another person's writing, and the twenty-five participants in the summer institute were well launched into the study of the writing process that was to occupy them for the next three weeks.

Much of the Writing Project's approach is expressed in the few simple activities of that first morning's work. We start writing within the first fifteen minutes of an institute because we have found that people learn to write (and to teach writing) most effectively not by listening to lectures about it, not by reading about it in textbooks or handbooks or grammar books, but by doing it—and then by reflecting on what they have done. We ask teachers to observe and report on what happens as they write because we have found that teachers (and students) who study their own writing processes begin to build together a body of knowledge about writing, knowledge grounded first in personal experience and later expanded to include the experience of others in the group and of researchers and theorists in the field.

We ask participants to read their writing out loud because we have found that reading out loud helps writers find their own voices and begin to hear their words as others hear them. We teach "active listening" (a way of responding developed by Carl Rogers and later refined by Eugene Gendlin) because we have noticed that writers who hear what they have written reflected in others' words are enabled to develop their ideas: to see where they have not yet expressed their meaning and to create, from what is still implicit in their writing, something explicit. We join participants in everything they do, from writing and revising to discussing the writing process and meeting in writing groups, because we know that we, too, learn through writing, and because we believe as well that the most effective teacher is a fellow learner.

On the third day of the institute, the participants approached their seats nervously. The first two days had been fun: the topics assigned by Sondra and Richard, the writing exploratory. Today, they knew, they were about to up the ante. They were to choose their own topics and begin drafting the pieces they would bring to writing groups, then revise and edit. This third morning, Sondra had promised, she would help them discover, if they didn't already have them, topics, issues, or themes they could explore in different forms or from different points of view for the next three weeks.

After everyone was seated, Sondra looked around the room. "OK," she said, "today's the day," and then more gently, "Somehow, beginning this assignment always seems so momentous. Finding a topic that matters to us, that we can be committed to, often seems like such a hard thing. In the Project, we've found that we can help make this moment a little easier. What I'm going to do is take you through an exercise we call "Guidelines for Composing."[2] Basically, it's just that. I'm going to guide you through your own composing process by asking you a series of questions. By the time I've finished, I think most of you will have found something you want to write about. If you already know what you want to explore for the next few weeks, I think you will find that you have deepened your sense of the topic. If you have paper, and you're ready, I'll begin."

As the teachers settled down, Sondra asked them to sit quietly, to relax, to tune out the distractions around them: the hum of the fluorescent lights above, the buzz of the lawnmower outside. Then, after several minutes of silence, she began.

"Ask yourselves," she said, " 'How am I right now?' 'What's on my mind?' 'Is there anything in the way of my writing today?' And," she continued, "when you hear yourself answering, begin to make a list."

As everyone began to write, she did, too. After a few minutes, she asked another set of questions.

" 'What else is on my mind?' 'Is there anything I might at some time want to write about?' 'Does a particular person, a place, an image come to mind?' "

The lists began to grow.

Five minutes later, she said, "Now review your lists and ask, 'Is there anything on this list that draws my attention right now?' 'Is there anything that reaches out, that touches me, that says, "Me, I want attention right now"?' If there is, circle it."

On and on they went, questioning, selecting, discarding, becoming more intent, becoming more engrossed. Soon the teachers had chosen items from their lists, had begun to ask themselves other questions: "What makes this so important to me?" "Is there an image or phrase that captures the whole of this issue?" "What haven't I said about it yet?"

And as Sondra came to the end of the questions, almost all the teachers dispersed to pursue whatever they had discovered for the rest of the morning. Of those who stayed behind, some had questions and a few had doubts, but eventually, on this morning and the mornings to follow, all settled down to write.

Once they had begun to write, the teachers found that their pieces grew and grew. Having completed first pieces, they went on to begin second and then third ones. But not on new issues or topics. In order to encourage them to explore and experiment with forms of discourse, with the genres available for writing, Sondra and Richard asked the participants to write at least three different pieces on the themes or issues they had selected that third morning: to find, for instance, a story within a poem, a poem within an essay, an essay

---

[2] A copy of "Guidelines for Composing" is included in Appendix A.

within a memoir, each related, in some way, to the original theme, yet each complete in itself.

Writing in the mornings, the teachers spent most of their afternoons in four- or five-person writing groups. They became increasingly confident as they read their drafts aloud. They refined their skills at responding, listening carefully to one another's writing, learning to reflect, to say back, the essence of what someone else had written. As the writers in each group responded to their listeners, they found themselves learning about revision. They hadn't quite written what they had meant. They had the sense they wanted but not the words. Maybe tonight or tomorrow they would. . . .

In the weeks remaining to them, the participants continued writing, responding to writing, and reflecting on the writing process. The first pieces from the guidelines gave way to second and third pieces—stories became essays, essays became poems. Practice with active listening led to longer and more detailed responses and to serious, heartfelt discussions in writing groups. Initial observations about the writing process became more acute, more finely tuned, and were recorded in ever-growing "process journals." Frequently the day began with participants reading to the group from their process journals, reporting discoveries made while writing or frustrations when words eluded them.

By the end of the three-week institute, most of the teachers had written more than they had in years; they reported themselves exhausted but exhilarated. Some found, once they got going, that it was hard to stop. "Three weeks is too short," wrote Diane. And Audre added, "This is the only class I've ever hated to see end."

During the following school year, teachers from the institute brought their enthusiasm for writing back to their classrooms. They wrote with their students, as Sondra and Richard had written with them; they experimented, invented, improvised. Some persuaded colleagues to sign up for the next summer institute.

In 1980, Sondra and Richard met another group of twenty-five teachers, each one, like those in the first group, with his or her own particular concerns. Reba Pekala, a first-grade teacher, found writing difficult and felt she wasn't good at it; she hoped the institute would help her find ways to make writing in her classroom "enjoyable, satisfying, fun." Ross Burkhardt, an eighth-grade teacher and Diane's husband, wrote often and successfully but wanted to know more about his own writing process. "I'm not aware of a process," he said. "I just do it." He hoped learning more about the writing process would help him help his students. Len Schutzman, a high school teacher on special assignment to teach third grade, had not written much before but had often thought he might like to. He saw writing as "a powerful method of focusing on one's own experience and being able to articulate it."

By the end of the second summer institute, one quarter of Shoreham-Wading River's two hundred teachers, representing most subject areas and grade levels, had become part of the Writing Project community. When Sondra and Richard returned for follow-up visits to the district's five schools, they were bombarded with comments and questions from dozens of these teachers wherever they went. Eager to share what they were doing in their classrooms, the teachers reported new surges of energy in their teaching. They were writing and talking about writing, sharing what they had learned with colleagues and parents. Their excitement about teaching and writing was spreading from one classroom to another, spilling over into the halls and invading the teachers' lunchrooms.

On these brief visits to Shoreham, Sondra found she didn't want to leave, and when she did leave, she found she couldn't stop talking about what she had seen. She wanted to know more about these Shoreham-Wading River teachers and their students, to understand the writing explosion that was taking place among them. In 1981, she applied for a grant from the National Institute of Education to enable her to study the teaching of writing in Shoreham-Wading River.

In the proposal, Sondra argued that ethnography, the research method pioneered by anthropologists, was best suited to the type of classroom research she wanted to undertake. Ethnographic methods, she felt, would enable her to arrive at an understanding of writing classrooms in a way no other research method could. Such methods would allow her to study writing classrooms in Shoreham from the inside out, as anthropologists studied the cultures they wanted to understand: by spending lots of time in them, by becoming, as much as possible, members of the cultures themselves, by immersing themselves in those cultures for prolonged periods of time, and then by stepping back to examine and refine—to make sense of—the lessons they had learned.

Hoping to arrive at the kinds of insights and understandings more detached observers often missed, Sondra planned to study the teaching of writing from the perspectives of teachers. As part of her plan, she invited Nancy Wilson and James Carter, experienced teachers from the New York City Writing Project, to collaborate with her on the research and extended an invitation to participate in the study to the seventy Shoreham-Wading River teachers who had been members of the summer institutes from 1979 to 1981.

Ten teachers volunteered to become part of the project, to allow researchers in their classrooms for an entire school year, to help Sondra answer her questions and their own. As it happened, four of the teachers were from the elementary schools, three from the middle school, and three from the high school. Four were men and six women. At the start of the study, most had taught for at least ten years, several for close to twenty. Three were former Peace Corps volunteers. Most were active in school affairs: served on committees, represented their colleagues in the Teachers' Association or the union, planned and organized special events, took some of the many courses offered by the district. Eight were married (two to one another), and all but two had children of their own. By the end of the study, two had become grandparents.

Since there were three researchers and three major school divisions, we divided ourselves accordingly: James Carter was responsible for collecting data in the elementary schools, Sondra focused her attention on the middle school, and Nancy spent her days in the high school. Together we formed a team: ten teachers and three researchers who were to work together for one, for two, and, in the case of seven teachers and two researchers, for the next three years.

Formulating Our Research Questions

Because we were Writing Project teachers ourselves, we never pretended—to ourselves or anyone else—that we were neutral observers. From the start, we were unashamedly partisan. We wanted to know not, "Does this approach have value?"—we were convinced it did—but rather, "How do teachers who see the value of this approach translate their beliefs (about writing, teaching, kids) into classroom practice?" The question of value, for us, would have been a false one. The question about practice was real.

We knew that most of the teachers who had participated in the summer institutes were using writing in their classrooms in new ways. We knew that some of these teachers were teaching six-year-olds and others sixteen-year-olds, that some were teaching English and others social studies, math, or science. We knew that these teachers shared to some extent our general views, but since the writing process approach is a way of thinking about writing and not a formula for teaching it, we didn't know precisely what these teachers were doing in their classrooms. In what ways, we wondered, would a first-grade writing class resemble a twelfth-grade writing class? In what ways would they be different? How would day-to-day classroom practice vary with the age of the students? With the philosophy or personality of the teacher?

To find out, we planned to study teachers and students in their classrooms, nearly every day, from September to June. Because we were to work long hours, often starting before 8 A.M. and ending after midnight, we didn't try to commute every day from our homes in New York City. Instead, we spent roughly four days a week in Shoreham-Wading River, staying in the homes of teachers and learning about the district through living in it.

The District

The drive from Manhattan to Shoreham-Wading River was a journey from one world to another. In the first year of our study, we made it every week. From September to June, we would leave the busy streets of New York, crowded with people and jammed with cars, and head out toward eastern Long Island.

We'd know we were getting close when the traffic thinned. Around Exit 62, Stony Brook, the Long Island Expressway would begin to unclog. By Exit 68, the turnoff to Shoreham and Wading River, few cars would be left on the road; on the William Floyd Parkway, heading north, hardly any. We'd pass scrub pines, a few scattered houses, a development or two; in the spring, dogwood trees in

flower. When we'd gone as far as we could go—when the parkway ended—
we would be there.

The communities of Shoreham and Wading River lie along the north shore
of Long Island. Shoreham, to the west, is more "suburban" in flavor; Wading
River, to the east, more rural. In winter, brown, leafless stalks of vegetable and
potato fields are visible from the road; in summer, high school students can be
seen picking tomatoes and potatoes and peaches. In June, joggers and cyclists
buy strawberries from roadside stands. In August, nearly everyone goes to the
beach.

We read about the beach before we saw it. It appears again and again in
the writing of Shoreham-Wading River students, works its way into stories, poems,
memory pieces. For some, it is a place to be with friends, to play and picnic;
for others, a place to be alone. The Shoreham beach is long and sandy, bordered
by grasses and, in summer, purple wildflowers. The beach at Wading River is
rocky, with houses at its edge and the green dome of the Shoreham nuclear
power plant behind it.

The power plant, too, appears in students' writing. It is the subject of editorials,
science reports, essays, and poems. Students attack or defend it in print or write
wild and chilling fantasies about what it might bring: glowing seashells, irradiated
rabbits.

About eight thousand people live among the sod farms, along the beaches,
and on the quiet residential streets of Shoreham and Wading River. Among them
are scientists from Brookhaven Laboratory, engineers from Grumman Aircraft,
teachers, fire fighters, police officers, and construction workers. Some work for
the Long Island Lighting Company (LILCO), many of these on the construction
of the nuclear power plant. Others work for the school district itself. A few run
the district's several small businesses: delis, gas stations, a general store, a bar.
People in the district describe themselves as "predominantly middle class." Over
half are Catholic, and nearly everyone is white.

There is no railroad station or shopping mall in the community. There are
no movie theaters. The nearest fast food restaurants are one town over, in Rocky
Point. Some teenagers who've spent their lives in the district have never, or
hardly ever, been to New York City, seventy-five miles away. Some call their
community "boring"; others say "peaceful," "friendly," "quiet," "safe."

The Shoreham nuclear power plant has been central to the history of the
school district. Before LILCO began to build it, in 1970, there was no unified
school district, only three elementary schools serving two sparsely settled communities. The building of the plant brought an influx of new population and
tax money to Shoreham and Wading River. Tax revenues from LILCO built the
middle school, the high school, and the public library; they pay the district's
teachers, support its athletic teams, and make its summer programs possible.
Ninety percent of the district's school budget comes from taxes on the Shoreham
plant.

By 1981, when our study began, the district had grown to comprise its present five schools. It employed approximately two hundred teachers and twelve administrators and served over 2,000 students. At the end of that year, a typical one in the district, 175 students graduated from the high school, 55 percent of whom went on to four-year colleges and 22 percent to two-year colleges.

Much of the public life of the Shoreham-Wading River community takes place in the schools. Kids and adults stay after school or drop by in the evenings and on weekends to play basketball, hold meetings, attend chorus rehearsals, watch films, take evening classes, and put on plays. Working late in the middle school, as we often did, we might find ourselves next door to a Japanese cooking class or a debate on the politics of nuclear power. Based in the schools, we were at the center of the community.

Another Classroom

In September 1981, in Ross Burkhardt's room in the middle school, a group of teachers met over coffee and cake to study and learn together. The Shoreham-Wading River study group was to meet after school on Tuesdays for nearly three years. In the beginning, there were thirteen of us meeting every week: ten teachers and three researchers, tired at the end of a long school day but ready to be revived by a joint inquiry. We started, to no one's surprise, by writing.

That first day, we wrote about, then read aloud, our goals for the project. Audre reported that she couldn't pin hers down. They were, she said, "forming every day," being reshaped as she reshaped her teaching. Ross felt uneasy with the whole notion of goals. "I am awed," he wrote, "by minds that probe deeply and delve bravely into dark corners." Ross touched on an aspect of the study the other teachers recognized, too: all there was to learn, to know. Diane wrote about it this way: "Every time I read articles related to writing research, I am struck by how much there is to know. ... How many teachers are like me? So caught up in the day-to-day business of the classroom that I take little time to reflect, to fit things into a total picture?" Diane hoped that the project would give her this time. Bill, too, wanted time to "look critically" at his own teaching. He hoped that the study group would "support [his] own efforts at change." All the teachers expressed excitement, felt as though they were "on the cutting edge," were eager to begin looking closely at the act of teaching.

As the weeks and months passed, the study group became increasingly important to all of us. It was a way for us to touch base, to cut across school boundaries, to examine what each of us was learning in one classroom against the background of another. Sometimes we researchers divided the large group into several smaller ones, to work intensively or to read our classroom write-ups to the teachers we were observing. At other times, we all worked together, examining student writing, listening to tapes of writing groups, discussing articles, challenging one another's assumptions, looking for commonalities.

Most often our inquiry took shape through writing. We researchers, in addition to keeping fieldnotes, wrote about our observations and our questions, our tentative "findings," and our moments of elation and discouragement. In fact, after spending six hours in school each day, we devoted most of our remaining time to writing and reading. We were all diligent notetakers, writing down as much classroom dialogue as we could in each class we visited. Then, to keep track of what was going on, to review for ourselves and to learn from one another, we read our fieldnotes to each other, listing points of interest— commonalities, differences—in a log, initiating a process we were to use over and over: using one set of data (fieldnotes) to generate another (a log book with emerging themes).

Six weeks into the study, we felt it was time to review notes, to synthesize, to step back and see what patterns had begun to emerge from our data. We knew no better way of doing this than to write. We did not, however, want to produce "analytic memos," the traditional ethnographic term for this type of writing, for we felt it was too early to set ourselves up as "analysts" of other teachers' teaching. Instead, we coined a term to fit our sense of what we were doing: we wrote "thinking-aloud memos," which represented our thoughts and perceptions in response to the question, "What have I learned about this teacher, this class, so far?"

In the midst of writing, we stopped short. We were just beginning to know these teachers' classrooms, but the teachers themselves had known them for years. So we set in motion another process that was to continue for the next three years: while we were writing, we asked the teachers, too, to write and join us in examining their teaching, this first time in response to the question "What are my implicit assumptions about teaching?" or "Why do I do what I do?" Then, in the study group, we met to explore, to construct together, from their papers and our memos, a shared view of the classrooms we were now all inhabiting.

In addition to answering particular questions of ours, the teachers were busy writing about their own concerns in teaching. They kept teaching journals in which they recorded their perceptions of classroom events, of their students, and their thoughts about teaching. They conducted case studies of students in their classes. Some revised these case studies for publication in professional journals; others wrote and revised articles on other aspects of classroom life. They wrote about their reactions to research in the field. They wrote about their reactions to having us in their classrooms. And we wrote back to them.

Over the course of the first year, our writing and theirs changed both in tone and scope. Our "thinking aloud memos" became longer and more complex. From two- to six-page reports on what teachers said and did, they became more thoughtful analyses, some of them thirty or forty pages long, of what teachers' behavior meant. We began to ask questions, to identify areas we didn't feel comfortable about, to probe. And, with each new round of writing, we included more. We wrote first of our perceptions, sprinkled with direct quotes from the teachers. Then we began to include excerpts from the teachers' journals. By spring, we quoted student writing as well. We kept widening our frame of reference, attempting to explore a broader range of issues from a more varied set of perspectives. We often likened memo writing to panning for gold—dipping the pan into the water, shifting and shaking until something appeared, saving what was useful, discarding what wasn't, and dipping back into the source, over and over again.

As the school year wore on and the teachers began to trust us, to see us not as "university researchers" or "classroom evaluators" but as fellow inquirers, their writing changed, too. In the early journals, we researchers appeared as outsiders looking in: "Sondra visited Social Studies B today . . ." "Nancy sat with Dave's group. She reported that . . ." Within a few months, however, in some cases almost immediately, "she" gave way to "you": "Did you notice . . . ?" "I've been meaning to ask you . . ." As the journals passed back and forth, and we began, gradually, to form partnerships in the classrooms, our replies, written in the margins or on sheets of paper stuck between pages, became part of the dialogue, and the journal entries themselves began to sound like letters. Len noted the shift: "I notice I have started writing this to you, Nancy, and at the beginning of the year I was writing it to myself."

The study group itself became an extended partnership. As researchers, we saw our task as different from the teachers', but we did not see ourselves as "knowing more" than they did. In fact, when it came to understanding their classrooms, we thought that the teachers "knew more" than we did, but often without knowing that they knew it. Our job was to tap their implicit knowledge, to work with them to make it explicit. To accomplish this, we needed to check our perceptions, again and again, against theirs. Memos, comments in journals, chats over coffee, and discussions in the study group—all became ways for each of us to ask each teacher we studied, "Am I seeing your classroom the way you see it yourself? Does my view match yours? If so, what can we add to it? If not, why not?"

Writing back and forth in the journals, circulating fieldnotes and memos, studying the data together, we were forging a research team. Our choice to include the teachers so fully was deliberate. We were doing ethnography not on a faraway island but in Shoreham-Wading River, close to home; we were studying not members of a culture strange to us but teachers like ourselves. We could not imagine behaving like traditional researchers, keeping our theories and interpretations to ourselves until the publication of a final report. We felt accountable to the teachers we studied. We thought they had a right to know what we were thinking as we sat in their classrooms. And we knew that, although at times it would have been easier for us to remain silent, had we done so we would have been giving up one of the most valuable aspects of our collaboration: the dialogue that would enable us to arrive at a common understanding of the classrooms, an understanding that would make sense not only to us but also to the teachers.

As the weeks passed, and then the months, our understanding of each classroom grew, and balances shifted. We researchers found ourselves spending more time in some rooms than in others, forming closer ties to some teachers than to others. In some classrooms, we remained primarily observers; in others, more and more, we became participants.

Sondra was most comfortable and most deeply immersed in Diane's classroom, Nancy most at home in Audre's. Was this a problem? we asked ourselves in research meetings. Should we be dividing our time more equally? Or should we let ourselves be drawn to these particular teachers by affinities we could not yet explain?

Deciding, eventually, that each of us would learn more by studying one classroom and one teacher deeply than by studying three or four classrooms superficially, we let our inclinations guide us. But always, we examined them. Why these pairs? we asked ourselves. What shared beliefs or sympathies have formed these partnerships? And since in ethnography the ethnographer is the primary research tool, we took notes on our answers. We couldn't and didn't try to leave ourselves behind when we sat in classrooms, but we kept on questioning and testing our biases to try to understand how they influenced what we saw.

By the end of the first year of our study, we realized that we had begun to put down roots in Shoreham and Wading River. We found ourselves sitting in the sun at softball games, making plans to attend school graduations, handing out our addresses to seniors who were graduating or second graders who wanted to send us postcards. We spent hours in front of the district's copying machines, duplicating teachers' journals and students' writing. Preparing to return to the city, we collected audiotapes and videotapes, interview notes, fieldnote books, and our own personal journals. As we loaded boxes of data into our cars, we wondered how we'd make sense of it all. What stories would emerge as important? And how would we ever compress the experiences of a year into the space of a single book?

Sorting It Out

During the second and third years of our study, the balances shifted again. Our visits became shorter. Roughly every other week during the second year and once a month during the third, for several days at a time, we visited the teachers in their classrooms. We looked forward to these visits. They allowed us to keep ourselves fresh, to keep looking, to follow leads, hunches, and even students from previous years. Often we were able to switch our focus and observe teachers we hadn't spent much time with in the first year.

Changes took place as well in the composition of the research team. After the first year, three teachers left the project, one to take a sabbatical and two to pursue other interests. The other interests were real enough; still, we thought it probably not accidental that the teachers who left were those whose classrooms we had visited the least often and who, therefore, may have felt that they were getting the least return on enormous investments of time and energy.

During the second year of the study, we researchers also faced some read-justments. James Carter realized that he would need to return to his full-time teaching job at the end of the year. Since Jamie would not be available to join us in collecting and examining the data during the third and fourth years, each of us took on the added responsibility of writing up one of the elementary school teachers he had studied.

We had, of course, spent time in the elementary school classrooms before Jamie left, but we had not given them the kind of time and attention we had given the middle school and high school classrooms. Now, in the time remaining to us, we were determined to absorb as much as we could, to learn from our own visits to their homes and their classrooms as much as possible about the elementary school teachers and their teaching. And so, in the second and third years of the study, we experimented with different forms of collaboration. Different kinds of partnerships emerged—less intense, but in their own ways rewarding.

We explored these partnerships in the classrooms and in our ongoing study-group meetings. The study group was smaller now—with only three elementary school teachers, two middle school teachers, and two high school teachers—and met less frequently. But as the time between our visits lengthened, the meetings became increasingly important. They were our link to the teachers, our way to reconnect, to discover what changes were taking place in their thinking, to let them in on the changes that were taking place in ours.

Away from the district, back in our office at Lehman College, data analysis began to take precedence over data collection. We sifted through the masses of notes and notebooks and folders and wrote to make sense of what we found in them. We organized the data in different ways: by sequences of events, by themes, by principles of the writing process approach. We wrote long narrative accounts of classroom events and short impressionistic "portraits" of teachers. We wrote theoretical analyses illustrated by anecdotes from classrooms. And always, as we had from the beginning, we told each other stories. "You've got to hear what happened in class today!" one of us would say. "Just listen to this. . . ."

We were bursting with stories. We told them in classrooms and at research meetings, in the study group and at conferences, to friends, husbands, and casual acquaintances. Our "findings," we realized, came encased in stories; our theories were expressed in them. In the end, we decided to write our research as a story.

The Story

We could not record it all. Years later, our fieldnotes—and our memories—are filled to overflowing with pictures of daily life in Shoreham-Wading River classrooms, too many to fit into this or any book.

Behind what you read lie the countless stories of students' lives: the braces going on in eighth grade and coming off in tenth, the friendships forming and reforming, the Junior Prom, the Senior Trip, the romance that, for a while, is more important to the students involved in it than anything that happens in class. Behind what you read lie the unpredictable upheavals of classroom life: the day the heat failed in the high school, and Audre and her students wrote valiantly on, in coats and mittens; the day an eighth grader cried when she discovered that her process journal was missing, and Diane interrupted class to comfort her; the day Bill's fourth and fifth graders brought their batik pillows back from art class, and writing took place amid explosions of blue and purple. And behind what you read lie the innumerable small distractions of a normal school day: the fire drill, the birthday party, the maintenance worker hammering the radiator pipes in the middle of writing group time.

We could not include more than a fraction of this richness of detail nor could we offer more than a glimpse of the human story behind our research: the gradual process by which "ethnographers" and "informants" became partners, became friends. Yet these stories, too, weave their way into our portraits of teachers at work. We lived in classrooms with these teachers and these students. Their stories are our stories, too.

Teachers Teaching

Chapter 2

Audre Allison
Eleventh Grade

In September 1981, on the first day of classes in Shoreham-Wading River High School, Audre Allison brought doughnuts and milk for the students in her housegroup. Everyone ate and drank—except me. I was too busy taking notes. I kept my head down, eyes on my notebook; I was afraid if I stopped writing I would miss something important.

I was desperate, trying to capture everything before it got away: the room, the students, Audre, what everyone said (verbatim of course), how they moved, what they were wearing, where they sat—everything. How could I catch it all? My muscles tensed; I frowned in concentration. By the end of the day I had a blister on the middle finger of my writing hand.

Audre was disconcerted. My fierce concentration on my notes was more than she had bargained for. She had known, of course, that I would take notes but had hoped, too, that I would be available for support if not practical help during what was to be, at best, a year of questions for her. There had been a departmental reshuffling since she had first agreed to participate in our study, and Audre, an experienced teacher of ninth-grade English, found herself this year teaching eleventh grade for the first time.

A new curriculum, new possibilities, new problems to be solved. She was willing to experiment, flounder, find her way through trial and error, as she always had, but she didn't know how it would feel to do it under the eyes of a researcher. At the end of a day full of minor crises—the wrong classroom furniture delivered, too many students in one class and too few in another, a rescheduling that upset her plans to team with another teacher—she listed frustrations in her journal, ending with, "—and Nancy writes furiously through it all!"

So I put away my notebook, from time to time at least. I began to make peace with the notion that, even if I wrote constantly through every class the whole year, I could not possibly catch everything. Whatever I wrote, the record would be incomplete, limited to what one fallible human being could observe through her own perspective; that was both the weakness of our method and its strength. For once I looked up from my notebook, I began to notice what only a human being notices: shifts in the mood and temper of a class, undercurrents between students, the atmosphere of the room. I went on taking notes but looked up more often to talk to students or to join a class discussion. Once Audre and I taught a class together; often I sat in on writing groups. Sometimes, involved in the work of a group, I couldn't take notes; sometimes, in the excitement of a discussion, I forgot to.

As the year wore on, the line between teacher and researcher blurred; sometimes it seemed to disappear. When students came to talk to Audre between classes, they often talked to me as well. The kids I came to know best began to see me as Audre's colleague, a teacher as well as a researcher; I thought of some of them, increasingly, as "my" students as well as Audre's.

My coffee cup joined Audre's amid the clutter of her desk; we talked for hours on end. We discovered shared ideas and shared passions. We compared ideas about teaching, about learning. We saw students the same way. We never got tired of talking about them.

I wondered, sometimes, if my growing closeness to Audre would prevent me from seeing her classroom clearly. I thought, at times, it might. But, for the most part, the gains from this closeness seemed to outweigh the losses. If I had lost the advantages of distance, of coolness, and of skepticism, I had gained the advantage of empathy.

Teaching Writing

Audre's classroom was high and sunny, with windows overlooking a pond, a parking lot, playing fields, pine trees up close around the school, pine woods in the distance. Its furniture was movable and often moved; its walls were lined with the comfortable clutter of classroom life: files stuffed with papers, bookshelves spilling over with books, blackboards temporarily obscured by displays of students' writing, a desk piled high with folders of more students' writing and more papers and more books. On a blackboard near the ceiling, where they would not be erased, stood the words of published writers: from Sidney Cox, "Write what you care about. Care about what you write." From Archibald MacLeish, "We have the answers, all the answers; it is the question that we do not have."

At 7:55 A.M. on the first day of school, Audre sent her housegroup students on their separate ways and arranged the room's seven tables into an open rectangle for her first-period class. By 8 A.M., the students had arrived: twenty-four eleventh graders, many in gleaming new sneakers, excitedly exchanging news about the summer and gathering at the windows to point out new cars in the parking lot. Audre greeted by name those who had been in her ninth-grade classes two years before and introduced herself to others. Then, after a brief introduction to the year's work and courteous (but very brief) answers to the inevitable questions about PSATs, RCTs and Regents (standardized tests taken in eleventh grade), she turned her attention to writing.

"We'll be doing a lot of writing this year," she said, "and writing *about* writing. Let's start by writing for a few minutes—five or ten—about why writing is important. Or maybe you think it isn't important, so write about that—why it isn't. Write freely as many thoughts as you can get down. You've been writers for a number of years now; I'm sure you have a lot to say about this. I won't ask you to hand it in, but I will ask you to share. . . . Spread out, get comfortable." She moved away from the rectangle of tables, to a small desk at the side of the room, explaining, as she pushed her chair back, "I find it hard to write when I'm sitting too close to other people." She picked up her pen and began to write. A few students joined her. Then a few more. By 8:25, all twenty-four were writing.

After ten minutes or so of quiet concentration, students began to look up, move around, talk to one another. Audre stopped writing.

"Who'd like to read what you've written?" she asked, taking her place again among her students; then, when no one volunteered, "Well—I'll read, even though I didn't get to write very much." She read haltingly, stumbling over words and apologizing for the inadequacies of her sentences.

" 'Writing is important for many reasons,' " she read, and then stopped. "But then I didn't like that," she continued, "so I crossed it out. 'The . . . ,' but I didn't like that either . . . 'The magic of writing intrigues me—watching a pen scrambling across a page casting gems along the way'—I wrote 'dropping' first, then changed it to 'casting'—'watching a pen scrambling across a page casting gems along the way is a mysterious phenomenon. How does it happen? Where does it come from and how do we dredge it up?' It's not really on the subject," she commented, "but that's what came out."

A few students read what they had written, the bell rang, and the first class of the year was over.

That night, in her journal, Audre reported, "Wonderful day—All write."

Audre Writing • Writing, for Audre, comes first, last, and in between. It is central to her life—and not only in the classroom.

In the middle of the second year of our study, in a note written to explain a gap between entries in her teaching journal, she described a busy season. She'd been in Mississippi over vacation, she explained, enjoying and taking care of her new granddaughter while her daughter studied for law school exams. Another of her four grown children wanted help finding an apartment. Another was having job problems. Her own mother had been ill. A friend had needed support in getting through a crisis. Her husband, a jazz musician, had just come back from a tour; she'd missed him and wanted to spend some time with him. And then, in addition to reading and commenting on her students' reading logs, writing journals, essays; in addition to planning classes, meeting with committees on the writing center, the poetry festival, the newspaper, peer counseling, she'd had other writing to do.

"I had to begin writing about issues important to me," she wrote:

> —my mother and what is coming—my self—my soul—I wrote two poems— mailed them to two ailing aunts . . . I have lists and lists of writing that ought to be done—but manage only letters to all my children, my mother, my aunts, my sister, my mother-in-law, my sister-in-law, former students, friends, etc., my private personal journal, . . . assignments with my students—and the two poems.

I smiled when I read her "only."

Writing, for Audre, is part of family life, of friendship, of learning, of everything that matters. It is for her at the core of a fully lived life. Her days are packed, sometimes to bursting, but whatever else is happening she goes on writing.

"Writing surprises me," she wrote in her journal,

> —sometimes disappoints me—but often clarifies what I'm thinking and it's as if I'm tracing over my thoughts that are already laid out ahead of my pen, like spreading a secret solution on invisible ink—this message appears—that "aha" moment. . . .
>
> Writing is so powerful—that once you know what it does for you—you will not let it go.

Writing, to Audre, is "useful" and "pleasurable." In her journal and in conversation, she compares it to playing jazz and walking on the beach, to cooking, to dancing, to riding a bicycle. Being in a writing group, she told me one day, was like "assisting at a birth."

As a teacher, she wants for her students what she treasures herself:

> I want kids to know the joy of writing—to know that it is something they can do for themselves, that real writing is a way of knowing themselves and their world—the power of writing for sheer pleasure and for energetic purpose.

Teaching English has always been, for her, a search for answers to one basic question: "How can I help my students discover this joy—this power?"

The year I joined her class, however, the change from ninth to eleventh grade forced her to reexamine her priorities in teaching. As a ninth-grade teacher, she had taught a course centered on writing. She had had questions, of course: How could she help students to respond better to one another's writing? And, always, "How can I lead—no, not lead—invite? encourage? aid?—students to make their own discoveries?" But, on the whole, she had been comfortable with her curriculum. Teaching English as a writing course suited her, matched her theories about writing, reading, and learning, and fit her personality and teaching style.

What she had learned in the 1979 Writing Project summer institute had confirmed what she already believed and extended what she knew. She had returned to her classroom that year with renewed enthusiasm for the teaching of writing and had continued to write and study writing with her students. Literature in her ninth-grade classes had been an enjoyable adjunct to the main writing curriculum, test preparation not something she needed to worry about.

Studying the eleventh-grade curriculum guide she inherited in 1981, however, she began to feel uncomfortable. The guide promised students, in literature, "a significant emphasis on literary analysis and interpretation," in writing, a concentration on "literature essays and shorter selections similar to those in Part II and Part III of the Regents exam," and, throughout the year, "considerable preparation . . . for major exams." The concerns addressed by the guide seemed far removed from her own concerns in teaching writing. Yet, given the pervasiveness of testing in eleventh grade, she wasn't sure she could dismiss them. In fact, given the circumstances, the approach outlined by the guide sounded reasonable— might even be useful to students. But could she live with it herself? Did she want to?

These questions forced her to look again at what she was doing, to ask herself all year what she believed was most important in the teaching of English and, once she had identified her beliefs, what teaching methods might best express them.

Writing in Class   •   Beginnings are important to Audre. As a writer, she loves the early stages of the writing process: the search for a spark, a discovery, an "aha!" moment. As a teacher, she reserves great chunks of class time for exploratory writing. When students are beginning new pieces, she acts as a guide to unexplored territory, often asking questions as the writing begins and joining in the search for topics. She speaks at such times of "stoking the furnace," "priming the pumps," "getting the mechanism going."

Sometimes she starts a writing sequence by reading from the works of published writers: a poem by Nikki Giovanni, for example, passages from Richard Wright's autobiography, or part of a memoir by John Updike, to help students recall and write about their own memories. More often she starts with questions.

On a Tuesday in November, she pulled seven rectangular tables into a large open square and gathered her students around it. "We're going to write in class today," she said.

The day before, she and her students had discussed passages from Edgar Allan Poe, Stephen Vincent Benét, and William O. Douglas, each describing a place of significance to the author, and had written one-sentence descriptions of places they knew themselves.

"What I want you to do now," Audre continued, "is to think about a place

... a place that has some significance to you ... that you can write about in your own real voice. Take out a piece of paper." She took out one of her own. "Find a comfortable place to work ... relax ... close your eyes. I'm going to take you on a guided tour of your place. We're going to try to loosen up, to see things from a different angle. This will be a prewriting session. I expect you to explore—really stretch out—find a fresh way of looking at something. We're looking for something that strikes a spark."

She took out a sheet of questions adapted from a set in Peter Elbow's *Writing with Power*.[1] "You can listen to me ... or drop in and out. I'm going to drone on. You can take notes. ... I want to see everyone writing. Right now, though, close your eyes. No one will get you, John. Close your eyes so that you can see this other place. In your minds, go to this place. Look around and see everything, everything that's there. Look up, look down, look very carefully. See and feel the time of day. What time of year is it? Winter? Take a deep breath and feel the quality of the air. What do you smell? You can start writing ...

"Now listen. What do you hear in this place? Listen very carefully. Is it a loud noise you hear, or are you listening to silence? Stay there for a while. How is your mood affected by being there? Now—here comes someone. Who is it? Who do you see there?

"What weather seems *just right* for this place? What mode of transportation ... a rocket? horse and buggy? scooter? ... Imagine that your body is the world. ... Where on your body is this place located? Now imagine you're someone who thinks this place is absolutely beautiful. Describe it. Now someone who thinks this place is ugly. How would you describe it? Someone who thinks it's boring. Just continue writing. ...."

Aside from a few snickers at "smell" and "body," the students were quiet, listening and writing. After a while, Audre let her voice trail off and picked up her own pen. Soon everyone was writing.

Shawn sat with his back to the room, feet up on the windowsill, notebook on his knees. Laura bent over her notebook, covering the page with her arm. Sandra sat upright and still, her back straight, only her pen moving as she wrote. Tom and Emil sprawled on the floor. Matt moved out into the hall. Audre, her sleeves pushed up and reading glasses in place, frowned over her own page at her favorite back table.

A murmur of conversation began in one corner, and Audre, distracted, looked up to say, "Let's quiet down so that I can write." The murmur subsided. The silence was broken only by an occasional sigh or a shifting of position, the ripping of paper, or the tapping of chalk on the blackboard of the classroom next door.

Halfway into the forty-five-minute period, Audre looked up. She had meant to stop the writing after about twenty minutes to bring her students together

---

[1] New York: Oxford University Press, 1981.

for a discussion of their writing processes; but, seeing the heads down, the pens moving, feeling the concentration in the room, she scrapped her plan. She returned to her own writing. "Since they were furiously writing ... completely engrossed," she reported later in her journal, "I didn't stop them until about five minutes before the end of the period."

> I hope all the concentrated writing is an indication that they were able to get something going that pleased them. Tom wrote for the whole period—Tom who usually chats nonstop. Third period did as well. It is a most wonderful feeling to be in a classroom with 24 brains clicking and pens and pencils moving nonstop—furiously across a sheet of paper—electrifying.

When Audre finally asked everyone to stop writing, students sighed, stretched, shook out their hands. As change-of-period noise swelled in the hall outside, they gathered their books together slowly, still partly under the spell of their own writing, reluctant to break it.

Cumhur, a recently arrived exchange student from Turkey, looked dazed. Lingering after class, he told Audre and me that he had had to pull himself back from far away. He'd been writing about his grandparents, he said, and about their village on the Black Sea. "There is so much to write in my mind. ... I could write for hours and hours. When the bell was ringing, I didn't want to stop."

Writing at the Core • Teachers often return to and remember with pleasure certain moments of teaching—talismans—to remind them on lackluster days of what they are aiming for: the moment a particular student made an important breakthrough, the day an unresponsive class came to life, a class in which, for a brief moment, everything clicked, and the air hummed with students' and teacher's shared purpose. I saw such moments in Audre's classroom when students and teacher were writing together. When Audre wrote with her students, joining them in the circle of tables, struggling alongside them to form a piece— "with us not above us," as Sue, a student, once put it—she seemed to me to be most herself; in her own words, "real, honest, a person, a writer in a class of writers." And, at these moments, the writing seemed to take over, the sense of it almost palpable in the room.

On the day in November described above, I too was caught up in the mood that swept the room. As Audre's prewriting questions set first one, then another, then the whole room full of students writing, I found my own thoughts drawing inward, toward memories of my own. I found a fresh page in my notebook and began to write—not fieldnotes but the beginning of a "place" piece. The air of discovery was contagious. I, the observer, became a participant; Audre, the teacher, stood back to let the mood ripen.

Audre's decision to postpone the next step, in the face of her students' absorption in their writing, was for me the pivotal moment of that class. When students wrote—when "the air was charged," as she described it, with the force of their thinking and discovering—all else, for Audre, fell away. Plans, schedules, class business, her own preoccupations, all could wait, all were pushed aside to make room for those moments she called "electrifying." "I love seeing everyone writing," she wrote in her journal. "It's always the best time."

Training Responders • Exploratory writing, however, is not usually an end in itself. Usually, although not always, it leads to "composed" drafts and then to revision, and revision presents different challenges. Audre, who often left pieces of her own unfinished, was well aware of them. "Searching for a topic expects and accepts wild forays into new territory and can be done with courageous gusto," she wrote as work continued on a new piece, "but revision is done with a critical eye. . . . The chore is more concrete, but the writer is more vulnerable." Writers in the process of revising, she believed, needed time, space, and, especially, support from their peers. As the work of writing groups got under way, she saw herself in class as "a trainer of responders."

"Revision is hard work," she told her students, "but it's exciting, too. It's where the *real* writing comes in, where you make the choices. Where you ask yourself questions, like, 'What if I didn't start, "The person I'm going to write about is . . ." What if I just started right in?' Or, 'Is this where I want to stop?' Or, 'Will this form help me say what I want to say?' When you revise, I want you to think, not just of cosmetic changes—a little powder and lipstick—but really take it around the track. That's where your group can help you—not to evaluate the writing but to help you decide what you want to do with it."

Before turning the class over to groups, she summarized the "Steps for Responding" she had learned in the summer institute (see Appendix B), emphasizing "sayback" and how important it is that the writer remain in charge. "Responders can tell you what they hear," she said, "and that can help, but *you are the owner of your own writing.* You can ask for and get advice, but it's up to you to decide whether you'll take it or not."

In the beginning of the year, groups took shape slowly, forming and reforming until most students had found congenial writing partners. In October, sitting in on groups as they discussed memory pieces, Audre thought she saw signs of live voices emerging in some of the writing and supportive responses from some members of writing groups. Her students weren't so sure.

Cumhur, following a train of thought suggested to him by an Updike passage Audre had read in class, had written a piece similar in theme to Updike's:

> I first saw her on the bus which takes us to school every day. She is a beautiful girl. Here I can't find any word to describe her beauty. She has blue eyes. But a different blue with green. . . . Every day as I enter the bus I see her sitting quietly on the first or on the second chair. I think for a while to sit beside her and talk. Then I hesitate. She might not talk to me. I say to myself that I don't want to use my chance quickly. I'll wait for tomorrow. Then I dream of how I can meet her. . . .

Dave was impressed by the honesty of the piece. "It's good," he told Cumhur. "You wrote about your real feelings. We all have those feelings, but most people don't write about them." Cumhur was pleased by Dave's response but wondered if he shouldn't be getting more advice. "My group liked my piece," he told Audre. "They helped me with punctuations and paragraphs. But they didn't find solutions to all my problems."

Audre smiled. "A group can't always find solutions, but it can help you, the writer, deal with problems."

Sandra, too, was looking for more direction from her group. She said group members had listened and done "sayback" well but "didn't look at the writing in depth." And, in fact, members of her group seemed to be at a loss as to how to respond to Sandra's writing. Faced, for example, with a first draft for an editorial that contained lines such as, "[T]he author is blatantly caustic" and "[T]he proclamations and generalizations take unfounded liberties in what is clearly undaunted prejudice, condemnation and stern pessimism," they found little to say other than, "It's good."

"Sandra's writing sounds so intelligent," they reported to Audre. "She uses all these big words. You don't know what to say about it." But Sandra herself wanted help, especially in dealing with an abundance of newly acquired vocabulary, swallowed whole and only partly digested. "I know I need to cut," she told Audre, "but I don't know where. I need someone to say, 'That word's got to go.' My group isn't doing that."

"Try asking them, specifically, about words you're not sure of," Audre suggested. She agreed to meet with Sandra between classes but cautioned, "I'll listen as you read the piece, of course, and give you my honest reactions, and if you like, I'll tell you which sentences put a strain on me as a reader, but I can't tell you what words to change."

"Sandra wants answers," she wrote in her journal, "—wants me to tell her what to do. I want to show her she can do it herself. I've never understood teachers who say, 'Cut out all that garbage.' It takes the learning away from the student."

In class the next day, Audre pulled up a chair to join another group, noting that its members were facing in slightly different directions. Walter was reading his piece, but Tom, Emil, and Matt were looking at their own papers or across the room, not at Walter. Audre, looking severe, interrupted the reading. "If you are talking, and I turn like this"—turning her back on the group—"what am I saying?" She added, "Show Walter you're interested. Give him some *help*."

Walter continued reading about the furnishings of his friend's "typical college room":

... The refrigerator that can have almost anything in it, from beer to last night's dinner. A stereo in the corner that didn't have a speck of dust on it. A desk that resembled a junkpile of papers, books, pencils and old coffee cups, that had probably been there for days, and a small desk lamp. ...

Matt said, "Sounds as if you're attracted to the free spirit of college life," and Walter nodded, adding, "I was there over vacation. I liked it." Tom asked,

"What kind of music might be playing? Do you want to add something about that?" and Walter answered, "Maybe." Emil suggested, "Instead of 'beer' and 'old food' in the icebox, what about 'a sixpack of Lowenbrau and a slice of old steak'?" Walter said he'd consider it, and Audre commented approvingly that Matt had identified the mood of the piece, and Tom and Emil had taken a "what if" approach. "You didn't say that Walter 'should' do such-and-such; that would make you the dictator of the piece. You asked questions so that Walter can decide himself what he wants to do."

Members of the next group Audre visited had stopped working and were sitting in silence, notebooks closed. Linda reported angrily, "My group put my story down. They should have consideration for people's feelings . . ." and then she retreated, "Just kidding." Members of the group chimed in: "We didn't put it down; we just gave advice. We told her it was confusing." Audre asked, "Did you tell her *it* was confusing, or *you* were confused? There's a difference. People's honest reactions can be helpful. If you tell Linda you were confused, she might clarify for you. But evaluations like, 'It's confusing' usually aren't helpful." Dennis protested, "People should tell you what's wrong," and Audre replied, "No, I'm convinced negative criticism is bad."

The group discussed this issue. Dennis maintained, "You should put your feelings out of the way; the group is supposed to be helping you," to which Audre replied, "Do you think you can do that? Put your feelings out of the way?" Dennis said, "Yes," but others disagreed. Audre turned back to Linda. "Do you think you know what to do with your story now?" "Yeah," said Linda, "I'll write a different story. I thought it was pretty stupid anyway."

"By the end of the day—I feel depressed," Audre wrote in her journal.

> As they report on their groups and how they worked, they seem to be saying, "Yes, it worked: they told me what I did *wrong*" . . . "They told me how I *should fix it*." . . . Over and over we go—the responder does not evaluate— the writer owns his/her own writing—over and over what that means. Why it's important. . . .
> Some seem embarrassed . . . unsure of themselves as writers—afraid someone will make a judgment about what they've written. We'll talk about that. How can we trust one another? How we must be able to trust.

As groups continued to meet, Audre brooded in her journal about those students who had

> not yet experienced the good feeling that comes with discovering that you've said something genuine and clear and said it in your own voice. . . . Kids who are unsure—have no voice, are searching for what others want and are con- fused because they seem to hear different things—are not listening to self—so can't possibly deal with trusting self. *Must establish belief in own voice*—that it is there and will emerge if the teacher leaves it alone . . .

One day during writing group time, Emil tilted his chair back until it fell over. Tim threw crumpled pages across the room, hitting and missing the wastebasket. Dawn, playing "a joke," she said, wrote "stupid," "boring," "puts me to sleep" in the margins of Eve's piece. Tina examined her purple fingernails, Kathy did her math homework, no one in George's group had brought a piece to read.

"I feel as if I've been hauling hod today," Audre wrote in her journal and reminded herself that "everyone can write." She looked more closely at those who thought they couldn't. "Linda just wants to get through the pain. Dennis just wants to get out of school and never have to write again. ...."

> It seems that we've spent years turning the writing process into an ordeal, one that came to be, for professionals, a truly solitary gamble, an endeavor only the bravest and most confident would set about—and who would be arrogant enough to say, "I'm a writer." Yet when we look back in time, we find magnificent letters from ordinary people. ...

More modeling, she hoped, would help. She went on circulating from group to group, "an available tool," as Sue once described her, trying to be of use to students as they found ways of being useful to one another.

As students gained skill at "sayback" and questioning, the "shoulds" began to disappear.

In January, Lynne read a piece about her parents:

> ... When you are thirteen you look at your parents as though they are villains. I know that I always thought my parents yelled at me for no reason, in my mind they were evil for keeping me blocked away from the outside world.
> But now I would like to thank them ... Everything that I had resented; not being able to go to parties, no teen rec, no car dates, I now appreciate ...

No one jumped on Lynne or told her her piece "didn't have enough detail" or "wasn't clear enough." Instead, Sue said, in an inquiring tone, "You felt bitter toward your parents," and Lynne, smiling and nodding, began to fill in the outline she had sketched. "Yes, I thought my father hated me. In the sixth grade I didn't want my friends to know my father wouldn't let me go to Teen Rec. I was embarrassed. I used to invent excuses so they wouldn't know. I thought my life was over." Sue, Cumhur, Laura, Sandra, and Dave laughed in sympathy. "Yeah, your life was over—in sixth grade!" In response to questions: What excuses did you invent? What happened then? How did you feel? Lynne scribbled notes for revision in the margins of her draft. "I was writing too fast to think of details," she said of this first effort. "I wanted to get the ideas down first. Now I'll go back and add the details."

" 'Sayback' helps you remember," members of this group agreed. "You go, 'Yeah, yeah, and besides that, there was this other thing. ...' "

Sandra had brought fragments of her exploratory writing to read to the group, as well as the piece about her grandmother that was beginning to emerge from the fragments:

> Dark windows let in streaks.
> Cane clutched well in a wrinkled hand with the vestiges of beauty. She is

wise, tall, stark. She is old and I am impatient. I am young and she is all of
it. The sun continues to shine.

The rays shone in the narrow windows ... She was magnificent, a face
showing the years yet alluding to the youth that once was and the wisdom that
had accrued. ...

I touched the bottom of her dress and looked up towards her face. It was
dim yet highlighted by the fresh rays ...

After an initial hesitation, Cumhur responded, "There is much love in the
story," and Dave agreed, "It's full of emotion." Sue said, "You mention the sun
a lot—again and again. Did you do that deliberately or didn't you notice?" and
Sandra, who had begun to take pride in making her own decisions, answered
firmly, "I meant to do it. I wanted the sun, the light, to be a theme." She made
notes on how to highlight this theme, to make it central in later drafts. "Maybe
I'll start, 'Rays of sun pierced through the narrow windows. ...'"

Some students still protested: too many group meetings, too much revision.
"It's boring to revise," said Emil. "I revised my piece about six times. I practically
memorized it. It got better every time, but it was still boring to do it."

Others, like Dennis, still refused to make changes in their first drafts. "So
many poor writers treat their writing as fragile," Audre wrote in her journal,

—afraid to handle it boldly—afraid it might vanish and never appear again—
That's not hard to understand. But if we could help that writer—those writers—to find the joy in building something slowly—that stands with substance—that would be splendid.

Unlike Dennis, however, many found that revision, supported by group work,
opened new possibilities to them. They added to their drafts, moved sections
from one place to another, threw out parts "that didn't fit." And Audre continued
to move among the groups, gently turning students' questions back to them,
helping them to locate their own answers. "What do you want me to write?" a
student asked, and Audre countered, "What do *you* want to write?" "How long
should it be?" "As long as it takes you to say what you want to say." And the
students followed her lead.

"You should ..." Dave began one day, but stopped himself. "No, I can't tell
you what you should do. But maybe you might. ..."

Group members are there, said Walter, "to draw the piece out of the person."

Students told each other what they heard in pieces and asked questions.
"Asking questions can make the writer understand and perhaps talk out the
intent of the piece," wrote Sue. "Ask questions ... be honest, if you can't
understand say so, say what you think but understand—you aren't in charge."

And Sandra, describing the effect of group work on her writing process,
wrote, "My group helps me define my message. It forces me to ask myself
questions and to discover things that would otherwise have passed me by ...
to make my own decisions about my writing ... to understand why I want it
that way."

Reflecting on the Writing Process • If writing produces texts to think about and change, it also produces experiences to reflect on. From time to time, as students took their pieces through exploration, drafting, revision, editing, and (sometimes) publication, the whole class gathered together to compare notes on the process of writing.

The day after starting "place" pieces, for instance, Audre asked her students to discuss how they had used the questions she had read while they were writing. "Did they help you find something to write? Did they get in your way? What did you do with them?"

"I stopped listening after the first few sentences," said Laura. "I'm on the tech crew for the play. I thought about being in the light booth, and I just wrote."

Cumhur said he, too, had stopped listening almost immediately. "One of the questions, it remembered me of something. . . . I flew away."

Dave reported that he hadn't written at all to start with. "A picture came into my mind, and I tried to draw it first. It was the lake at Lutheran Youth Camp. When Ms. Allison asked, 'Where is the light coming from?' I thought, 'The light is from the faces.' I saw my friends' faces clearly in my mind. I made a list of their names on the side of the drawing, and then I began to write. It's mainly impressions still—not really a piece. I've put in the trail markers, but there's no trail yet."

Debbie said she'd gotten stuck. "I didn't like what I wrote in class. When I got home, I decided to write something else. But when I put my pen to the paper, my mind just went blank."

And Audre said, "I had trouble too. I couldn't concentrate in class while I was reading the questions—had too many different things on my mind. I went all over the place, wearing myself out. At the end of the day, all I had was this crazy-looking list." She held up the list. "I was worried about not having a piece to bring to class today."

Dennis, incredulous, asked, "You worry about *that?*" and Audre answered, "Oh yes . . . I woke up at 4 A.M. worrying about it. I started thinking about Hilton Head—a place I like a lot, that always makes me feel good—and I realized I had a poem. . . . jumped out of bed and wrote the first draft—for my pleasure of course—then a second. It made me feel good to write it."

Kim said the questions had helped her find what she wanted to say about the beach. She'd written a process note about the experience of writing in class:

> As we continued to write, Ms. Allison read things aloud. It gave me ideas and
> lots of ideas. I described it so well, I thought I never could. I loved the piece.
> I couldn't believe that I wrote it myself.

Audre and her students spent a lot of time talking shop—writers' shop. They compared notes on how and where they liked to write, how they made decisions, and how they felt about their writing. They swapped stories.

"We had a lot of fun comparing craziness," Audre wrote in her journal after a particularly freewheeling discussion:

> It is amazing how discussing process stirs excitement—I guess there is always excitement in finding out about ourselves—Sue said it: "Talking about your writing process is talking about yourself; everybody likes to do that."

Audre describes her own writing process as "messy," "idiosyncratic," "unpredictable," "volcanic." She shared it with students all year, both as she wrote in class, and when she reported in class on those parts of her life as a writer she pursued at home.

Early in the year, she brought an old process journal to class, choosing to read an entry which began, "I'm blank." When she brought poems to class during a poetry unit, she also brought a folder fat with drafts of one short poem she had been working on "for years." "And they're still piling up," she told the class. When a poem she read one day seemed so "finished" to students that, apparently intimidated by its polish, they seemed hesitant to comment on it, she found another, in rougher form, to share with them.

She shared, too, her worries about reading in public. Although she would stop students who prefaced their reading with "It's dumb," reminding them, "Don't evaluate yourself," she often began readings of her own work by saying, "This isn't very good." Once she said, "Mine stinks."

"The first time Ms. Allison read in class, you could see how nervous she was," Sue said later. "I figured if she could be that brave, maybe I could too."

Audre's nervousness became part of the class, freeing students to admit their own. Kris said one day she was afraid to read a poem because "people might think it's peculiar—or I'm peculiar." Others chimed in, "People might laugh . . . or snicker . . . or think it's boring . . . think it's stupid." Audre nodded. "Everyone feels that way. You remember that time I brought in that story I was working on? Remember how I said maybe you wouldn't be interested, that the subject might not be interesting to high school kids? I was protecting myself, I guess, in case you didn't like it."

When Emil wrote, in a short piece about talking to himself, "Sometimes it's a good idea to get your thoughts out without anyone *knowing about it*. . . . This way no one can criticize me," Audre wrote in her journal:

> As he continues of course it's clear that he means he *speaks* to himself in a clear and honest voice because no one is going to attack him. When he writes, readers can attack—We all know the feeling.

Audre "knew the feeling" from her own experience as a writer and shared that experience with students as she shared her flounderings and thrashings around and moments of exhilaration. Trading writing stories with her students, she reminded me sometimes of a seasoned traveler, one who has dared great adventures and survived to tell of them, sitting around the fire with other, younger adventurers, exchanging tales of narrow escapes and hard-won triumphs, gathering strength before setting out again.

Writing "for Selfish Reasons" • "Strange things happening," Audre noted in her journal toward the end of December. A number of students had begun to bring in, in addition to the writing they were doing for class, pieces written for themselves or for friends or family or teachers or others important in their lives; pieces written to express confusion, anger, love, or—sometimes—sheer exuberance. Audre described the phenomenon as "a rash of writing sweeping through my classes." It continued for the rest of the year.

Kristen, an experienced volleyball player who had recently taken up basketball, wrote an angry account of a basketball game, describing what she saw as unfair treatment of the second-string team:

> ... I had understood the situation as far as playing time was concerned, and it was okay, it didn't bother me. Although it was an unimportant scrimmage, I understood that the coach might want to have her first string to practice as much as possible. ... It's just a fact of life that the five substitutes happened to be all inexperienced people who had never played in a varsity basketball game in their life. ...
> What I can't understand is why, when there were only ten minutes of scrimmage time left, she proceeded to put the inexperienced string in, and then she left.
> The second string was lost on the court. ... When we finished, no one was around. ... We walked into the locker room, and there was the first string, laughing and eating cake. That was okay, because I'd lost my appetite by that time anyways.
> Why was I there in the first place? Am I a number? Am I needed to fill in the drills? Excuse me for misunderstanding, I had thought my job on the team was the more menial one of player. And I thought that entailed consideration and support for other players, no matter how insignificant they may be, or how little they played. I guess I was wrong. I'm sorry. I didn't understand.

Kristen's piece ran to five pages, and she revised it three times. She gave the final version to the coach, who didn't comment but did stay to watch the next time the second string played.

Glenn, a student who until December had written as little as possible, heard that his former girlfriend, Alicia, had written a short piece about the events leading to their breakup. Incensed by Alicia's account, Glenn wrote one of his own. In six pages, rewritten twice, he presented his side of the story. His piece began:

> This is my version of a personal problem between Alicia and I. I'm the one in her "biggest change" story. Alicia can see this for all I care, it's the truth not a bunch of BS like hers,

and ended, "Sounds like a Dear Abby letter, huh? I had to get this off my chest."

Glenn's friend Greg, another reluctant writer, told Audre he thought Glenn's story was "great—like a soap opera," and proceeded to write his own six-page account of what had happened between Glenn and Alicia. It began:

> It's going to be hard for me to tell about this delicate situation Glenn wrote about because at the time some of the events that he wrote about took place we weren't on speaking terms. What I will try to make clear in this paper is: what was, what is, and what will never be. . . .

Greg's piece, carefully recopied, covered six pages.

Laura, riding the Orient Point–New London ferry, noticed a scene that struck her imagination, grabbed the nearest piece of paper (which happened to be the ferry schedule), and wrote it up on the spot. Later, describing the experience, she spoke of the pleasure it gave her to write on impulse: "It wasn't for an assignment . . . I didn't have to do it . . . I felt released; everything flowed."

How widespread was this phenomenon? Audre and I wondered. Were other students writing for purposes other than "school"? If so, how many? And what were they writing? We began to ask them, informally, as we met them in the halls or talked with them between classes.

Many told us they kept journals. Dave said he took his journal with him to the beach and on camping trips; Kym said she kept hers in poetry. Cumhur kept two: one in English, which he shared with Audre; the other in Turkish, for "mean and nasty" thoughts he didn't want to share with anyone. Kristen sometimes used her volleyball journal, read by her coach, for working things out but also kept a private journal at home, "which *nobody* sees."

Other students wrote poems, letters, stories—some private, others shared. John kept poems in a bulging folder hidden at home; Walter wrote poems to and about his girlfriend and gave them to her as gifts. Karen and Kim told us they had been exchanging notes, poems, and stories for years. Denise wrote letters to her parents, who wrote back. A number of students had started stories or poems in class, then gone on adding to or revising them for themselves, long after the class had moved on to other things. Erin, among others, said she wrote every day. "I could have had the worst day of my life," she explained, "but if I sit down and write about it—maybe a poem—I feel better."

"It's all the talk about process," Audre thought. "Talking so much about writing—about how we write—about how other people write—makes it all right or even desirable to write for real reasons—outside of school assignments." Students who had written secretly for years felt free to claim their writing. Students who hadn't, Audre observed, were beginning to sound "forlorn, left out"; they wondered if they were missing something. After a particularly lively class, she wrote in her journal:

> Some kids were awed when others read today—didn't have a notion about this immersion. Brian—very cute—looking dumbstruck after Amy shared says, "I think I'm doing this wrong"—Kids protest—can't be wrong— he says—"Well I didn't do it anything like they did—They get so *emotional*."

"Write selfishly—for selfish reasons," Audre told her students often, smiling, half-joking but (as her students knew) meaning it, too. She had come to believe, she wrote, that "there is no such thing as teaching writing to someone who does not yet use writing selfishly—for his or her own purposes. ... This comes first—*must* come first, whether we're beginning in first grade or in twelfth."

When students discovered their own uses for writing, Audre was excited. Some were finding, she thought, that writing could be

> utilitarian—like Greg and Glenn—they hated writing, wrote little snippets of phony BS. But when they hit upon a real life situation, a dilemma, the writing comes pouring out. ... They are hoping to be able to sort out real thoughts and they write three drafts of a six page paper—and then Kristen, Walter, Kym—so many others ... I love it! This is what real writing is made of.

As Audre and I delighted in this explosion of writing, I wrote a series of memos about what seemed to me to have allowed it to emerge: the way writing and the study of the writing process were woven into Audre's teaching, the way Audre herself became part of the community of writers in her classroom.

Audre was pleased by my description of her classroom. "You see what I see as important," she told me. "You wrote about my class the way I would have." She began to feel she could trust my perceptions; I began to feel I could trust them myself. For Audre and I, I had begun to realize, were much alike, both in our reactions to students and classroom events and in our reactions to teaching itself.

The Process of Audre's Teaching • Before I watched Audre teach, I thought other teachers—the ones I passed in the halls—moved smoothly from one high point to another, never breaking step, never doubting direction or losing sight of goals or wondering if their students were learning anything at all. My own teaching, of course, was seldom so smooth. I kept teaching journals filled with doubts and questions, seesawing between elation and despair. But surely the teacher next door rode a steadier course?

Audre's classroom, with its ups and downs; her journals, with their honest recording of highs and lows; her raging, her laughter, and her tears were a revelation to me. Reading her journals and observing her classroom, I found, as in the messy manuscripts of published writers, evidence of a process more complex but, in the end, more worthy of respect than the smooth sequences I had expected to see.

Audre's journal charted the ebb and flow of classroom life and her reactions to it:

> —Wonderful day—all write.

> —Lovely day listening to kids talking seriously about their writing.

> —Low point I'm working so hard to get seriousness ... If only Dennis would care about his writing. ...

—Ed is not writing—keeps looking at what Tom has written. . . . Some put pens down, fold arms, close up shop . . . Too many loll away a beautiful afternoon and I decide I'm not a teacher.

—If I could remember that it is not a continuous process, but occurs in spurts, it might be helpful . . .

—Some days bring malaise—it spreads like canned cake frosting—sickly over everything—The kids sink down in their chairs—ooze over the sides—smear across the table—and we get nothing done. Other days are crisp as fresh zucchini.

Audre often stopped to observe her students and to change direction in response to what she observed. Although she had a rough idea in September of what she wanted to do during the year, her day-to-day plans changed frequently. "I don't know what I'll be doing in January," she wrote, "—or, sometimes, tomorrow." She often decided what to do next by writing in her journal about what was happening in her classroom. Why does this group work better than that one? she would ask herself. Have we spent too much time on this piece of writing? Too little? Would a list of questions help Ed, who doesn't seem to know what to say about another student's writing? As she described it:

> The struggle comes in trying to decipher what is happening—Is the talk of Saturday night crucial to growth in my class (and of course—often it is—as all talk is). But is there a balance of interest, talk, struggle?—is the stand-still really a recouping?

As her students continued with their "place" pieces, for example, through drafting, revising, meeting in writing groups, editing, and publishing (in rexographed booklets), Audre reflected on the time it was taking:

> Everything is working in period 3 today. I wonder why? Is it because I've slowed down? The thought of speeding up in order to begin a new assignment before next week made me feel ill, and so although this seems a long time spent on one composition, it may be worth it. Some kids just don't seem to crank up easily and then (perhaps) I get nervous about their inactivity and press them with "Well, a final's due tomorrow." Do I do this?

In response to the pressure of high school life, with its packed schedule and many demands on students' and teachers' time, she wrote, "I hate having to rush through work—not to be able to give them time to do it well . . . I like to be in things wallowing not zipping through . . . Sometimes I think what we need is the whole semester on one piece of writing." She reported with pleasure on a slow-moving lesson, "We didn't cover much ground, but we dug deeply," and ended up pleased with her decision to allow extra time for the "place" piece:

> Everyone shares piece with whole class. They listen appreciatively and it is wonderful. Even Doug, Steve, and John read. I love today! I feel it has been worth the time. If some have taken advantage of the freedom in order to goof

off—others have taken the advantage-opportunity to work and re-work their writing into something they like.

A teacher's ability to change plans from day to day—sometimes from moment to moment—is one of the main attractions of teaching for Audre. She wrote of the "sheer pleasure" of

> doing something that feels so right—being in a position to experiment when it begins to feel wrong—to change directions and to really *find* what one is looking for.

She referred to her planning and teaching process as "not planning and not teaching," compared it to her writing process, and noted that keeping a teaching journal had helped her

> to understand my seemingly disorganized approach and to alleviate the guilt— same guilt I used to feel for not having an outline before I began to write. Like gestation—exploratory period in writing, and until it's down on paper and communicated to audience—it is always "in process" and subject to revision— or a junking.

"Exploratory periods," in teaching as in writing, suit Audre's style. In class, she frequently makes new starts, changes direction, sometimes contradicts herself, accepts her own contradictions. She relies on her reading of her students and her own strong sense of what matters to tell her where to go next. "For all her doubts and constant searching," said Sue, "Ms. Allison trusts herself."

In Audre's first year as an eleventh-grade teacher, the anchor of her curriculum was not so much a sequence of lessons—those were constantly in flux, constantly changing to meet the needs of the day—as her clear sense of what she wanted to see happening in her classroom: students reading, writing, exploring their own ideas, making their own discoveries, finding their own voices, finding joy in writing and reading and in themselves. When those things seemed to be happening, Audre stayed with whatever she was doing; when they didn't, she tried something else.

In the year I spent with her, as in any other year, Audre wanted to be free to follow her students' moments of inspiration wherever they led, stopping only to observe and describe the process of writing and revising as she and they engaged in it. But the eleventh-grade literature curriculum still worried her— and the eleventh-grade tests.

Writing About Reading

Reading, to Audre, is first of all "something you do for yourself." From the start, she and I were in perfect agreement about this. Both readers for whom reading is joy and necessity, we traded novels over coffee, compared favorite writers, and complained to each other when we didn't have time to read for pleasure.

Much of what Audre believed about writing she believed about reading as well: that you learn to do it best by doing a lot of it; that an understanding of literature, like skill in writing, needs ample time to grow; that the attention to language and meaning from which it grows arises most naturally from extensive reading "for selfish reasons." "Enjoyment must come first," she wrote in her journal. "It is [the reason for] engagement with texts."

As a ninth-grade teacher, Audre had, she said, "had fun with" the literature curriculum. She and her students had rewritten stories from different points of view, composed their own "epics" while reading Homer's, been playful and gay and shared their enjoyment of the works they read in class projects, art work, imitation, and spoof. But literature in eleventh grade, Audre's colleagues warned her, was serious business.

Another eleventh-grade teacher ordered a book called *Literary Analysis*. Parents asked for class time to be devoted to literary criticism in preparation for Regents. And Audre's students themselves, the same students who were writing and boldly revising their own pieces, became tight with anxiety in the face of those works of other writers we call "literature."

Many students told us they had stopped reading for pleasure. They looked back wistfully at the books they had read as children and at the leisure they had had to read them. Not any more, they said; they felt overwhelmed by the demands of a packed curriculum, by extracurricular activities, sometimes by after-school jobs, and nearly always by worry about and study for PSATs, SATs, RCTs, and Regents. Another book to read, however carefully chosen by Audre, however enticing, felt to many like another burden. Students for whom reading was difficult to begin with groaned at the announcement of each new set of novels from which they might choose. Fluent readers worried about the next step: "Are we going to do literary criticism now? Is this what they want on the Regents?"

Audre was disturbed. "Literature looms," she wrote in her journal. "I love it—I know its value ... It informs the center ... It teaches us what it is to be human." Yet to be taught by literature, she believed, a reader has to be open to its messages. As she chose plays, poetry, essays, and short stories to be read in class and novels for students to read at home, she wondered how they would read them. Students worrying about what "they" want on the Regents; students looking for "right" answers, afraid of being "wrong," paralyzed by anxiety as they read—how could such students read with the full power of mind and emotion that brings a text to life?

Most teaching methods she had seen (and tried) seemed to her to interfere with rather than promote students' full responses to what they read. "All those questions that follow stories in literature anthologies—to what purpose? Yetch ... They ask the student to find out what the teacher already knows. It is a kind of puzzle which sets the student groveling to put the pieces together in just the way the teacher expects." She distrusted the custom of teaching eleventh graders formulas for writing about literature:

Just as textbooks treat writing as though it were an object to construct—thesis statement, 3–5 sentence paragraphs, topic, outline, etc., etc., etc., so we teach reading—literature—plot, theme, character, setting: know these and you have your instant ready-made response—the Brand X response, yours in one easy lesson—What is missing is—*the whole experience.*

Writing literary criticism in eleventh grade, she thought, many students skipped the most important step:

If they want to try [literary analysis] because they have made a passionate response, I will let them, of course, but this so seldom happens. I don't believe I ever felt compelled to "analyze." I have experienced great satisfaction in writing about literature, but I don't think that comes until there has been a great deal of experience ... perhaps not until you've experienced craftily putting together a piece, making delicate choices, paying attention to form yourself.

"Passionate response," for Audre, came first; soon after, from crafting your own writing, attention to other writers' craft. Then—later, if at all—the more formal study teachers call "analysis."

Making Connections • "Reading is very subjective—like writing," Audre told her students in class one day. "That's how it is—how it ought to be. The pleasure in reading comes from your own individual response, from seeing connections that have meaning for *you.*" Writing about literature, she added, can help you "to discover the impact it has on you. If you write freely, you begin to understand what you think about something."

Early in the year, after listening in class to a tape recording of professional actors reading *Death of a Salesman,* Audre and her students wrote about the play. Audre read her response aloud:

This play is having a very profound impact on me at this time. I suppose it's because my father just died and I remember how over and over he comforted himself by recounting all the things that had gone well in his life. How lucky he was to have married my mother and how lucky he was to have 2 wonderful daughters who married 2 wonderful men, and had wonderful children, and how lucky he and mother were to live in Florida in such a wonderful town with such wonderful friends and on and on.

I suppose it's very important to have made a fine life for yourself. I suppose we all feel a burden to do so. It is an obligation—to dream, to aspire, to work toward a goal, to reap rewards—all as confirmation of self as if you are what you achieve.

How does one *begin* to feel guilty if life has not heaped reward, if the nature of the society makes victims of some—like Willy Loman. Charley says nobody dast blame this man. Is that true? Do we blame those who don't succeed? ...

Despite Audre's example, however, students' responses were for the most part short, thin, and written in a language not natural to them (or anyone): "I experienced much enjoyment while reading the play ..." and so forth.

Audre, frustrated, tried with her next literature assignment a technique she had used successfully when teaching ninth grade. She asked students to rewrite episodes from the novels they were reading from different points of view or in different modes. But she reported that she was "not completely satisfied" with the results. While the diaries, dialogues, and musings of imaginary characters based on *Main Street, Babbitt, Daisy Miller,* and other selections from the eleventh-grade American literature curriculum were livelier and more imaginative than the responses to *Death of a Salesman,* they seemed to Audre to lack depth. Eleventh graders, she thought, could go further. "[How can I] help students to listen carefully to themsleves, to be aware of their own perceptions however slant or from whatever angle, to stay alert to knowing and feeling and expressing what is true?" she asked herself.

Questions, she thought, were at the heart of the matter. Not textbook questions, directing the student to what the teacher or textbook writer already knew, but rather the kinds of questions that run through an exerienced reader's mind as he or she encounters an unfamiliar text. What were those questions? she asked herself. How could she encourage students to ask them? She examined her own reading process: what questions did she ask *herself* as she read? She tried translating some of these into focusing questions for students:

> What do you like? How does it make you feel? ... How does the character talk? ... What does it make you think of? Remind you of? ... Listen to the sounds and the rhythms of the writing. What do they add? How did you feel while reading the book? Were you frightened? envious? happy? hopeful? disappointed? depressed? Explain that. ... Why did you remember the parts you remembered? ... Did any one of the characters remind you of yourself in any way? Which one? Why? Did you like him or her? ...

"Ask yourselves these questions," she urged her students, "and soon you'll be learning to verbalize your responses. Look back at what you've written. Think about it. Treat your writing with respect. Expect to find answers there."

But, while a few students began to write honestly about what they found in books, most continued to hand in plot summaries or rather stiff, bloodless essays. In January, Audre showed a videotaped version of *The Scarlet Letter* in class and invited students to write their responses to it while watching as well as afterward. A few warmed up but many, again, produced plot summaries: "The name of the movie was *The Scarlet Letter.*" "Hester was a lady who broke the law of the land by having a child with a man she was not married to." "Many things weren't clear until the end." Audre found these responses disappointing and described them in class as "slim pickings." In March, to head off the retellers of plot during an in-class reading of *A Streetcar Named Desire,* she passed out a guide sheet:

> Summarize if you must, but only for a bit. What questions occur to you as we

read the play? Can you answer them? How does Williams reveal his characters to us? ... As you reflect on the action of the play so far, what connections do you make? To your own experience? to your other reading? to other people you have known? to movies you have seen? ... What can you predict will happen? ... Let your writing go wherever your ruminations take you.

In class, she asked her students to keep writing as they read and heard the play, "so that you really *have* something from it—not just a vague, fuzzy memory." "Concentrate your energies on seeing what an author says," she added. "The more you look, the more you will see. Ask yourself questions and answer them. Trust yourself. You may see something the most sophisticated critic has missed. Don't try too hard to figure out the author's meaning. Just trust your instincts and let yourself respond to the work."

To encourage students to take their responses seriously, she started each class by asking a few to read from what they had written the day before. The readings led to discussion: of alcoholism and insanity, of family relationships, of people students knew and characters in novels and other plays; on one occasion, to a comparison between Blanche Dubois and a character on "General Hospital." Discussion got livelier. Voices began to emerge from the journals.

Todd, for instance, started stiffly,

> Throughout the first scene, the reader is introduced to the three major characters. From their dialogue you can determine a great deal about their personality and background. ...

but unbent as he went along:

> Blanche begins a long lie in how she received a wire from a millionaire friend who invited her on a cruise in the Carribean. The story of course does not fool Stanley in the slightest, but perhaps it is not really Stanley that Blanche wants to fool. She needs more than anything to convince herself that there is a future, and that her life will not be forever filled with disappointments, running, deluding, and hiding. ...
>
> Blanche rambles in her common dreams of gentlemen and elegance ... then Stanley comes. He mentions the name Shaw to Blanche. She tenses and recoils strangely. ... What is it about "Shaw," "Hotel Flamingo," and "Laurel" that raises Blanche's blood pressure, and what secrets are hidden in such places and people?

Sue speculated:

> Stanley seems like this really street smart tough guy ... I think he and Blanche are very similar, yet very opposite at times, so there might be a lot of upcoming conflicts, because both are such strong characters. ...
>
> Stanley's ill manners and crudeness and machoism really come out in this scene. Blanche tries to snow job Stanley about her background and Stanley is no dummy; he can see it. ... Poor Stella, it looks as if she's going to get pushed between these two, bumped back and forth.

John, like Sue, recorded his observations in lively language not usually found in school writing:

Scene VII. Uh-oh! Stanley's got the poop on Blanche, and the shit's going to hit the fan! At least that's what I think. Now Blanche is going to be forced to accept some kind of reality. I guess singing "Paper Moon" in the bathtub while Stanley was rattling off all those things about her was supposed to be symbolic.

Scene X. Now I'm really confused. Why, after treating Blanche like dirt, would Stanley want to go to bed with her? And why on the night his baby is going to be born? I know he's a bit dumb, but still, how could he? ...

Steve asked questions, answered some, left others unanswered:

What would Stanley say or do to Blanche after he hears what she thinks of him? The author doesn't show you, yet, what Stanley will do. ...

Why does Blanche keep lying? Maybe she doesn't want to blow her "last" chance at a decent life. Will Blanche leave with Mitch and marry him. This was not answered yet. ...

Why didn't Blanche leave when Stanley gave her a chance to? Not answered. Why does Stanley rape her? Not answered ...

Stella is sending [Blanche] to a mental hospital ... Where will Blanche go? Will they treat her right? Will Stanley, Mitch, or Stella ever visit her? None were answered.

Lynne reflected on changes in her own reaction to the play as she read. At the beginning, she reported her indignation at Blanche's behavior:

Is Blanche an alcoholic? She seems to have a serious problem. Blanche is rude even to her own sister. Why is Blanche shaken up and nervous? What happened? Is she always that way. Blanche constantly critizeses Stella "Oh, you've gained weight." I think that's an awful thing to say. ...

Stella seems polite and quiet, she is Blanche's opposite. ...

I think that Blanche may cause trouble, between Stanley and Stella. I mean she tries to act sweet when she throws out her rude comments. The thing I don't understand is that Stella doesn't say anything back, she just takes it.

Blanche tells Stanley that he's simple, straight forward and honest, but a little primitive. Stanley doesn't fall for her compliments and I like that.

By the end, however, she had come to see the characters quite differently:

I really feel that Stanley raped Blanche. I have such pity for her now. I feel so sorry for her I can really understand her how all that flirting was just an act, deep down inside she was hurting and she knew that she was living in an imaginary world. ... How could Stella have her sister put in an institution? Is that right? Was Blanche brought to some kind of mental institution? that's what I thought happened. How could they do that? ...

I liked Stanley in the beginning and now I hate him. It is all his fault. I blame him for Blanche's breakdown it wouldn't never gotten that serious. And I don't like Stella either, I think she's dumb and naive, I think she should've listened to Blanche. Boy did that ending bother me. It made me hate everyone but Blanche.

Listening to and reading these responses, Audre and I began to get excited. Something had clicked. Students were speculating, daring to make new connections, asking new questions, willing to live with uncertainty as their answers emerged.

Many, like Steve, were willing to leave questions unanswered at the end. Many, like Lynne, were intrigued by the idea of recording, instead of answers, the shifts and complexities of their own reading processes. Audre wrote in her journal of her hopes for her students' reading:

> By asking students to listen to themselves as they read, in the same way I ask them to pay attention to their process of writing, to pay attention to the process—to recall—reflect—question—explore—connect with past experience—the aim once again—just as in writing—is to get in touch with what you know—to open yourself enough to hear what is in your center (what you feel and know)—to guess at what you don't—to see that you connect with your own experience and that the synthesis makes reading or writing the wonderfully pleasurable thing it ought to be. ... This play of knowledge—discovered—shared—translated—and transformed into your own experience—is so full of joy and wonder. ...

Reading through the *Streetcar* responses, Audre noticed recurring phrases, questions, students' ways of making their own connections to the play. As students were choosing from another set of novels to be read outside of class, she gathered some of these together, added others, and came up with a new set of directions for responding to literature. On a sheet she eventually titled "Wonderings and Wanderings," she abandoned her "teacher's" questions, even the broadest and most open, in favor of unfinished sentences that, she hoped, would invite students to ask their own:

1. I began to think of ...
2. I wonder why ...
3. I know the feeling ...
4. I noticed ...
5. I love the way ...
6. I was surprised ...
7. I really can't understand ...
8. I thought ...
9. I can't believe ...
10. If I had been ...

"As you are reading your novel," she wrote at the top of the sheet,

> keep a daily log where you discuss the ideas in your book. In this way you will begin to connect these ideas to your own experience, making the novel your own, a part of your storehouse of knowledge. As you reflect, ruminate, and question, listen carefully to yourself and attempt to describe the effect the book is having on you. This is your reading process. Examine it and take note of what you do with the material you read. Write honestly, respond deeply, admit confusion, expand on the author's ideas, attempt to discover your own.

Halfway through this next set of readings, Audre collected the logs to see what her students were doing. Almost immediately, we both noticed something different about this writing: unlike reports on literature from earlier in the year, it made good reading. We found ourselves passing notebooks back and forth to each other, reading passages out loud, calling one another's attention to moments of insight, humor, honest questioning. Students, we noticed, asked themselves questions we would never have thought to ask—would not have known how to ask.

Eve, an infrequent reader who described most books as "dumb" and "boring," accepted Audre's invitation to "admit confusion" as she tried to make sense of *The Great Gatsby:*

> I can't really keep up w/ this book. I feel like I [am] reading one thing and all of a sudden it starts telling about something else. For example: I[t] said how beautiful Toms wife is and how huge and great Tom is, then it will switch to how his house looks like an eyesore compared to Gatsby's house. . . . I don't understand why the characters will be talking about one thing in a sentence and then start talking about someone else. For example, when Mrs. Wilson was talking to Mrs. McKee, they were having a long conversation about feet and all of a sudden something about a dress came in the conversation which didn't make sense. . . . Why was Gatsby nervous about Tom being there? Did I miss something? . . .

Eve seemed to see reading as a test she was constantly in danger of failing ("Did I miss something?"). She felt totally at sea in her novel; asked question after question, quoted sentences and whole passages she couldn't understand at all, floundered miserably. Audre and I admired her courage and perseverance. We thought she was on the right track, asking the questions she needed to ask, and told her so. She pushed on and was rewarded:

> There's something wierd about Tom. He seems to want Daisy more than ever and now she's just coming to her senses (it's about time) and seems really to be leaving Tom this time. I change my mind I just realized she was having a more serious affair with Gatsby than I thought. . . . For the first time in the book I understand what is going on.

Other students tackled confusion by finding the familiar in what was new to them. James found a way into *A Farewell to Arms* through a special interest, "gas masks and guns." Emil thought *The Sun Also Rises* was "boring—but the bullfights were great." Lynne, who liked to watch soap operas on TV, read *The Great Gatsby* as a romance:

> I can't wait till Daisy sees Gatsby. What will she say? or do? . . . Gatsby has a lot of love for Daisy. I'm glad. I hope they get together and she leaves Tom. I never liked him. And I don't think Daisy ever really loved him. . . . I'm so glad that Daisy's been seeing Gatsby. I think it strange that Daisy kissed Gatsby when Tom was right in the other room. Does Tom suspect anything? It doesn't seem as though he does. This whole thing is weird, very very weird. . . . I can't believe it! Daisy told Gatsby that she loved him and Tom saw. Now what? This is getting to be ridiculous. . . .

Intent on romance, Lynne was impatient with distractions ("I don't want to read about Dan Cody and his dumb yacht") and excited by discoveries ("Daisy and Gatsby used to be in love . . . I knew it!"). Involvement in the romantic plot,

however, did not prevent her from reaching a conclusion a more experienced
or sophisticated reader might have expressed in more academic language:

> I feel so sorry for Gatsby. Why did he have to die? I wanted him and Daisy to
> get together. I'm so mad! Daisy and Tom seemed to mess up everyone's lives.
> And they ended up with no problems but the people they were involved with
> died. That's a real shame.

Other readers wrote of feeling angry, hurt, elated, or despairing as they
followed the fates of the characters in the books they had chosen. Sandra, for
instance, taking off on her own to read *The Portrait of a Lady,* wrote early in
her reading of a strong identification with Isabel Archer:

> ... Isabel has done much reading and is not overwhelmingly modest by any
> means. She is too intelligent and does not feign otherwise, yet one can already
> see how the author intends to develop her simplistic pedantic intelligence
> into that of a mature intellectual. This is no simple growth, one which I am
> anxious to see and hope to experience myself. For all her knowledge from
> books Isabel is still quite naive and has yet to learn from reality. ...

As she saw where Henry James was leading her, however, Sandra became dis-
illusioned and then angry:

> ... how astonished I am. Isabel, I feel like ripping her out of the page, rough-
> ing her up and saying I told you so. But no she married and stayed with that
> idiot Osmond. Perhaps there is something here which I do not see. But I
> wonder why she stays with this man who robbed her of everything that made
> her significant. ... Perhaps I misconstrue this however and the author is
> showing Isabel's strength in facing a bad situation rather than running from it.
> Nevertheless I have doubts. ...

Sandra recorded a double vision: on the one hand, she was passionately
involved in the fate of Henry James's Isabel, on the other she was constantly
aware that James, the author, had created Isabel and used her for his own
purposes. Recognizing that the writer's intentions might have been different
from her own, she ended her log sadly:

> I wish I could say I enjoyed the novel as much as I thought I would. ... I
> have lost almost all my love and respect for the heroine. Maybe the author has
> made a point in this.

Cumhur let Hemingway's *A Farewell to Arms* suggest broad questions to him:

> In the war lots of things change but there are things which don't change.
> Frederick and Catherine find love during the war. Especially the days which
> they spent in the hospital for the whole summer was very good. Being together
> all the time, talking about love, making jokes, sitting on the porch on the
> breezy summer nights and watching the city. It sounds lovely, romantic. But on
> the other side the war is going on. People die ... soldiers attack, soldiers
> retreat ... yet under all these adverse conditions we can find love. ... What is
> the meaning of love for man and woman? ... should we restrict our freedom

when there is war; is it fair to please ourselves when the rest of the people suffer?

At the end, he described and examined his reaction to the book:

> The end of the book effected me a lot. I felt sorry when Frederick did, I felt melancholic when he did, I felt excited; and finally felt I lost everything that I have when Catherine died. It was as if I were Frederick and I had all the experience he had. … The reason might be because I wanted to feel in the same way. … Besides this the events which occurred at the time when I read the [book] shaped me to behave in that way. I'd felt lonely, lost; was very sensitive too. Therefore when all these effects came together, I felt sorry, excited, melancholic, and lost everything I had.

To which Audre replied, in a note in his log, "Yes, this is the way in which we all connect. Your experience with the experience of the novel creates something unique, your own, and yet it is also shared."

Attention to Craft • When Audre read, with her students, the works of published writers, she worked hard, she wrote, "to help them see the writer behind the writing—a writer like themselves."

She had never drawn a clear line between literature and students' writing—in fact, had drawn no line at all. As far as she was concerned, the community of writers included Shakespeare, Nathaniel Hawthorne, Flannery O'Connor, and Ed, the student in fifth period who'd flunked English last term. All, in her eyes, were writers: all participants in a process that begins, often, in confusion, proceeds to discovery, and ends, if possible, in the sharing of a published piece.

She often spoke of students' writing and of literature in the same breath. One day, Emil, who said he "hated to write" and wrote infrequently, produced a poem about football. It ended with a line about the players' uniforms—that they were "colorful, and getting dirty." Beth said she liked the line about the uniforms—"how they were getting dirty." Emil responded, "Yeah, you can tell by the uniform if the guy played or not," and Audre said, "That last line surprised me. Something wonderful about the language is that you can keep on using it in new ways. Shakespeare took the language and just burned it up." Emil and Shakespeare, both writers, the similarities between them more important than the differences.

Stories, poems, and essays by published writers were woven into Audre's teaching of writing. Sometimes she used them for inspiration, like the poems and memoirs that helped students get started on their memory pieces. Sometimes she chose passages for comparison: descriptions by James Agee and Alfred Kazin, among others, to compare with students' own evolving "place" pieces. When students were writing poems, they read poetry; when they were writing stories, they read fiction.

Often Audre read aloud in class, letting her voice linger over the rhythm of a line, pausing to laugh out loud at a well-turned phrase or to repeat and savor a well-chosen word. "Ms. Allison gets turned on by words," said Steve. I liked his phrase and repeated it in class. Steve was embarrassed, but Audre was pleased. "Words are my life," she quoted from Emily Dickinson and wrote it on the blackboard. Often after reading she would draw her students' attention to the source of the pleasure produced. "How did you feel when you heard that?" she would ask. "What did the writer do that led you to feel ... ?"

"Kids get excited by the discovery that a writer is consciously ensnaring the reader," she wrote in her journal. "When they discover the craft of a story, an 'aha' occurs not unlike the 'aha' we feel when our own writing begins to do what we want it to." As Kym said, awed, "How did Salinger ever *think* of that?"

Beyond that, however, and constantly, as she and her students observed, discussed, and wrote about their own experiences as writers, they compared these experiences with those of other, published writers. When Audre brought in Diana Chang's "Woolgathering, Ventriloquism and the Double Life," for instance, students identified with the author as she described herself wrestling with drafts of her novel:

Denise: She had her idea, but she couldn't get it down. .... Guess she was too uptight.

Audre: She was stuck until—What happened?

Steve: It hit her.

A voice from the back: Boing!

Matt: She was bugged by it. Then she was walking down the street and it came to her.

Emil: I'm like her. You can't try too hard. Sometimes when I'm writing I'll get an idea and I'll write it down on the side of the paper so I won't forget it.

The one day Audre and I taught together, we brought in copies of drafts by Hemingway, Virginia Woolf, Stephen Crane, and other writers to compare with students' own work in progress. That day Ann, a student, took notes:

> Kris is telling how James Joyce added a lot to his paper. Lauren said that she does the same exact thing as James Joyce. Kym said that Ernest Hemingway can't make up his mind on what he wants to say in one sentence. He has 4, 5, or 6 startings. Kym said the first sentence is the hardest for her, too. Stephen Crane crossed out a whole page. Lynne says she starts something and then restarts it. ...

As the year went on, students wrote longer and more detailed accounts of their writing processes. When they read what published writers had to say about their struggles with writing, they identified with the writers. As Audre wrote in her journal, "They compared, moaned, contrasted, explained ... The study of process makes them proud to be stuck, to be freed, to be impelled, to share quirks, to *be* a writer." And she added, "It can help them to see literature."

Greg, reading *The Great Gatsby,* thought about the process behind the decisions of a fellow writer, F. Scott Fitzgerald:

Nick and Daisy cousins. Why did F. Scott do that? I don't think it was a good idea. I didn't like the way F. Scott delayed on the information on people and who they were like Jordan Baker, the other lady mentioned in the beginning of the book. She has to go to some tournament, but F. Scott doesn't tell what for. That bothers me. . . .

I like the way F. Scott finally made Gatsby and Nick meet. I thought it was funny. . . . I wonder why F. Scott jumped from Nick telling a story to Miss Baker . . .

Edris, reading *A Farewell to Arms,* recognized in Hemingway's use of a recurring phrase a technique she had enjoyed first in the work of another student:

On page 134, the top paragraph, reminds me of John's story, the one with "are pine needles edible," do you remember? I started laughing cause it reminds me so much of his story except Hemingway uses the expression, "they were all cooked," "he said it was all balls." What a thing to remember.

Emil, who found writing even short pieces "boring," asked himself why Hemingway had written a whole book, *The Sun Also Rises,* and came up with an answer:

I realized that in 30 or 40 years I could be acting like Ernest Hemingway and looking back on my life to write a [book]. . . . This discovery made me realize what Hemingway was doing. He wasn't writing for my benefit but for his benefit. If I liked his book and bought his book it was a bonus, but the main purpose of writing it was to satisfy his inner self and his own mind.

"It's the discussion of process," Audre wrote in her journal after a class on "A Rose for Emily,"

—that makes them aware of the craft or skill or art of putting a piece, a story, a novel, etc., together—see the genius of Faulkner's time manipulation—why he did it—what the effect was—see what is to be appreciated—It helps them think seriously—enables them to participate in the selection a writer must make in choosing point of view—and to understand why and what the effect could be—what the benefit of that angle is. It's the bike metaphor again—you can't really appreciate the skill of a racer (who may be 1000 times more skillful than you are) unless you ride a bike. You can't really appreciate the light, graceful and seemingly effortless execution of a grand jeté unless you've worked at ballet yourself.

Studying their own writing processes, Audre thought, led students to appreciate the craft of other writers. Lynne agreed. She'd noticed that herself. She wrote about it in an unassigned piece she shared with Audre:

Do writers have special powers? Some people believe that experienced writers have no problems with writing. People think that words just come to famous authors. Or perhaps the most creative authors have some special powers that enable them to write so wonderfully.

I have found from my own experience with writing that it isn't all that simple. In beginning to write a children's novel, I rewrote the first six pages six or seven times. Crumbled papers filled my garbage pail until I was satisfied with my writing. I never thought that it would be so difficult to write a book. . . .

I have found now that I can actually picture the characters in my head. I know how they will react in any situation. I know where they live, what they like and dislike. It's as though they are real and in my mind I can picture everything they do. . . . I am glad that I realize that writing isn't something that just comes to you.

Writers and Readers • By the end of the school year, Audre's teaching of literature had merged with her teaching of writing; you could no longer tell where one left off and the other began. When Audre and her students wrote, they saw themselves as belonging to a community of writers stretching beyond the classroom to include the authors of the books they read; when they read, they brought to their reading an awareness of craft and a depth of response informed by their experiences as writers.

Lynne, through her own struggle to write a novel, came to understand that "writing isn't something that just comes to you." By becoming a writer herself, she gained a new appreciation of the "famous authors" she read. Others agreed that writing and studying their own writing processes helped them to understand their reading. Stacy wrote:

Knowing a lot about your own writing process and responding and working with writers in a group helps you to appreciate how difficult it is to really write a good piece. So when I read now I'm always looking for what made it good—same way I do in my writing group.

Writing in reading logs, many thought, helped them understand a writer's craft, as writing in writing process journals helped them to understand their own. Ken put it this way:

When I get involved in writing about what I read sometimes I'm amazed at how the piece works. It helps me to see the writer as a person—as another writer like me.

But, most of all, writing about their reading in reading logs enabled students to make their own connections to the books they read—to make their reading their own. "Trust yourself," Audre told them, again and again. And most began to.

There were exceptions, of course. Emil's log remained skimpy, Dave never wrote one, at least a few students used their logs mainly for plot summaries, and Matt wrote an essay about *The Great Gatsby* instead of a log. Matt's essay, extolling the virtues of Fitzgerald's novel, seemed forced. I asked him about it. "Actually, I hated the book," he told me, "but I could see what was *supposed* to be good about it, so I just wrote that." When I asked, predictably, why he hadn't written about what he'd hated, or why he'd hated it, he replied, honestly, "Too much trouble."

But, by and large, students rose to the challenge and reported that it was worth the effort. Kevin wrote:

> I don't like to read just to answer the teacher's questions because then I'm always nervous about what I should pay attention to and I never know the right thing to look for. Writing in my reading log helps me to pay attention to what *I* like or don't like, not what somebody else likes or doesn't.

And Carol:

> Writing in my reading journal helps my reading to be mine. Now I don't just read so that I'll find the answers to someone else's questions but I get myself involved in my own reading so I'll find my own questions and then I'll work hard and enjoy finding my own answers.

By spring, the reading logs had given birth to a new excitement about literature. Students recommended books to one another or joined Audre and me to compare favorite writers between classes. Eve reported proudly that, after nearly giving up on it, she had finished and for the most part understood *The Great Gatsby.* "It was writing the log that kept me going," she said. Sandra told us that she had begun to keep logs on books she was reading outside of class— and on paintings and lab experiments in science. "I write to see what I can discover," she wrote of a set of responses to Flannery O'Connor's short stories. "Surely these things have been noticed before. Yet I noticed them myself. What power!" And Lynne wrote:

> I used to find reading boring … most of the time after I'd read a novel I'd forget what it was about. But when I started to keep a log I began to ask myself questions about what I was reading … I began to understand what I read … I began to love to read. Now I write about everything I read … Writing about reading has opened a whole new world for me.

For many students, the "passionate response" Audre had been looking for had come with a rush. Passionate response, attention to craft, and, here and there, the seeds of what might, for some students, lead to analysis of literature. But it was the excitement in the logs that excited Audre and me. Passing them across our coffee cups, laughing, exclaiming, we stopped worrying about more formal literary criticism—that year at least. For by then it was May.

Next year, Audre promised herself, she'd start the logs earlier: right away, in September. She'd form reading groups, use logs in class discussion, use them to guide the writing of more formal essays. Next year, she said. But this year we had this year's logs to read. We went back to reading them.

The Question of Tests

"But what about the tests?" The question is familiar to any eleventh-grade teacher. Whatever else is going on in school, students, teachers, and the parents of eleventh graders worry about "the tests": Preliminary Scholastic Aptitude Tests (PSATs), Scholastic Aptitude Tests (SATs), Regents Examinations in New York State, and, for students thought not likely to pass the Regents Examinations, Regents Competency Tests (RCTs). Audre's students were no exception.

Doug captured the tension many felt:

> 11th grade is one of the most important years in your life. This year will set up your education . . .
> The better grades you get, the better college you can get into.
> You have your PSAT test and your Regents exams at the end of your year. . . . This year will tell you what kind of career you will have.
> Everything you do now will set up your future.

Given that definition of eleventh grade, it was no wonder anxious students pursued Audre with questions: Can we do more Regents prep in class? Can we do the PSAT book for homework? Are you going to teach us to do literary criticism before Regents? What's my grade? ("Damn grades!" Audre wrote in her journal. "But try telling that to an eleventh grade student.") No wonder parents, too, felt the pressure: they showed up on Open School Night to ask that more class time be given to test preparation; they kept anxious eyes on grades and practice test scores. "A parent no longer asks, 'Did you learn and understand algebra this semester?'" wrote Matt, "but rather, 'What was your math grade?' Isn't this the wrong approach to learning?"

As school got under way, the students, many of whom saw the year as an obstacle course strewn with hurdles, were impatient; understandably, they wanted to begin practicing hurdle-jumping as soon as possible.

Another eleventh-grade teacher, as Audre's students were quick to inform her, had started Regents prep on the first day of school. Students in other classes had test prep for homework. Audre, new to the grade and flustered, cut short her first writing asssignment to make room for a Regents essay practice and then regretted it. With her strong commitment to a curriculum based on writing and literature, she faced, as she wrote in her journal, "a slight dilemma. Shall I—the green eleventh grade teacher—ignore the pressure for test prep? Do I really believe I can?"

Test Practice • "Can we go over a Regents pronoun review?" Todd asked early in September. Audre, who had made it clear from the start that she thought grammar, usage, vocabulary, punctuation—the things standardized English tests claim to test—were learned best through reading and writing, agreed to help students who wanted to try one. Several groups met over an exercise containing sentences such as, "In the front row of the orchestra sat Robert and (he, him)," "I shall ask my father to let Louis and (he, him) come with us to the beach," and "It was (they, them) who objected to the decision."

Audre: "If someone in your writing group read a sentence like 'It was they who objected . . . ,' what would you say?" Todd and Kristen responded, "Simplify. Say, 'They objected.'" Audre: "You wouldn't use clumsy sentences like these in your own writing. Sometimes it helps to rephrase the Regents examples in your head in the simplest way possible."

Matt, Tom, and Emil looked over a test together and read examples out loud. "It must be (them, they) who ride their bicycles to school." "I don't listen to gossip about anyone (who, whom) I know." Matt protested: "These are horrible sentences. We don't speak like this." Audre joined them and agreed: "Some of the 'correct' answers are archaic usage. How could you rephrase that last one?" Students: "You wouldn't say, 'anyone whom I know'; you'd say 'anyone I know.' "

Emil said he'd discovered a formula that worked for usage questions. "To take this test, you read the sentence out loud, and the one that sounds right, you take the other one."

On another day, students reviewed a vocabulary test. There was a buzz of words in the air: "laconic," "pithy," "garrulous." Sandra asked Audre and me for help with "eleemosynary," which, it turned out, neither of us knew. We consulted three dictionaries before finding a definition: "concerned with the giving of alms."

Others compared notes on a puzzling example of test language: "The speaker tended to be *redundant*.   1. wordy   2. boring   3. well-spoken   4. embarrassed." Several students figured out that the right answer was probably meant to be "wordy." "But that's just wrong!" said Dave. "I don't believe it!" said Tom. Matt, who had missed only one out of fifty answers on the last vocabulary review test (I'd missed two myself), explained how you have to think about these things: "Test-makers use language differently. You have to forget what you really know about it and try to think like the test-makers. You ask yourself, what does this word really mean? And then, what does it mean to the test-makers?"

And, all year, as they wrote personal essays, editorials, poems, stories, responses to literature, and accounts of their own writing and learning, students worried about Regents compositions. In fact, the more writing they did, and the more confident they became as writers, the more uneasy they were with the requirements for Regents essays. Laura and Sandra, both competent writers, explained the problem:

Sandra: There's no time to revise. . . .

Laura: You don't dare to try anything that isn't really concrete on a Regents. . . . You have to have an introduction—you know—[*grimace of distaste*] the middle paragraph—and the little end. . . .

Sandra: The topics aren't even that bad—you could make something interesting out of them—but on the Regents you're afraid to do that: there goes thirty points.

Laura: When I read what I was supposed to do [in a practice] I came in one morning and I said to Ms. Allison, "I couldn't do it," because here was this essay and I was sure it wasn't what they wanted, because it was something like what I'd normally write, and she was saying, "Well, gee, that's okay," and I was thinking, "No, it's not; it doesn't sound like the ones in the book."

Audre brought "the book," a Regents prep manual, to class. Her students didn't think much of the model essays. "He bull-crapped his way through it,"

Emil said of one; of another, "He didn't say anything." Sandra described the "best" essay, "the one they gave 30 out of 30," as "the dumbest one in the book." Laura translated the criteria for grading: " 'Thought coherence is excellent'— That means it's so boring you fall asleep between sentences."

Yet, despite their reservations, Audre's students clamored for test practice. And Audre, vacillating between anger at the testing system and sympathy for her students' dilemma, gave in to their demands at times—sometimes against her better judgment. What if they do badly on the Regents? she worried between classes. What if they don't do as well as students who've been practicing tests all year?

Trying to decide what to do about the tests, Audre took another look at them. She reviewed the RCT reading selections ("Prairie dogs are important in the diet of the black-footed ferret"), the Regents essay topics ("Forward Leaps in Science"), and the prepared outline another teacher had provided to help students produce essays written to the RCT formula: "My first reason is . . . My second reason is . . . In conclusion, I think that. . . ." In her journal she revolted.

The creators of these tests, she thought, were asking students "to write like a bubblegum machine."

> The kind of prep we do for tests makes writing strictly a concrete operation. "Take these building blocks, that *I* have discovered (not you) and stack them in this way—carefully—so that the stack doesn't topple"—It is a paint-by-number method that inhibits writing.

She worried about students learning the formula. Even if it worked on the test, she wrote, "how will they find their voices again?"

I shared Audre's distress. Reading over my notes in preparation for writing another memo, I was struck by the number of times classes had been interrupted by tests or test preparation. I had had similar experiences in my own teaching and, like Audre, had been frustrated and enraged by the demands of standardized tests. Identifying with Audre, I wrote with heat:

> . . . Test prep invades writing group meetings . . . plays havoc with the pace and timing of Audre's writing sequences . . . does violence to her plans. . . . Reading and writing units are rushed, crammed into what space is left between test practices. . . . "I don't like what I'm doing," Audre writes at a low point. . . .

I quoted from Audre's journal, choosing passages she had written in rage and frustration. I meant, in using such strong language, to offer support—but Audre didn't feel supported. On the contrary, she felt exposed.

She could hardly bear to read what I had written, she told me; it made her feel "awful." "Your memo . . . troubles me," she wrote in her journal. " 'Play havoc'—'do violence'—and 'invade'—gad—please don't share that one with anyone. Sounds like the Holocaust in my classes."

Was test prep doing *that* much damage? she wondered. Was I blowing the whole thing out of proportion? Was she? "I wanted you to feel my frustrations," she wrote to me, "and I know I can be dramatic ... but somehow seeing my rantings in print causes pain. ... It seems to give this one small part of my teaching life a life of its own—make it more real than other parts."

"I never meant to cause you pain," I wrote to her. And so we wrote and talked, back and forth in journals and between classes, until we had come to understand one another's reactions to the issues my memo had raised. But, despite our talk and writing, the tests remained an issue, and Audre continued to be troubled by doubts about test preparation.

She tried, as the year went on, to make test prep serve other purposes as well. She organized writing groups to work on practice Regents essays, reminding students that even a Regents essay could be "real" writing and could be written in an honest voice. She encouraged students to think through PSAT analogy questions by exploring them in writing and then meeting in groups to compare and debate their answers. She read and evaluated model Regents essays with her students, encouraging them to think critically about the definitions of good writing offered by the test-makers—and about their own. But her heart wasn't in it. For all that she wanted her students to feel prepared for the tests and comfortable when they took them, she couldn't see much value in vocabulary lists (although she gave them out, on occasion) or usage quizzes. Writing skills, she kept reminding her students—and herself—are not acquired overnight, in a vacuum, but rather gradually, through practice, and through the careful attention to structure, choice of words, phrasing, and form that comes with investment in writing. "If you care about it you'll *want* it to be correct."

She resented above all the narrow definition of literacy that leads to the testing of measurable skills:

> Why can't we teach using only the methods we really believe in? What a silly question—Who can trust me to *know* what is best. But why do people demand "Back to Basics" in English as if we were not capable of going farther and deeper (more basic). ... Can you imagine an outcry to science—let's get *back* to basics? I suppose that whenever the complexities of any learning are revealed, it seems like chaos to anyone not steeped in it and "basics" sounds so simple. The problem is—what is referred to in that cry is far far from basic when it comes to language.

She worried, too, about the values reflected in the testing system and about the implications of practicing test-taking in school. What messages are we giving kids? she asked herself.

> Are we training them: To figure out what sells? To figure out what people in authority want? To figure out what people in authority think is true, useful, interesting? To succeed? To adapt? To perform? Do we reward their shrewdness and ability to conform? or, do we encourage them to find their honest centers—to release their own creative energy—to love themselves?

The more she thought about it, the more she resented using class time for test practice. At best, the practice exercises were irrelevant to what she wanted to do; at worst, they sabotaged it. Either way, they siphoned off precious time that could have been devoted to reading, writing, talking, learning.

She returned to her planning with renewed determination, relying more and more, as the year went on, on her own clear sense of what was important. In the face of pressure from outside the classroom, she held her ground with increasing firmness. When students were caught up in the excitement of reading and writing, she would *not* interrupt them for test prep—unless she absolutely could not avoid it.

The two weeks before PSATs, she knew, would have to go for PSAT practice, the week before RCTs for RCT practice, and the last month of the school year, just before Regents, for Regents review. But beyond that she would make few concessions. Responding to the concern voiced most frequently by students and their parents, she would make room in the curriculum for vocabulary work (in the form of study groups set up to tackle the official lists), but the rest of her students' time, and her own, would be spent on writing, on reading, on discovering and making meaning.

"It's all part of the same thing anyway," she reassured her students, hoping—believing—that what she said was true but wishing she were entirely sure of it. "The reading and writing we're doing isn't *for* the tests, but it can't help but help you on the tests, too. A Regents composition is just another piece of writing, after all, and you already know how to do that."

Lynne agreed. "Lots of the Regents topics are like what we've been writing all year: write about a place or a memory. . . ." Karen pointed out "Nightmares" on the Regents list of suggested topics, and Lynne, who had revised and revised a "nightmare" piece, beamed. "I hope they use that one; I've written it five times!"

The Tests "for Real" • As the end of the year approached, tension mounted. January's RCT scores had been encouraging: all but one of the fifty-six students who had taken the test had passed, and the one who hadn't had hardly ever been to class. Regents, however, were more formidable. The forty students who were taking them were nervous. Most knew other eleventh graders who had spent more school time on formal test prep. Yet, when the tests were graded, their fears turned out to have been groundless: their scores were at least as high as those of students from other classes. Of the forty, ten scored in the 90s and nearly half over 80; only three scored below 65. Audre breathed a sigh of relief. She had refused to teach to the tests, but her students had not been penalized for it—even by the narrow measure of the tests themselves.

For her own final exam, given to students not taking the Regents, she prepared an assignment that drew on the year's work. It had two parts: a short story to explore in writing and the opportunity to revise a piece completed earlier in the year "to make it say more of what you want it to say."

The students went to work with enthusiasm. They speculated about the story (Tillie Olsen's "I Stand Here Ironing") and returned with fresh vision to memory pieces, place pieces, even to essays from the very beginning of the year. The results, Audre thought, were "wonderful." "I had such a good time reading them," she told me. "I'm embarrassed by how high the grades were—but the kids deserved them. They really worked. They thought deeply about the story, they made their writing the best it could be, they *cared* about what they wrote." She said that, reading the papers, she could practically feel kids making new discoveries as they went along.

The exam had given students a chance to demonstrate skills they had been learning all year and then to learn others as they were taking it. And that, Audre thought, was what an exam should do.

Back to Writing

By the end of the school year, students were reporting excitement, pleasure, and pride in their accomplishments. They spoke of their writing with passion.

"Todd said he felt 'joy' when his river piece came out the way he wanted it to," Audre wrote in her journal.

> I have never in any other year heard kids talk about the "joy" of writing—
> perhaps we can create a vogue—a fad—The Joy of Writing—Lingering on
> the process of writing allows for the joy to be experienced—There is some-
> thing so much more basic in its value than in the value of a product. ...

One day toward the end of the year, taking a break from anxiety about Regents and finals and last-quarter grades, Audre skimmed through a batch of "place" pieces students had written in May. As she turned the pages, Audre and I began to remember together other pieces that had been important to students over the course of the year. Comparing notes, we realized that we could think of dozens of kids, each of whom, at least once since September, had become excited about a piece of his or her writing: perhaps a reading log or a part of a collaboratively written story; perhaps an essay or a poem or a piece of writing about writing; perhaps something written outside of school. Nearly everybody, we thought, at one point or another.

Ending with Writing • On the last day of school, Audre brought grapes to class, and I brought strawberries. All of us—students, teacher, and researcher—ate fruit and laughed together, all of us wrote—"about writing in this class this year"—and nobody took notes.

After class, reading through students' hastily composed reflections on a year's worth of writing, Audre and I noticed how many wrote of their pleasure in it and of writing as a permanent part of their lives. "I like my writing," student after student wrote. "I enjoy writing." "I've done my best writing ever this year."

"Sometimes when I'm all alone and have nothing to do," wrote Kim, "I'll start writing, which I've really never done before."

Kris wrote, "I feel good about the way I write and I'm going to do some over the summer."

Sandra looked back on her earlier skepticism:

> ... as I am sure you know by now I came in with an attitude that was less than positive. "Writing groups? Process? What kind of junk is this," I thought. Well, by the end of the 1st quarter you had won me over. ...

She would continue group work, she wrote, "throughout my life as a writer."

> Perhaps we can start a revolution, and soon there will be a writing group in every college dorm, later in the executive offices of IBM and soon every family will have its own writing group during prime time. ...

Cumhur, too, described a change in attitude:

> ... Writing was simple at first, just plain. There was no understanding of it, not the struggles, nor the pain which satisfies at the end. ...

His writing, he reported, had been "partly censored" at the beginning, but, by the end of the year, he had written about "everything": "It was learning myself through my writing."

> As I got into writing more I understood it more. The process, the importance of self-evaluation. It was not simple anymore. Writing now was a complicated process which needed not only feelings, but also intelligence and experience. ...

He ended wistfully. "I'd like to say that I'm a good writer now but I can't. I might write better than I used to, I understand better than I used to but there is so much more to learn."

And Audre, too, reflected on what she had learned:

> I've discovered what is most important to me—in teaching writing with emphasis on process. True, the product is better—but that is not what is important. The importance lies in what happens to the students—how they grow—in confidence—in self—in coming to see writing as useful, as a means of pleasure even ...
>
> It's an awakening—which some never experience. I have a feeling that I know more about it—it is not as mysterious this joy. This joy that comes from making concrete that which exists in the air—thoughts—reaching out—in—down—over—to grab them spilling them out onto a page. Shaping a new experience. ...
>
> So it is not what they produce, but what they go away with—that feeling that writing is what you do for yourself and the knowledge that if you do it for yourself—you'll get pleasure—The ability to generate our own pleasure. How strong and courageous it makes one feel.

Teacher and Researcher • As writing, especially the informal, exploratory writing best described as "thinking on paper," is central to Audre's life, so it is to mine, and so it was to our partnership. I came to know Audre through her teaching journals at least as much as from observing her classes; she came to know me through the notes I wrote her about her journals and through my memos about her teaching. Each of us liked the way the other used words.

I loved reading Audre's journals, considered myself lucky that reading them was part of my job. I would have read them anyway, for pure pleasure, like novels or poetry.

Audre's journal-keeping was erratic. She wrote in bursts of inspiration, when and where the impulse hit: in a car, in a restaurant, under the dryer while having her hair permed. She recorded her teaching life in flashes: bright illuminations of the moment, sometimes pursued, at other times left hanging. Her journals, like her teaching process, appeared chaotic on the surface. The entries were seldom dated, and sometimes there were long gaps between them or sudden leaps from one subject to another. Exotic images burst from their pages, punctuated by dashes or not punctuated at all, her punctuation personal, idiosyncratic—blasting away the rules to capture stress and pause and emphasis.

But reading and rereading these journals, luxuriating in the richness of Audre's images, I began to be able to identify themes as they recurred. Parts of the journals felt to me like poems in which the same themes occur again and again, seen from different angles or through new images, the growth of meaning cumulative, a deepening of understanding gained from looking in new ways at the same events. I wrote about these themes as I discovered them.

My writing, Audre said, "gave" her her teaching. Sometimes, as when I wrote about the tests, it upset her; more often it made her feel proud. Either way, she said, seeing her classroom through my eyes allowed her to understand, in ways she hadn't before, what she had been doing all along.

Partly, we agreed, this was because, by writing about classroom events, I had stopped time for her, had preserved, for her to look at, moments which would otherwise have been lost. Responding to a memo I had written about students and their reading, packed with excerpts from students' logs, she wrote:

> A gift! I feel I've just been given an irreplaceable, "unduplicatable" gift. To see the fruits of our effort! My God, this is something that never happens to teachers. We rarely give ourselves time—or have the time—to wallow in or bathe in the delights—rarely time to thoroughly digest and then reflect. The moments of delight are smothered by . . . work that often buries them. But now I have it to hold on to. . . .

It was not, however, my stopping time alone that made the difference to her, Audre said, but rather that what I stopped—the "bits" I held up for her inspection—were "the very bits" she wanted to see. I was "looking for the same bits," she said, and I agreed.

For if Audre felt I had given her her teaching, I felt she had given me mine. We were so alike—in our values, in our struggles and flounderings and questions and doubts—that in studying Audre I studied myself as well. Writing about Audre's classroom, I came to understand my own. When Audre wrote, on the back of one of my drafts, the beginning of a poem, she spoke, as she so often did, for both of us:

Her writing so close to—
experience so close to mine—
that her writing makes order
out of my chaos.

Watching Audre experiment and flounder, I stopped worrying about the unevenness of my own teaching. Good teaching, I could see in Audre's classroom, didn't have to be smooth. Like Audre's writing, her teaching was continually evolving—continually, as she wrote herself, "in process."

Like her students, I could see that it didn't bother Audre to take chances, make mistakes, stumble, and recover. She knew from previous experience that she would eventually "get it right"—or nearly right. And that for her, as for her students, the pleasure would come in the quest, the questioning, the making of discoveries; it would come, as she put it, "not in the treasure but in the hunt."

As Audre's students took courage from her example and became themselves more willing to experiment and flounder, I too took courage. Through Audre, I came to accept my own trials and errors, my own vulnerabilities—to see my own classes as Audre saw hers: as partnerships of students and teacher learning together.

Chapter 3

Reba Pekala
First Grade

First-grade teacher Reba Pekala is a reluctant writer. She approaches writing hesitantly and assumes that most teachers, certainly those who teach English, write with greater ease and more facility than she does. Yet, every day, this nonwriting teacher, as Reba calls herself, initiates young children into the mysteries of writing. Under her guidance, six- and seven-year-olds become energetic and enthusiastic writers almost overnight. Delighted that her students show so little of her own hesitation, Reba marvels at how quickly they take to writing. The year I studied her teaching, in fact, she was so inspired by her students' growth that she determined to join them as a writer in class.

Reba's first-grade curriculum was not always infused with writing. At one time, Reba assumed that six- and seven-year-olds could not write, certainly not before they learned the alphabet and the sound-symbol relationships. As a result, she rarely taught writing, or when she did, it was by encouraging students to dictate their stories. After one year of using the "Dictation Method," however, Reba was disturbed. "Something was lacking," she wrote. "It was sufficient, good, but not enough—for me anyway." She explained it this way:

> [When I moved from upper elementary to first grade,] I had the children write every Friday in the morning by dictating stories to parents. As the year progressed the children began to copy their words right below the parents' writing. From the beginning the kids had drawn pictures to accompany their stories. At the end of the year, I felt a need to change this. Yes, their stories were pretty good—but the kids were very dependent on the parents. The parents were more in charge so if a parent asked a question of a child, he would

agree to change his story just because the parent had questioned him. The child had no real investment in his work.

Reba wasn't sure what she wanted to do. An elementary school teacher with ten years' experience, she had been teaching first grade for one year when she heard that the district was offering training in the teaching of writing. She was wary at first. "Writing and English were my worst subjects in college," she explained, adding emphatically, "I was not eager to write at all." Eventually, however, she convinced herself to take the summer training, not because she wanted to write but because she wanted "more information on how to teach writing to young kids."

In the first weeks of the summer institute, Reba doubted that what we offered her would work with young children. A traditionalist by training and inclination, Reba thought that writing—real writing with drafts and conferences—should be reserved for the upper grades. No matter how much I reassured her, she remained unconvinced. I asked her, however, to suspend judgment until after she had talked with Lucy Calkins, the consultant we had invited to work with the elementary school teachers. Reba remembers the day well:

> Lucy discussed this whole approach to writing very enthusiastically. But I still didn't believe my kids could do it. Yes I know she did it with 1st graders—not that I thought she was fibbing—but my kids were different. You know how researchers are—they always look at the bright kids—I thought, "What about the slow or average kids? The bright ones will learn in spite of what we teach, but the others need our *best* guidance!"
>
> At lunch she showed us video-tapes of kids writing. I remember munching on an apple and my words were—"Just amazing!" Her kids looked like my kids—Yet they could write—I could hardly believe it—what she and Sondra had been saying did make sense, did apply to my kids—"By golly I've got to give my kids this chance."
>
> That was the moment of my awakening! I now felt obligated to learn more, to figure out a way that I could use this project in my class—next year— there was no time to waste. I was determined to outline it on paper—time schedule and all—I was convinced—the only questions I had were in management, not in the ability of my kids to handle it. I just *knew* they'd be able to do it!

Reba's "awakening" occurred in the summer of 1980. Ever since, she has worked to create in her classroom a writing environment that feels "safe," where her students feel comfortable and free to compose. And each year, she tinkers with the schedule and her management system, working to match the needs of her students with her understanding of what it takes to implement a process approach in her classroom.

In 1981–82, the year we began the research project, Reba originally fit writing into a thirty-minute slot between mid-morning snack and outdoor recess. In November, she made writing time longer, and it became the first thing students did each day. This was not an arbitrary decision. It came after she began to pay close attention to what her students were doing as they entered her classroom.

Several consistently wanted reassurance. "Mrs. Pekala," they asked day after day, "are we going to write this morning?" Others ran straight to their writing folders as soon as they came in the door. Reading a message in their behavior, Reba changed the schedule. The kids loved the change. Beginning the day with writing gave them time to settle in, to write, to draw, to chatter with one another, and their immersion in their work was not cut short, as it had been before, by the appearance of the recess monitor at their door. Reflecting on the change, Reba commented, "My kids think school starts when writing time ends."

Now, whenever visitors enter her room between 8:50 and 9:40 A.M., they see fifteen to twenty kids hunched over desks, sprawled on the floor, seated in corners or at the conference table, working on their writing. Since students work at their own individual pace, they are generally at different points in the process. Annie might be seen beginning a new piece by stamping her booklet with the "rough draft" stamp. Mike and Darryl might be off in a corner, collaborating. Mike likes to write the words, while Darryl prefers to draw the pictures. Joey might be found at Reba's side at the conference table, reading his handwritten draft out loud to her. Together they will decide if his piece is finished or if it needs more work. Kim might be illustrating her "published book," the one Reba typed from Kim's handwritten draft the night before. And all of this goes on from the beginning of first grade as naturally and uneventfully as if it had always been so. But how did it begin? Where did Reba start?

Introducing Writing

On the fourth day of school, Reba took a deep breath and walked to the front of the room. Standing by the chalkboard, she knew she was about to do something scary for her: she was about to write a story. Quickly, she drew a sketch on the board and asked, "Can you tell me what I've drawn here?"

The kids chimed in, "A bed!" "A pillow!" "Is that a dog?"

Reba responded, "Did you know I have two dogs at home and that they like to sleep on my bed?"

Reba then drew six dashes under the sketch and said, "I'm going to write something about the picture."

Cindy, a student repeating first grade, recognized the activity and blurted out, "You're going to put one word on each dash. That's how you write."

Reba smiled. "That's right, Cindy. Now, what should I say here? How about, 'My dogs sleep on my bed'?" She repeated the sentence again, pointing to a dash for each word. Turning to the class, she continued, "If we wanted to write this, what would we do? How would we write it? What letters can we put for 'my,' Cindy?"

Cindy said, "*M* and *I*."

Reba responded, "*M* and *I*? OK, I'll put that on the first dash," writing *MI* above the first dash on the board. "How can we write 'dogs'? Mike?"

"D–O–G–S," Mike said, voicing each letter deliberately.

"Good." Reba wrote it in. "Now, how can we write 'sleep'?"

"*S*-s-s-s *P*-*P*-uh," said Joey.

"Thank you, Joey. We'll write *SP* on the third dash here!"

Kim contributed *O–N* for "on" and Maureen suggested *M–Y* for "my." The class had one word to go.

Reba continued, "So, 'My dogs sleep on my bed.' 'Bed'—how can we write that? Alison?"

"*B–I–E–D*," spelled Alison.

Reba, "All right, let's put *B–I–E–D* on the line."

Reba now read "My dogs sleep on my bed" written as *MI DOGS SP ON MY BIED*. She said, "Let's read this together now, class," leading the recitation by pointing to each word as the group pronounced it.

Rick, always looking for a laugh, chimed in, "Cats sleep on my bed!"

Glancing again at her drawing and frowning, Reba acknowledged, "Anybody can see that I'm not the best person to be drawing." Turning to address the class, she continued, "If I were going to write about my dogs, this could be page one. What could I write next?"

"Your dogs chew on your shoes?" asked Kevin.

"Talk about their names!" suggested Kim.

"How about, your dogs play frisbee?" offered Rick, leaning over his chair and giggling.

Reba smiled and addressed the whole group. "I have a story inside me about my dogs. How many of you would like to write a story today?"

With this simple beginning, Reba launched her students into writing. She had their nine-by-twelve-inch construction paper booklets ready and a "rough draft" stamp at hand. She explained that rough draft meant, "It's not real good yet, it's my first try, and I could probably do something to make it better." When Darryl discovered that the students could stamp their own booklet covers, he jumped up and began stamping his eagerly, at least nine times. While a couple of children laughed, most were already off drawing or writing.

Finding My Way in First Grade

"Mrs. Pekala, what if I don't know how to write the word I want?" "I've finished my rough draft, Mrs. Pekala. Where do I put it?" "Please, Mrs. Pekala, can you conference with me now?"

Within a few days, Reba's students find their own rhythm within the routine. They learn Reba's answers to questions because she is consistent. "If you don't know how to write a word, just put down what you can—as close to the sound as possible." "Rough drafts go in the conference bucket. When I get to yours, I'll call you over for a conference."

In 1982–83, the year I visited her classroom and studied her teaching, I noticed that I quickly became as accustomed as the kids to the rhythm of her classroom. I expected to find Reba in her room before school began, organizing the day's activities, checking over her plan book. As soon as the students arrived, I expected her to move to the conference table and begin talking with students about their writing. I knew how she would greet her students and the type of questions she would ask them. I knew how excited she would be when students had published one of their books; at times, I could even picture her delighted smile long before it appeared on her face.

Initially, though, I was bored by the predictability of her classroom activities. Every day, the same routine: writing, conferencing, illustrating; then, after attendance and the pledge of allegiance, letter practice, snack time, reading groups. Wasn't Reba bored too? I wondered. But slowly, eventually, I began to see what Reba's routine allowed for: consistency, safety, knowledge of what to expect. And when I took my eyes away from Reba and looked at the kids, I began to understand why she liked it.

The kids were not bored. Reba's consistency gave them boundaries. And, within the boundaries, they were free to explore. The results of Reba's teaching, I realized, appeared in her students' work. And so, after checking in with Reba, I began to sit next to children to observe more closely what happened as she encouraged them to find their own way.

It was difficult at first to focus my attention. So much was always going on. Students at various tables would be working on pieces in various stages of completion. Some would be talking, others drawing. A few would gather near Reba. One or two would be staring into space or wandering around. As they became accustomed to me and my interest in their writing, several would come over, lean against my arm, and shyly slide their papers in front of me. Others would run up, shove their drafts in front of my face, and declare, "This is what I'm working on. Wanna conference with me?" They loved to accompany me to the main office whenever I made copies of their work. Slowly, I became an accepted part of classroom life. One week early in the year when I had missed several classes, Reba reported that the students wondered where I was. "Where's that lady who watches us write?" they kept asking.

After several weeks of moving around Reba's classroom, I felt the need to organize my observations. Random chats with different kids were interesting, but they would not, I felt, tell me as much in the long run as a sustained look at one or two. If, in addition to studying Reba's teaching, I wanted as well to examine the growth of her students, then I knew I needed to study several writers over time. As hard as it was to choose—every child was compelling in his or her own way—I selected two for close scrutiny.

Willy appealed to me because he was different: a loner, he seemed uninterested in writing and difficult to know. The only way I was able to study how he wrote was by watching him obliquely out of the corner of my eye. Annie was just the opposite. Articulate and outgoing, she basked, as any child might, in the attention I gave her. Together they provide an interesting contrast, and together they will accompany me as I describe Reba and the way I came to understand her teaching.

The Students Begin to Take Off

In the beginning of the year, Reba kept the pace relaxed. By 1982–83, her third year using a writing process approach, she knew what to expect:

> So far the children are progressing as I thought they would. They are asking to write at various times during the day, and Alison even suggested that I conference with her during her free activity time.
>
> Some are still not trusting themselves with their own writing, while others are free from restrictions.
>
> No one (this year) is uptight about using invented spelling. Only occasionally will someone ask me how to spell a word. I will respond only by sounding out the word—I then remind them that it is the rough draft.

Together we began to examine what students were writing. In September, for example, we noticed that one-third of her twenty first graders filled almost every page of their five-page booklets with letters and beginning sounds. A few put down a dash for each word but weren't ready to include the letters. Others drew pictures.

In the fall, E.T. and Pac-Man seemed to make it into almost everyone's writing, but in very different ways. Joey drew several elaborate pictures and then placed a little Pac-Man before the text each time Pac-Man was speaking. His letters, although occasionally reversed, were clear and well-spaced (Figure 3-1).

Figure 3-1 • Joey's Draft on Pac-Man, September 1982

I am going to eat you.

I am going to blow you up.

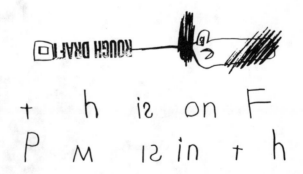

The helicopter is on fire.
Pac-Man is in the helicopter.

Continued

Figure 3-1 Continued

Pac-Man found E.T.

Rick's drawings were bold and full of color. He scribbled his stories, preferring to run around the room and make noise. His first draft was about his new baby brother, who in this draft grew up rather quickly and managed on the way to play Pac-Man (Figure 3-2).

Figure 3-2 • Rick's Draft on His Brother, September 1982

Chris is a baby 6 weeks old.

Chris is now 6 years old.

Chris is a big man. He has a house.

Continued

Figure 3-2 Continued

Chris is playing Pac-Man.
Chris gets a big score!

Chris gets ten million!

In his first draft, Willy put E.T. in the hospital. Not an elaborate illustrator, Willy spent more time on his letters, but, like many beginning writers in first grade, he left very few spaces between them. Willy also consistently reversed the letter *s* so that his *s*'s were written as *z*'s (Figure 3-3).

Figure 3-3 • **Willy's Draft, "E.T. in the Hospital," September 1982**

E.T. is getting operated on. E.T. is getting his tonsils out. E.T. is sleeping.

E.T. is sleeping for one hour.

Continued

Figure 3-3 Continued

ETIPDRDITBD
AHE YOC UP N
2 HIZRPDL HEHUTO
CLE HIZ BD

E.T. is puddling in the bed. He woke up in his puddle. He had to clean his bed.

ETHICJ 22ORC
TF8 ONtheND

E.T. took a glass of soda and poured it in the can.
The end

I first saw Annie's first draft on September 29 when she had a conference with Reba. Following her over to the conference table, I sat in and listened as she and Reba began work. Mainly concerned with helping Annie decipher what she had written and with establishing basic conferencing procedures, Reba asked her to read her draft out loud so both she and I could hear it.

Annie turned to the first page (Figure 3-4). Slowly, she read, "I take piano. [*5-second pause.*] My teacher's name is Miss, Miss, Mrs. Rohrig. I like piano."

Annie stopped, frowned, pointed to the row of letters following "PAN" on the bottom line, and commented, "I . . . I think I have to cross that one out 'cause I'm not sure what this says."

Reba left the composing decision up to Annie. "I'm not sure either," she responded. "What do you think it says?"

While Reba was working with Annie, the noise level in the room increased. The students, not yet entirely able to work on their own while Reba gave most of her attention to one of their classmates, were becoming rowdy. Quickly, Reba turned to the group and made a request. "Boys and girls," she said, "please whisper. Annie and I are having a conference and it's hard to think. Inside voices, please."

Turning back, she discovered that Annie had scratched out the confusing letters. Reba then wrote Annie's three sentences on the side of the draft, repeating each sentence as she went along. Reba explained what she was doing to Annie: "This way when I get ready to type your rough draft, I'll be able to read it."

Figure 3-4 • Annie's Draft, "Piano," September 1982

I take piano. My teacher's name is Mrs. Rohrig. I like piano.

Figure 3-5 • Annie's Draft, "Piano," Page 2, September 1982

My sister takes piano and my sister's name is Mary-Beth.

When Reba finished writing, Annie turned to page 2 of her booklet (Figure 3-5). Annie read this as "My sister takes piano and my sister's name is Mary-Beth." Reba then put her finger on each letter on the draft and Annie crossed out what she didn't need, concluding with the words, "The End."

The draft completed, Reba moved on to the next part of the conference, the Goals Book and the summary. Here Reba records the date, the title of the story, whether it is true or "made up," and any goals she and her student set together. Annie titled her story "Piano" and was very pleased to announce that it was "all true."

Writing as a Social Event

In Reba's classroom, students talk about their writing. They discuss their topics, lean across the table to read each other's drafts, and comment on each other's ideas whenever they feel like it. Sometimes one child starts a rhyme, and another spontaneously finishes it; at other times, someone brings in stickers or cut-outs and these, too, find their way into drafts. Occasionally, one child calls out, "Hey, who wants to write a story with me?" and another answers, "Please be quiet, I'm trying to write my own!"

By October, the kids were accustomed to borrowing and extending one another's ideas. When Scott said the name of his story was "Pac-Man," Rick immediately added, "Mine is called 'Pac-Man and E.T. Are Friends.'" Overhearing, Kevin told them, "Hey, you gave me an idea. I'm going to write about E.T., too. But it's not actually going to be E.T. It will be E.B."

In his second piece of the year, Willy began to fill up more of the page, making his letters and drawings larger and bolder. He also began to leave spaces between words, indicating his dawning recognition of the conventions of writing. In his story called "The Baseball Game" (Figure 3-6), he formed his *s* correctly, but he now reversed the letter *g*. Also, in this draft, his most important sentence, "I hit a homerun," is followed by four exclamation marks.

Figure 3-6 • Willy's Draft, "The Baseball Game," October 1982

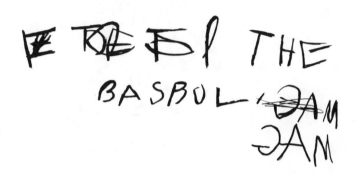

The Baseball Game

I hit the ball. It went rolling.

Continued

Figure 3-6 Continued

I hit a home run!!!!

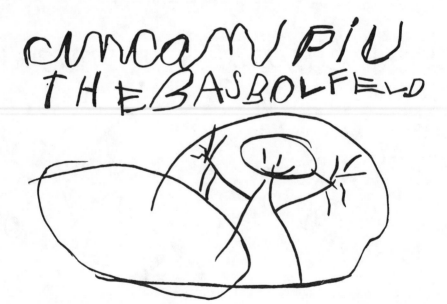

King Kong picked up the baseball field.

In October, Annie announced, "I'm doing a story on E.T., too!" She had already drawn a picture of E.T. on her page.

Rick, glancing at her draft, raised a skeptical eyebrow: "E.T. doesn't look like that."

But Annie, who had already learned that, in writing, whatever you want to put down is fine, retorted, "There's no right way to draw E.T., Rick."

She continued to draw throughout the morning, talking as she went along: "E.T.'s holding Reese's Pieces 'cause that's what he likes. You know how the bags have a little space so you can see inside? That's what I'm drawing now. OK. Reese's Pieces. I need yellow here. Hmm. I think E.T. is sort of a lightish-brownish."

The next day as I sat down next to her, Annie showed me her first page: a drawing of E.T. and underneath, the words "Hi E.T." She whispered, "I have a picture of E.T. in a magazine that I'm going to bring in and staple into my book." Then she began composing page 2, bending over her paper and talking to herself. "E.T. went through the woods and. . . ." She stopped to reread what she had written, then continued, "and hunters, huhnnters. . . ." She reread again, "and hunters were in the woods."

She turned the page and began another drawing of E.T. All of a sudden, she turned to Rick sitting nearby and said, "Rick, you don't like my drawings of E.T. I'll bring in one that looks exactly like him." Then she continued drawing, then erasing, drawing, and frowning.

I asked her what the problem was.

She responded, "I can't make him. His head has to be like this [she gestured big] and his neck smaller. When his neck is up high, do you know what it means? It means he is scared." To get out of this dilemma, Annie roughly sketched two trees with E.T. peeking out from behind one of them.

Annie continued to draw and compose throughout the rest of writing time. She had E.T. running, hiding, and eating Reese's Pieces. Pleased with her draft and excited about the idea of publishing it ("In the real book," she confided, "I'm going to put in the real picture of E.T. from the magazine. It's gonna be sooo great!"), Annie grandly placed her work in the conference bucket.

Unfortunately, Annie did not see her draft again until November 1. It took Reba that long to extricate it from the pile of drafts that had begun to accumulate. By the time Annie sat down at the conference table, she could barely remember what her story was about. But all was not lost. With Reba's encouragement, she began revising on the spot. The *h* for hunters became a hideout. Reese's Pieces became E.T.'s favorite food. And while Annie was recapturing her text, she was also learning some lessons about revision: how to add, change, and delete words from her draft when she needed to. Her revised draft is shown in Figure 3-7.

Already I began to see change. In September, Annie used only one letter per word. By early November, she was using two or three letters to represent one word, and some words ("and," "is," "love") appeared in their entirety.

Figure 3-7 • Annie's E.T. Story, October–November 1982

Hi, E.T.

E.T. went to find a hideout and he found a hideout.

E.T. ran and ran. E.T. hid behind a tree.

E.T.'s favorite food is Reese's Pieces. E.T. loves Reese's Pieces.

When looking over her first four drafts in order to choose one to publish, Annie commented that all the other ones she had written, "Piano," "Halloween Night," and "Thanksgiving," were "boring." She wanted to publish "E.T." because, she explained, "At least I have a real picture of E.T. I should pick 'E.T.' then because what would I do with the picture?" As she planned illustrations, she said, "It's going to take me a long time to make all these Reese's Pieces."

Learning About Conferences

In Reba's room, conferences occur frequently. They are for her one of the most efficient and effective means of assessing whether and how her students are progressing. Working individually with students at the conference table, Reba is also able to teach or reinforce the specific skills she thinks each writer needs.

Her procedures for organizing conferences are straightforward. The year I observed her class, students put their "completed" first drafts in the conference bucket and waited for their turn to be called to the conference table. Once there, they read their rough drafts to Reba as best they could. If she found that there were too few letters on the page for her to recognize the word the writer was attempting to spell, she wrote the correct spelling or sometimes the entire sentence along the side of the rough draft booklet. Students quickly recognized the difference between their invented spelling and Reba's standard one, and they were thrilled when she no longer needed hers but was able to decipher their writing on her own.

When students had completed four separate rough drafts and had had conferences on all four, they chose one of their drafts to publish. This meant Reba would type what they had written onto white paper, changing their invented spellings into standard orthography as she went along. Reba would then insert these typed sheets into cardboard covers and return them to the students for illustrating. Since students remembered what they had written on the rough drafts, they "read" their published books with little problem, although in the beginning of the year, reading was more akin to reciting a memorized text. As the year progressed, they became increasingly able to decode the standard spelling of words they could once only guess at, truly becoming readers of their own writing.

During her early conferences, Reba generally worked on two aspects of the writing process: making the meaning clear and establishing sentence boundaries. She asked questions of students, guiding them but always letting them make the final decision.

As the year wore on, her conferences became more complex, and she began to rely on skills the students had already learned. By November, she began to focus systematically on end punctuation with most of her students. Her conference questions were variations of the following: "How would you like to end that sentence?" "Do you want to put a period there?" "Do you want to show a lot of emotion?" "Remember that new thing we learned called an exclamation mark? Might you want to use that here?" And she was delighted when kids noticed the features she was highlighting in conferences in other reading material.

From her journal:

> At storytime, the kids have been bringing in their brothers' and sisters' published books. I've read them and Rick today noticed that one of them used an "!" which he used in his first book.
> Mike said that sometimes there are "!!!"—three of them in a row—he had seen this in a book at home.

In November and December, once her students showed her that they were ready, Reba also began to pay more attention to the sequence and development of their writing. She began to respond to what children had written by using active listening, repeating back to them the gist of their stories. At other times, she questioned them directly, asking, "Is there anything you want to add?" "Is this finished?" or, even more pointedly, "I'm not sure I understand what you are saying here. Is there something you can add to make it a little clearer for me?"

By December, Reba and her students had the conference format down pat. Before they were eligible to have conferences with Reba, the students had to confer with one another. During these mini-conferences, one student read aloud while another listened and occasionally asked questions. At the end of the conference, the listener had to sign the writer's cover. At this point, the writer could place his or her rough draft in the conference bucket and wait to be called to Reba's conference table. Because the backlog was becoming greater and greater, Reba began to work with two students at once. While the first read aloud, the second reviewed his or her draft. While the first revised, the second read aloud. While the first discussed goals, the second revised.

From December until the following June, then, conferences took on a comfortable familiarity. Reba always asked similar kinds of questions, never threw anyone off base, always appreciated what was down on the page, and waited patiently while students remembered an idea or painstakingly revised a sentence. It seemed to me that the students eagerly awaited conferences. They puffed up their chests on the way to the conference table, seemed to enjoy sitting next to Reba as they read their drafts aloud, seemed to appreciate the support, praise, and encouragement they received for their work.

Reba saw her job as a conferencer to point out what the writers in her class had done and to ask them what they thought they needed to do next. From her first conference on, she left decisions in the writers' hands. She was comfortable accepting the students' own spellings for the words they were trying to write, and if she offered information, it was generally to help the students hear the sounds they were trying to vocalize. Later on, as students became more confident, Reba questioned them more directly. She assumed that they would want to answer her questions about their texts and that they would want to insert whatever information was missing. Generally, they did, but when they didn't, Reba still left the choice to them.

The major problem with conferences was time—there was not enough of it. The students produced drafts more quickly than Reba could respond to them. In December, she brought this difficulty to their attention:

Reba: We have to talk about a problem we've got. It's the problem of the overflowing books. What are we going to do with that stack of rough drafts in the conference bucket?

Kids [responding with suggestions]: Get more buckets! Get more helpers. Yeah, ask the mothers to come help.

Kim [*responding with a suggestion for Reba*]: You could say, "When you write, slow down."

Reba: How can kids do that?

Kim: Don't draw scribbly pictures.

Annie: Yeah, you can say, "Take your time on the words and sound them out."

Kevin: Yeah, don't go hyper.

Rick: Don't write like a pig.

Reba: Those are all good suggestions, but what should we do about the basket now? Should I throw these out?

Kids: NO!

Sharon: You could throw away the ones that don't have names.

Annie: You could look through them carefully, see the sloppiest pictures, ask those kids if you could throw them away.

Reba: Well, why don't I pass them back to you, and you can see what you've got. Make two piles. One is the pile you like and want to keep, and the other is the pile you don't like.

This procedure helped the students weed out the drafts they no longer cared about or could no longer read from those they wanted to discuss in conferences. Throughout the next month, a student would occasionally wander over to Reba during a free period and ask, "Do you want to conference with me now?" And some kids gleefully volunteered to have conferences during math.

Learning to Slow Down and Talk About Writing

By December, publishing had taken over. The kids knew that after they had written four rough drafts on four different subjects they could each choose one draft to publish. Soon kids were rushing through three drafts so they could publish their fourth. Reba's concern, which surfaced in her journal, showed me that "feeling free to write" was only the first of many goals she had in mind for her first graders:

> I'm concerned. Darryl and Mike and others are sort of cheating on the 3
> rough drafts that they don't choose to publish. They aren't doing their best,
> just quickly writing anything. This occurred last year, so I'll do what I did then.
> From now on, I'll look at all four stories instead of only the one they want
> to publish. It takes more conference time, but I'm now beginning to look at
> quality, and not only at the fact that they are feeling free to write.

It was exciting for me to watch as Reba's kids began to feel "free to write." But sometimes their freedom to improvise as they wrote led them to invent new uses for their writing materials. On the day Robbie covered himself with red ink from the rough draft stamp, Cindy, Scott, and Brian discovered that the hot air from the heater floated their writing folders across the room. Disconsolate, Reba wrote:

I don't know what I want to do tomorrow, but something's got to give—I
was unhappy with today's writing session—
            too much noise
            too much play
            too much goofing off!
I had a terrible headache this morning.

That night, Reba resolved to change the pace. Thinking that a whole-group activity might work, she decided to bring everyone together for a sharing circle to discuss what each writer was doing. Having never tried one before, she wondered how her students would respond.

Early the next morning, Reba asked the students to bring what they were working on over to the rug. "It's time to share our writing," she announced. As she, the kids, and I gathered together on the floor, she asked, "Would anyone like to read something or to tell us what you are working on?"

Darryl and Mike, sitting close together, waved their hands in the air.

Darryl: We're starting a story about a submarine.

Reba: Could you tell us something about it?

Mike: We can't do that! We don't know! We only have the first page, and that's the picture.

Maureen [*going next*]: I finished this book and the name is "I Lost My Tooth." See. It's all true. [*Maureen opened her mouth and showed us a gaping hole.*]

Kim: Mine is called "The Ghost with the One Black Eye." It's not true. [*She giggled.*]

Annie: I don't know if everyone will laugh. But mine's going to be *so* funny. I'm starting a new one on Strawberry Shortcake.

Kevin: This one is about the spaceship that crashed.

Rick: This is E.T.'s house.

Kids [*looking at his drawing*]: What's that brown?

Rick: It's a volcano. And here's Pac-Man with a top hat and a bow tie on.

Robbie: I've finished two rough drafts. I'm on my third. It's about I'm going to Boston. The first one was I'm going to space.

Joey: Are you really going to Boston?

Robbie: Yes.

Rick: Are you really going to space?

Robbie [*in an exasperated tone*]: No, that's made up.

Reba was pleased with the success of the circle and decided to hold one at least once a week. It gave the students a chance to pause, to stop in midstream and talk, to share stories, to listen to and learn from one another. Recording her impressions in her journal, Reba wrote:

> Today, I tried a "sharing circle." Since I wanted the kids to come out with their own ideas—I really didn't know how the discussion would shape itself. We began with Mike and Darryl and quickly the children started sharing their

ideas. As we went around the circle, we would stop along the way and talk. The 25 minutes flew by.

The Kids Inspire Their Teacher

In January, a few kids unknowingly placed Reba in an awkward position. They asked her when she was going to write a book. She was taken aback. In the summer institute, she had chosen not to submit a piece to the class anthology, feeling too shy to make her work public. In the research project, she was keeping a teaching journal, but only because she had agreed to. In addition, I was encouraging all of the teachers in the study group to examine their teaching more closely and to begin thinking about articles they might write for publication. "Now on top of everything else," she groaned, "my students are asking me to write too!" It just seemed like too much.

But, Reba wondered, how could she let them down? They were so eager, so willing to try. How could she possibly admit to them that she didn't like to write? Besides, she wondered, what kind of an example would she be setting? So she took a deep breath and told them that she would begin soon, using some of her conference time for producing her own rough draft.

As she began writing her story, "The Day I Got Mad at My Sister," the kids came by to peek over her shoulder. They were very excited, watching her work, seeing the pages pile up. Sometimes they just stood there quietly; at other times, they interrupted her to ask questions: "Is this your first story?" "Is it true?" "How long is it taking you to write it?" "Where did you get the idea from?" "Are you really going to publish it?" As she answered them, Reba became increasingly pleased with her decision. It put her in her students' place; it gave them a chance to interview her, and she was delighted to discover that many of the questions they asked her were the same ones she used in sharing circles. For a moment, she even entertained the thought that writing wasn't so bad. But mainly, she was pleased that the kids now saw her as a writer among them:

> Today I wrote with the children. They accept my writing now and no longer feel that I'm not doing my part with conferencing. And next week, I'll be ready to have them conference with me.

Even more important than their shared adventure, however, was Reba's sense that she was teaching her students an important lesson. Thinking of the slower students, she wrote, "Perhaps some of them will see that not all of us have an easy time writing a book."

Examining Growth

Reba's becoming an author was not all that changed in her classroom in January, for we had now reached the time of year she has come to think of as "the growth spurt." After several months of working on an even keel, her students each January seem to leap ahead, to demonstrate major breakthroughs in their drafts. Nowhere was this more true than in the writing of Willy and Annie.

In November and December, Willy continued to produce drafts at about the same level of proficiency as those in September and October. But in January, I saw the dramatic change Reba had predicted. In his draft, "Muffin and Sam" (Figure 3-8), I came across an explosion of words, covering two-and-a-half pages. The story about his lost cat, he said, "was true."

Figure 3-8 • Willy's Draft, "Muffin and Sam," January 1983

Muffin and Sam

One day our cat Muffin ran away.
This is Muffin.

Continued

Figure 3-8 Continued

Ramaway ~~to~~ Then we got a new cat ~~call~~ c a Red Sam. he is grey and Whitean the is 2½ muns and very! good

Muffin ran away. Then we got a new cat called Sam. He is grey and white and he is 2½ months old and very good.

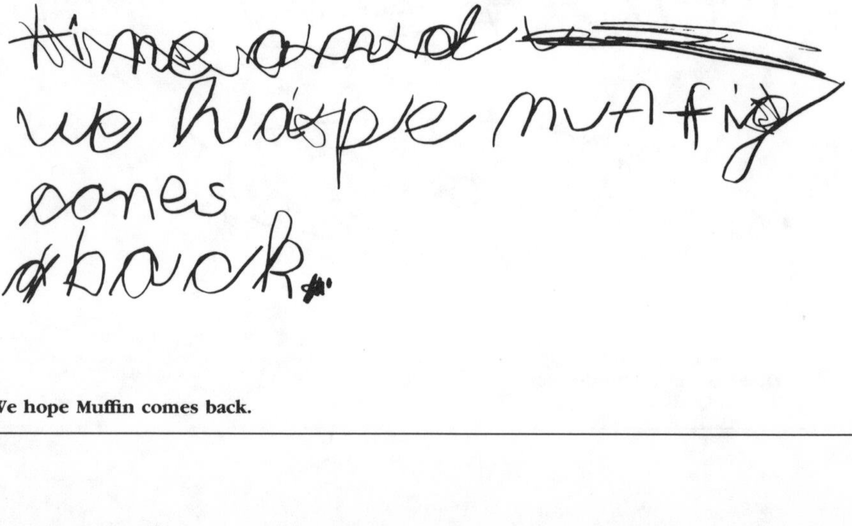

~~time and~~ we hope mufin comes back.

We hope Muffin comes back.

Like Willy and other first graders, Annie also continued writing at the same even keel for a few months. And, once again, it wasn't until January that I saw another breakthrough, another explosion of words. A total of eight pages and eleven sentences, Annie's story (Figure 3-9) is a detailed description of a lunch she had with her sister and grandmother, complete with "7 lur [layer] and black fors [forest] cake." She called it, "I Went to the Mill Ridge Inn."

Figure 3-9 • **Annie's Story, "I Went to the Mill Ridge Inn," January 1983**

I went in my car. I picked up my grandma. We went to the Mill Ridge Inn. I like the Mill Ridge Inn!!!!

Continued

i Had a Han Brg
and a 7: LUR cake.
My sit Had a skin.
pag. and 4 BLACK Fors-
it's cake WiaT iS BLUK
and Hast WiT FoST
and chars!

I had a hamburger and a seven-layer cake. My sister had a hamburger and a black forest. It's a cake which is black and has white frosting and cherries.

thene we wbek
and look at
the shops. my
sanna Bot us sik
~~of~~ of likris.

Then we went back and looked at the shops. My grandma bought us sticks of licorice.

Continued

Figure 3-9 Continued

*I tak my yanna
we waits
to my
uat and My ud*

*we tak ure yandmore
to my ats and
uack*

We took our grandma to my aunt's and uncle's.

*thene we wait
hom*

the   end

Then we went home.
The end.

Publishing Student Writing

At the end of the sequence of rehearsing, drafting, conferencing, and revising comes publishing. Providing students with both a goal to work toward and a way to see their invented spelling in standard form, it is more than anything else a way for students to celebrate their accomplishments.

Almost every day, one of Reba's first graders came up to her and asked, "Mrs. Pekala, did you type my book yet?" They too had come to know the sequence, and they too looked forward, as any author might, to seeing their work in print. Once Reba finished typing the rough drafts, she returned both the drafts and the typed, bound pages to the authors. The students then read what they had written to themselves and began their illustrations. When the books were fully illustrated, the writers practiced reading them out loud and then, usually at the end of the day, read them to the whole class.

The group was always attentive as one of its members read a published book, sitting in the same chair and acting the same way Reba always did when she read to the class. There were claps, laughs, pauses, and "oohs" and "ahs" as kids read and held up their illustrated pages. After the reading, the writers took their books home to read to parents and friends. The next day, they returned the books to the class, adding them to the growing stack of student-written books in the class library. At this point, anyone in the class could check out a book to take home.

In 1980, during my first visit to Reba's class after the summer institute, I was charmed—and amazed—when first graders came up to me and asked, "Can I read you my first published book?" After spending one year in her class, I became accustomed to children coming over and announcing, "I got my published book back today," or "This is my *ninth* published book. Wanna hear it?" or "Can you stay today to hear us read? Maureen and I published a book together."

However, as delighted as I was with the apparent success of publishing and the pride kids took in their work, I could see the toll it took on Reba. In March, she wrote about her exhaustion:

> I'm getting tired of typing books every nite—its been over two years now. I really feel that if my enthusiasm is low—which is happening—then it must reflect on my students.

Reba found two ways out of her dilemma. She located a teacher's aide in the school who was willing to type the students' rough drafts on a large-type typewriter. To help the aide, Reba rewrote the kids' invented spelling on a single sheet, admitting that "not typing each book is making it better, mentally, for me." But she also had some misgivings. Since she was no longer typing each word herself, she was no longer as intimately aware of how the students' spelling/encoding and handwriting skills were developing. She missed the close scrutiny that typing forced her to give to each text. On the other hand, though, she sorely needed a break from typing.

Reba's second way out was to take a complete break from publishing books and to focus on writing in other areas:

> Well I've realized that in the last few weeks I've enjoyed *not* typing and *not* binding books. Yes, we've been writing in class—but our purpose hasn't been in order to publish books. I now realize that as important as it is for the kids to publish books, its equally important for them to explore other forms of writing. Letters and science projects have widened their experiences.

Writing for Other Audiences and on Assigned Topics

While students in Reba's first-grade room wrote chiefly to record their thoughts, impressions, and ideas on paper, occasionally, writing took a more structured form. Every few months, Reba assigned a topic or suggested a project for students to work on. The year I visited her class, she found herself sympathizing with the plight of Julian Thurston, an eight-year-old British boy who came to New York for a life-saving spinal operation. One morning, she read the newspaper account of Julian's illness to the class, including his request to receive mail from American children. Her students responded immediately, working on rough drafts of letters, then having conferences and revising them. Reba was pleased with their response and marveled at the questions they asked him: "Do you use computers?" "Does it snow in England?"

Reba also began to notice that, for some students, the letters to Julian seemed to occasion better writing than their own published books. "Sharon wrote a beautiful letter to Julian," she said. "Her own stories have not reflected the insight into herself that her letter did." And, Brian, too, "who usually wanders around the room a lot, had a super question to ask Julian—and usually his stories are not that 'invested' either."

When I asked Reba if I could have copies of the letters, she looked surprised. "Oh," she said, "I guess because we didn't do them during writing time, I forgot to think of them as writing—you know, the kind of thing you're interested in." Embarrassed, she admitted, "I've already sent them to Julian."

Reba's admission was an important reminder. It showed me that no matter how important "the data" were to me, it was the real life of their classes that mattered to the teachers. As careful as we tried to be, reminding the teachers to save drafts, take notes, record "everything," certain drafts, conferences, and exchanges eluded us when teachers made decisions that put students' needs ahead of ours. If, for example, Reba planned to tape-record a conference and the tape recorder wasn't working properly, the conference had to go on. Or if a student had completed a rough draft and was so excited he just had to take it home to show it to his parents, he would, whether or not we risked losing it as a piece of data.

But I was not the only one to make a discovery during the letter-writing episode. "I guess I'm realizing that it's important for students to write for many different audiences," Reba commented in her journal soon after she had read the students' letters. Then she noted how the frequent writing they had been doing seemed to have an impact on this assignment. "I also think, though," she wrote, "that because my students do a lot of writing and have the freedom to explore their own topics, then when they write for a different audience or purpose, they have a depth of understanding they wouldn't otherwise have."

As Reba began to see connections between different kinds of writing, she also began to wonder whether she could draw on the students' accomplishments in writing to enhance their progress in other academic areas. She had already been excited by the way this approach to writing quickly led her students to learn sound-symbol relationships and how it enabled them to become more active readers. Soon she was wondering, could writing help them learn more about science?

In mid-March, Reba began a science unit in which the students planted seeds in plastic cups. She planned, several weeks later, after the seeds had sprouted, to take the students outside and show them how to transplant the seedlings in the school garden. But while the seeds were growing, Reba noticed that the kids couldn't take their eyes off the cups that lined the shelves and window ledges of their classroom. Each day, they bombarded her with questions: "What's happening?" "What do the seeds feel like?" "How long will it take for the seeds to become beans?" One day, she began to wonder what would happen if the children began to write—about the seeds themselves.

Early one morning, she gathered the kids around her. Sitting on the floor near the windows where the beans were growing, she began: "Boys and girls, perhaps you could write a story about the beans. Pretend you are the seed that you planted. Close your eyes. How does it feel to be planted? What's going to happen to you?"

As students recalled the experience of planting the seeds, they called out ideas. "It's cold down here in the mud," said Robbie. "No," said Maureen, "it's warm and mushy." "I poured water on my seeds, so I'm going to have a pool party down underneath the soil," offered Elizabeth. Brian said, "It's cold down here, so my beans are going to have a snowball fight." Chrissy said, "My beans are going to grow up and get eaten."

Reba's students, already familiar with writing, had no trouble entering the world of the beans and imagining both serious and humorous events. Reba was so pleased with the results that she couldn't resist typing the rough drafts and helping the kids make a classroom anthology of their bean stories. They called it, "Those Incredible Seeds."

The students' stories were varied. Rick continued his Pac-Man theme. Playing the role of the bean, he wrote that he died because Pac-Man caught and ate him—complete with illustration (Figure 3-10). Joey's draft took the beans through

Figure 3-10 • Rick's Bean Story

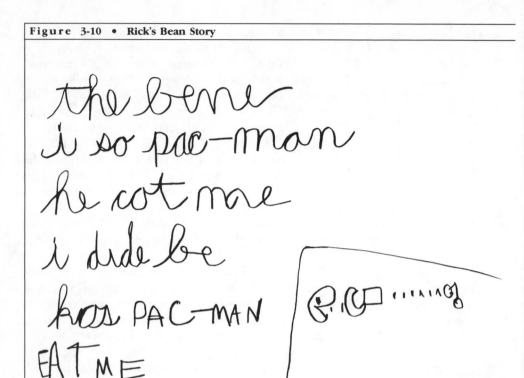

The Bean
I saw Pac-Man. He caught me. I died because Pac-Man ate me.

the whole life cycle. They had a party, they got wet, they died, they had babies, the babies grew up, had another party, and as Joey put it, "it wen [went] on and on!!!" (Figure 3-11). Willy's bean story (Figure 3-12) reflected a struggle against odds: "There was a boy. He found me. He wanted to plant me. He didn't give me any water. I grew [even] if I didn't have any water." I could almost hear Willy say, "So there!"

Writing Development in First Grade

The bean stories were written in March. When I compared them to the drafts students had written in September and October, I was amazed to see how far Reba's first graders had come. A few had entered first grade with little or no knowledge of letters and the sounds they represented. The majority were familiar with the nine letters taught in kindergarten. A handful were able to recognize much of the alphabet from watching "Sesame Street" or from reading at home with parents. By the end of first grade, all successfully wrote the letters of the

Figure 3-11 • Joey's Bean Story

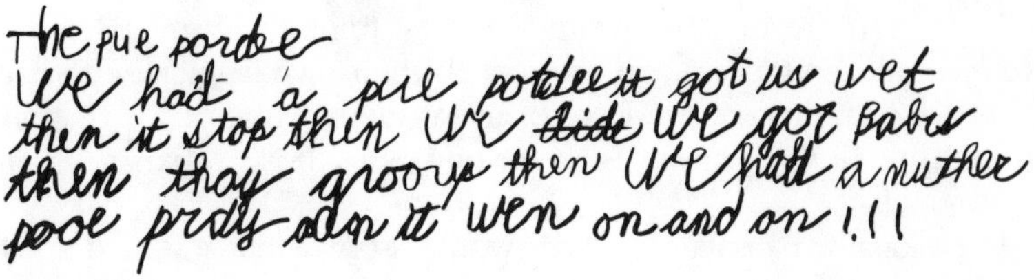

The Pool Party
We had a pool party. It got us wet. Then it stopped. Then we died. We got babies.
Then they grew up. Then we had another pool party and it went on and on!!!

Figure 3-12 • Willy's Bean Story

The Bean
There was a boy. He found me. He wanted to plant me. He didn't give me any water.
I grew [even] if I didn't have any water.

alphabet, and each had come to see that writing entails using the letters of the alphabet to form words which convey messages.

This development was the result of many activities. It seemed to me that the hour or more of writing time the first thing every morning was crucial. It gave the children time to explore actively their own language resources. Because during this time they were free to invent the spelling of words, they took risks and did not limit themselves to writing only those words they already knew how to spell.

Occasionally, parents or visitors would ask whether invented spelling fostered "bad habits." Reba's opinion, mine, and that of the other first-grade teachers in Shoreham who used it was that it fostered *good* habits. It became obvious to us after seeing the growth in child after child that when students' efforts at writing, however minimal, were respected, they began to enjoy writing and they took pride in their work. They knew their invented spellings were approximations, and they worked toward greater accuracy as the year progressed. The typed versions of their drafts provided them with the standard spelling of the words they had chosen to use, and, as a result, they seemed to learn many more words than they might otherwise have learned had they never risked inventing the spelling in the first place. Perhaps more important than anything else, the students never doubted, because Reba never did, that they would and could write.

Writing and Reading

Reba was convinced that the process approach to writing helped her students become confident writers. She also believed that this approach complemented the more structured language work she did in reading. I was less sure.

Every day, after the children returned their rough drafts to their writing folders, they returned to their seats for attendance and the pledge of allegiance. Then they turned their chairs toward the chalkboard where Reba stood, quiet and confident, ready to introduce them to a new letter. In the early morning, she had become accustomed to letting her students play with language. Now, however, following the district's mandate, she showed her students how to examine each letter of the alphabet closely, to listen to its sound, to practice writing it—to learn it, in essence, through practice and drill.

Skills in isolation. Workbooks. Basal readers. My heart sank. Hadn't I heard that elementary teachers were experimenting, finding ways to use writing to teach reading? Weren't they putting their basals on a back shelf, relegating phonics to the broom closet? What had happened in Shoreham-Wading River? I wondered. Was it possible that the writing program in the elementary schools was fundamentally at odds with the reading program? The writing program, as I understood it, was based on a meaning-centered approach. It assumed that language users were purposeful, that they had real intentions to communicate, that they would discover and invent meaningful ways to reach out to others and to understand. The reading approach, as far as I could tell, seemed just the opposite: words broken down into syllables, syllables into sounds, sounds into letters, letters into shapes. Did all those discrete bits ever add up to anything? Where was the meaning? I wondered.

I found myself in a dilemma. Not an expert in the teaching of reading, I was beginning nonetheless to have reservations about the reading curriculum as I was coming to know it in Shoreham-Wading River. My preference would have been to have reading and writing taught together: the students' published books used as reading material and trade books and children's literature enjoyed and discussed as examples of good writing. Reba, however, like other first-grade teachers in Shoreham, taught them as separate. My job, I knew, was not to change what Reba did (any more than my presence already affected whatever went on) but rather to document what she did. So, after an hour or so of writing every morning, I frequently sat, often with mixed emotions, through an hour or more of reading.

Interestingly, when I began to look closely at what Reba was doing, I began to notice things that might have escaped my attention had I completely dismissed these lessons. First of all, Reba never taught the students how to print. If they came to first grade already knowing how, they could continue. But if they didn't, they wouldn't learn printing in her class—or in any other first-grade class in Shoreham either. For while Reba and the other teachers were teaching the alphabet and its sounds, they were also teaching their kids script—or cursive writing, as they called it.

Reba's students seemed to like "learning cursive" and to think of it as fun. They didn't know that in most school districts first graders didn't write books, let alone use script. They were always volunteering to rush to the board to practice the letter of the day ("That's right," Reba would say, "with the letter *l*, you curve it up, then loop it over and come down straight and tall"), and they loved practicing their names once they knew all the letters and their formations. Christine had a great time since hers was the longest name in the class.

I also caught myself glancing at the area above the chalkboard as soon as I entered Reba's room. This was where she posted the new letter she was introducing, and I realized that I was never sure which letter it would be. She began with *c*, then *o*, then *a*, followed by *d* and *g*, and on and on, in no order or pattern that I could decipher. One day I asked her about it and discovered a history I had been unaware of.

It seemed that the district had been influenced by the work of Phil McInnis.[1] Using his "Assured Readiness" program, the kindergarten and first-grade teachers in Shoreham-Wading River introduced letters to students using a variety of

---

[1] Philip J. McInnis, *The McInnis/Hammondsport Plan* (New York: Walker Educational Book Corp., 1977).

kinesthetic experiences. Besides drawing letters on the board and practicing them on paper at their seats, the students outlined the letters in sand, sculpted them in clay, traced them with string. And the rationale behind the sequence? Shape. Those letters that were easiest to draw or write were learned first. Those with similar shapes followed.

McInnis asserts that cursive writing is easier to learn than print. With printing, students have to lift the pen from the page for each letter. With script, letters are joined, making the act of writing smoother. And, by learning cursive writing in first grade, students were saved the occasional agony of switching to it some time in the later grades. All in all, it seemed a rather sound and strikingly innovative approach.

I was less intrigued by Reba's reading groups, which always followed letter-writing practice. During this part of the morning, the students worked in groups of four or five and moved every twenty minutes or so from one "station" to another. At each area, they had a different task to perform. At one group of tables, they were expected to complete their workbook pages for the day, identifying and coloring in pictures whose labels started with the letter they had just learned. At the next, they worked with clay or string, molding it into the shape of the new letter; at the third, they ate their mid-morning snacks; at the last, they met with Reba to read.

At the reading table, Reba organized reading matter according to the students' abilities, providing each group with its own copies of a preprimer or a basal reader. Then, taking turns, the students read aloud from their books, pausing to answer Reba's questions as they went along.

The stories were instructive, to me at least. As a result of my stay in Reba's classroom, I had begun to become absorbed in the controversies surrounding the teaching of reading. One side, those I came to think of as the "meaning" theorists, argued that work on phonics and decoding was a waste of time, detracting from and at times impeding the development of "real" reading skills: the meaning-making skills we all use to make sense of texts we want to understand. The other side argued that work in sound-symbol relationships and decoding was appropriate, even necessary, for the development of reading skills, especially for children in grade one. Proponents of the Shoreham-Wading River reading curriculum said that it wasn't an either/or issue, that "something could be said for using both approaches." I understood their argument, even sympathized with them over the complexity of the isssue, but the longer I sat at Reba's reading table, the more I began to understand why so many meaning-centered reading theorists disliked the skills approach. Time and time again, I came across such sentences as "Mr. Pap put his cap on the mat near the cat." The meaning was contrived so all the sounds could fit in. Slowly, I began to understand why so many students, brought up on a diet of nonsense sentences, thought reading was silly.

Watching Reba's students make their way through their readers, I began to wonder what they thought about their work in reading. When I asked them about it, most agreed with Kim, who said, "Oh, this stuff is really cinchy!" And, to many of them, "figuring things out" was what life in classrooms was all about. One day, I watched as several kids played school when they had finished their "real" work. Maureen stood at the board and wrote lists of nonsense words. The other kids had to guess what they were.

From time to time even Reba tired of the basals. At those moments, she turned to the students' published books. She and the kids never seemed to tire of them. At other times, Reba let the students convince her that they needed writing conferences. If someone really wanted to work on a rough draft, she wouldn't draw hard and fast lines. After all, she said, "It's all reading, isn't it?"

Reba, I saw, wanted to do what was best for her students. She didn't want them to miss out. She hung charts with "sight words" on the walls and held up flash cards so that they would be sure to have a "second-grade vocabulary" by the time they left her class. She taught structured reading lessons not only because the district asked her to but also because she believed that such lessons had their place in first grade. The students accepted it all, yet they also seemed able to distinguish between the two very different uses of writing in their classroom: the spontaneous, meaning-centered work they did first thing in the morning and the more structured work they did a little later on in the day.

Looking More Closely at Willy and Annie

Willy was a shy boy with light hair and big round eyes. In class, he kept to himself but was willing, I noticed, to participate whenever he was called on. When he wrote, he wrote quickly, covering his page with letters and occasional pictures. His strokes were bold. Beneath the scribbled surface of his drafts, I often thought I detected a touching message.

By the end of the year, Willy had completed thirty-eight rough drafts and published nine books, second only to Rick, who published eleven. Three-quarters of his stories were fiction dealing with the fantasy themes common in Reba's room: E.T., Pac-Man, Space Invaders, missile blowups, Jaws, King Kong, and ghosts. One-quarter were based on experience and dealt with friends, animals, and memories.

In March, Willy returned to writing stories about E.T., publishing "E.T.'s Fun Day," a story in which E.T. drowned (Figure 3-13). This time, he switched back to print, and since Reba never insisted that her students use script in their drafts, he continued to print for the rest of the year. In this draft, written in all capital letters, Willy first worked carefully, taking his time with each letter. By the middle, however, he began to rush. On page 3, his printing degenerated; on page 4, he exited as hastily as his main character.

In March, Willy produced a bean story along with his classmates (Figure 3-12), and, in April, he wrote "The Bowling Alley" (Figure 3-14). His final story of the year, "The Dentist" (Figure 3-15), was my favorite. In bold letters and

Figure 3-13 • Willy's Draft, "E.T.'s Fun Day," March 1983

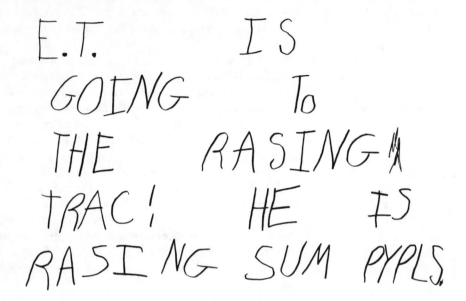

E.T. is going to the racing track! He is racing some people.

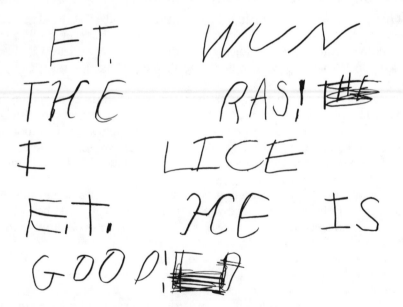

E.T. won the race! I like E.T. He is good!

Chapter Two
E.T. meets the swimming company.

E.T. drowns!!!

Figure 3-14 • Willy's Draft, "The Bowling Alley," April 1983

I made lots of scores!

Continued

Figure 3-14   Continued

I lost some scores. I got mad!!!

I took a bomb and I blew up the whole bowling alley!!!

I did not die. I had a costume on. It was metal.
The End

with lots of exclamation marks, Willy told what happened to him when he went
to the dentist. I was struck by the narrative technique, the acute detail ("It felt
like my tongue was cotton!!!"), and the sheer energy that this piece exuded.
Although I never spent a great deal of time with Willy, I was struck by how far
he had progressed, working very quietly under Reba's guidance.

Figure 3-15 • Willy's Draft, "The Dentist," June 1983

The dentist put me in a chair.

The chair went backwards!

Continued

Figure 3-15 Continued

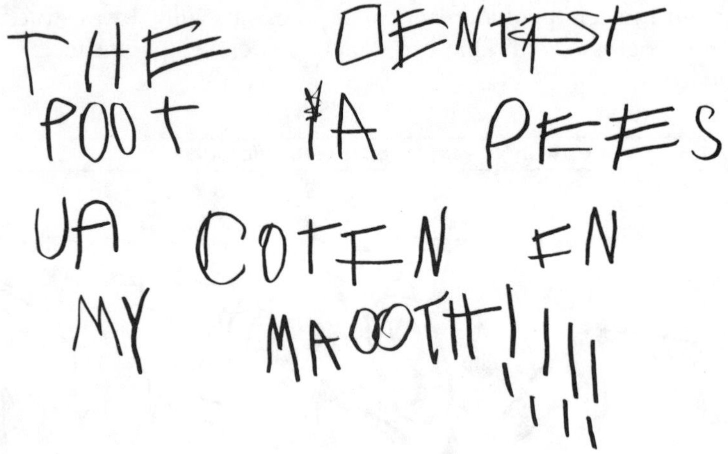

THE DENTIST
POOT A PEES
UA COTEN EN
MY MAOOTH!!!!

The dentist put a piece of cotton in my mouth!!!!

HE TOOK THE
COTN OUT!!!!

He took the cotton out!!!

HE GA ME
A SHOT!!!!

He gave me a shot!!!

IT AEELD LIKE
MY TUNG WVS COrmll

It felt like my tongue was cotton!!!

THEN IT STOPD
HRTENG!!!

Then it stopped hurting!!!

While I often observed Willy obliquely, I observed Annie directly. The first grader to whom I gave most of my time and attention, Annie showed me how one first grader learned to write.

Annie took to writing immediately. As soon as she grasped the idea that each word could be represented by a beginning sound, she began to fill her rough drafts with big printed letters. A prolific writer, she produced twenty-five rough drafts during her year in first grade and published six, a little above the class average. This is an instance, however, in which numbers are misleading. Annie's production was lower than that of many other first graders, but her drafts were longer, she took more time with them, and, by the end of the year, she frequently had twice the number of words on each page.

In March, as I sat down next to her, Annie said that she had no ideas for writing. Quietly, I watched her as she looked around the room. Noticing the Apple II computer, which her class shares with two other first grades, she had an idea: to write about the turtle who moves across the computer screen in the

Logo program. She added, "Logo doesn't really speak to you, but I'm going to pretend he's speaking."

She began composing, "I am . . . I am Logo . . . Logo is . . . a tur—[ten-second pause while she looked at the bulletin board above the computer] turtle. He— I'll just say it's a he—he looks like . . . like . . . like [two-second pause] a . . . Instead of writing 'triangle,' I'll just put this—" and Annie drew a triangle. Then, quickly sketching the computer, she got up, took the bathroom pass, and left the room.

When she returned, she sat back down and matter-of-factly returned to work. Then she looked at me and said, "When I get up, sometimes I forget what I have done." She reread what she had written, added some details to her illustration, and commented, "Logo has two question marks."

Rick interrupted, "No, he has four."

Annie retorted, "I know. I'm not putting in all the boxes." She then turned the page and continued. "You . . . y-o-u . . . push . . . push . . . but-buh-t-ons . . . to get it to muh-ooo-ve. Now, let's see what I have here. I'm talking so much, I don't even know what I have." She reread and commented, "The End." Figure 3-16 is a copy of her draft.

Figure 3-16 • Annie's Draft, "Logo," March 1983

About Logo
Hi, I am Logo. Logo is a turtle. He looks like a △.
Your Board

You push buttons to get it to move.
The End

Compared to many others I observed, this episode was brief, but it illustrated clearly many of the skills Annie brought to the task of writing. She knew that topics for writing were not mysterious, that she could begin with whatever struck her fancy—a trip, a television show, or some object or person her eyes happened to chance upon. She was comfortable making a range of stylistic decisions for the sake of her text, from allowing Logo to talk to deciding that Logo was masculine. She was flexible enough to allow for interruptions, and she had learned to reconnect herself to her text by rereading.

One final draft showed me how far Annie had come during the year. In April, she produced her longest piece, eleven pages with three chapters, entitled "I Went to Washington, D.C." (Figure 3-17). Describing the trip her family took over spring vacation, her draft starts out readable but falls apart a bit toward the end. On the cover, she has drawn the Washington Monument and the White House.

Annie was excited about this piece and asked me to conference with her as soon as I entered the room. As she read through it, she told me about her trip. She loved the American History Museum and explained that the objects in her drawing include "the real rubber ducky from 'Sesame Street' " and "Dorothy Hamill's dress." When I asked her why she used chapters, she commented, "If I didn't split it up, it would be like in one day we went to the whole entire thing."

Since we were having a writing conference, Annie watched me carefully, checking to see, although in this draft it was hardly necessary, whether I had written the words she did not know how to spell along the side of the page. She explained, in case I didn't know, "Someone else has to type it, and they need to understand."

In this session and in many others, when I sat by Annie and watched her write, I was struck by the easy, relaxed rhythm she established. Sometimes she sat, hand on chin, and looked out the window waiting for a thought to come. At other times, she hunched over, her face only a few inches away from her page, and painstakingly drew a picture. She scowled at something that didn't

Figure 3-17 • Annie's Draft, "I Went to Washington, D.C.," April 1983

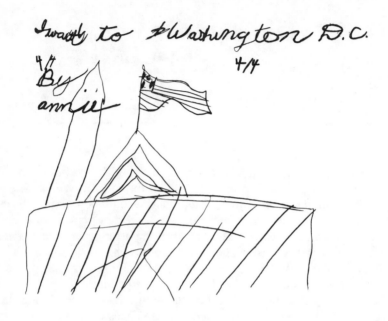

I went to Washington, D.C.

At five o'clock in the morning we got in the car. We got our stuff. We put it in the car. Then we got going. We are in New Jersey.

We are in Washington, D.C.

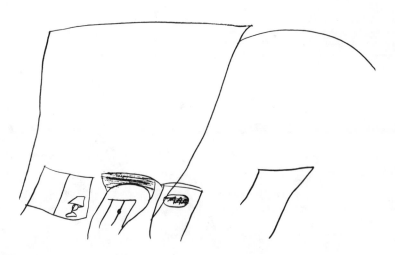

We got in the hotel.

Continued

Figure 3-17 Continued

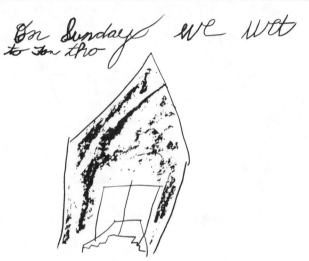

Chapter 2
Ford's Theater

On Sunday we went to Ford's Theater.

This is where Abraham Lincoln got shot.

Chaste theee
Nashnal Geegafick &
amncn Histoee &
Dtancaegrde

Chapter 3
National Geographic &
American History Museum &
Botanical Gardens

THe Biggest Gob'in amnao
Butancee gus   is Buful,!!!

The biggest globe in America.
The Botanical Garden is beautiful!!!

We saw Judey Gras Shoes
& fos Jackit
in & I saw them
amnalctr

We saw Judy Garland's shoes and Fonzie's jacket. I saw them in the American History Museum.

Continued

Figure 3-17 Continued

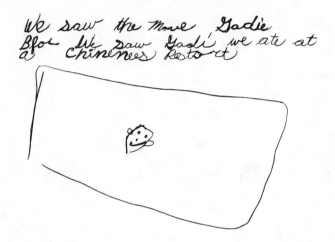

We saw the movie *Gandhi*. Before we saw *Gandhi* we ate at a Chinese restaurant.

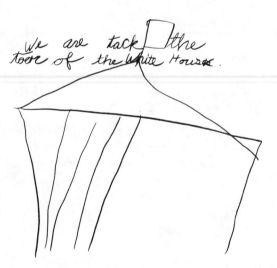

We are taking the tour of the White House.

We got home!
The End

please her and talked nonstop when she found something that did. By the end of the year, she was, in my eyes as well as her own, a writer who understood a lot about the writing process.

Celebrating the Students—and Their Work

By June, Reba's reading corner was overflowing with books published by her first graders. The year I visited her classroom, twenty students published 107 books for an average of 5 books per child. In prior years, smaller classes produced many more books, but 1982–83 was the year Reba "let up" on typing and began exploring the uses of writing in other areas. The question for Reba, however, was never how many books her students produced but rather how satisfied they were by engaging in the process. Their satisfaction, their accomplishment, and the recognition that each of them had become a writer was celebrated when Reba and her students gave an authors' brunch.

In the third week of June, the children invited their parents to come to school. While Reba and some students prepared cookies and breads, others rehearsed reading their favorite books out loud. On the appointed day, everyone's eyes were shining as each author was called to read his or her book to the crowd of parents and peers. Reba, gracious as always, stood off to the side, quiet and proud. Applause greeted each writer at this last sharing circle. Afterwards, the parents and the published books went home.

Teacher and Researcher

Reba came to the research project a willing, if somewhat reticent, participant. She arrived on time to all of our meetings, kept a teaching journal for two years, even managed to complete several articles on the teaching of writing in her classroom. But throughout the entire project, she was never completely comfortable with her written work. As our time together drew to a close, she wrote, "The research project has been draining on me only because I feel so incompetent with my writing." She saw herself, she said, as "not measuring up to everyone else."

How strange, I thought. Reba was the only teacher in our original group of thirteen who admitted to having such a strong aversion to writing. Everyone else liked to write, some of us had been writing for years, and nearly everyone kept some kind of journal by choice or wrote poems, letters, or notes. Yet when I examined my own thinking, I began to wonder whether we were the unusual ones. How many teachers, I wondered, were like Reba? How many were reluctant to write, uneasy about picking up their pens and making themselves vulnerable? My experience in summer institutes and workshops had shown me that Reba was not alone. It began to dawn on me that she was unusual not in her hesitation in the face of writing but rather in her courage in pursuing it. A "failure at writing" in her own eyes, she did whatever she could, which included participating in a study group after school for almost three years with writers she saw as more skilled than she was, in order to learn more about helping her students to write.

I began to see that Reba's supposed failure was a powerful teacher. Constantly aware of what it felt like to be the least skilled in the class, Reba made sure that everyone in her own classroom felt comfortable. No one was going to get lost. No one was going to feel diminished because he or she was not as skilled as the next student. And once I knew how to watch her, I began to see how these concerns shaped her teaching.

Reba was a protector. She watched over her kids; she made sure that everyone's work—however minimal—was appreciated. Uneasy with writing herself, Reba wanted her students to feel comfortable with it. She gravitated toward the process approach not, as other teachers did, because it confirmed the role writing played in their lives but precisely because it did not. Through this approach, Reba found for the first time that writing could be "nonthreatening." She took to it because she felt that it enabled her to create a classroom in which "each child is accepted for what he can do, and each has a place in the writing community."

One of her papers for our study group was entitled, "The Struggling First Grade Writer." It began with a description of how excited she had been when she first saw her students writing. But three years' experience with this approach had taught her that not all students, not even all first graders, can write immediately with ease and confidence. If Reba had any message for other teachers, it was to make sure that they gave enough attention to and understood the needs of those students she called "the wanderers" and "the avoiders." "The Annies of the world will always do fine," she wrote. "It's the Willys I'm concerned about—the ones that sort of slip by."

Not much slipped by Reba. As I watched her during writing time, I noticed that she watched the whole class. While conferencing with one or two students, she also kept track of what the rest of the class was doing. She knew who was conferencing with whom, who was off writing in a corner, and who was wandering around. Her tolerance was a result of her practiced eyes. They had shown her repeatedly that the children who were drawing, talking, or even wandering around were often inventing useful strategies when they were not quite ready to write.

Through her own experience as a writer and a teacher, Reba came to see that growth—in writing or anything else—took time. Recalling a visit by some administrators who had heard about the Writing Project and were interested in the writing that was going on in first grade, she wrote:

> One very snowy winter day some school administrators visited us from Connecticut. They had driven in bad weather, stayed in a not so great place for the night, fought the icy roads out to our school early the next morning, just in time to see my kids writing. They didn't move from their original standing positions, never asked questions of me or the kids, and gave the impression of disappointment in not seeing an earthshaking event taking place.

Reba was disappointed when visitors to her class did not see her students' growth as clearly as she did. In her words, "It's the 60 minutes each day that is building. If viewed by a single day, it doesn't seem like a great deal is happening. No, it happens in such small bits you have to know the large picture in order to appreciate the smaller, daily parts."

It is the "smaller, daily parts" that matter to Reba. At the beginning of the research project, she wondered whether we would see what she saw. She asked, "Will the growth be as apparent to the researchers as it is to me?" and frequently, she implored us to "see the kids as people—individuals with strengths and weaknesses." She felt strongly that we "had to get to know them, to see that the talker was a talker during math, music, gym, science, as well as during our writing period. The kids don't leave such traits behind when they leave writing time," she said, encouraging us to broaden our view and visit her room for entire days.

In fact, for Reba, writing comprises only a part of the school day. "Writing is much more important to me than ever before," she says, but she is also quick to state that she is equally concerned about "math, social studies, science, workbooks, listening skills, directionality, and most of all—learning how to learn." Reba was delighted when I was able to spend whole days in her class and when I came to know the students on my own. She was pleased that I got to know "the whole child," that I "watched them work in all the curriculum areas," and that I came to glimpse learning from "their points of view."

She was not so sanguine, however, about her own learning. She still viewed writing as "a huge weakness." She still did not write except when assigned a topic in the study group. She still felt, even after having a paper accepted for publication,[2] like an unskilled writer. In fact, Reba admitted, when she volunteered

---

[2] "By Popular Demand," *Elementary School Journal* 84 (September 1983): 25–27.

to be part of the project, she had not expected to write. "I sort of thought you or Jamie would be in my class watching, talking, and writing. I really didn't expect to play an active part—more the one being observed." But, in reflecting on the project, she also came to see what she had learned:

> The project came at a good time in my teaching career. Moving from a higher grade to first grade had already taught me that little kids have a lot on the ball. They ask honest questions, many of which I can't answer. This writing approach has convinced me even more that young children can reason and work independently. Even at their young age, they like to have some control in their lives. One of the things I've learned is to let them have more choices.

And while all her work in the project never brought Reba any closer to feeling successful as a writer herself, it did help her understand that even timid and uncertain writers can be valued in a community of peers. As she explained it in a letter written to me at the end of the study, "Now, I'm even more convinced that I'm not a writer, yet you, Sondra, still put up with me. I hope to generate the same feeling in my students—that no matter how unskilled they feel, they still know that their ideas are worthwhile and they can find help in getting them on paper." Reba, a reluctant writer, had, with the support and encouragement of the study group, managed to write papers and even to publish one. And if she could do it, she felt, then others could—even if they were scared.

Chapter 4

Ross Burkhardt
Eighth Grade

This is the story of a successful teacher who had a bad year. It is the story of Ross Burkhardt, an eighth-grade English and social studies teacher with twenty years' teaching experience, who found that, in one particular year, he could not connect with his students. It is a story of small successes and lots of anguish.

Not that Ross's year was a complete failure. By outside standards, he was quite successful: his students wrote, worked in writing groups, revised, and edited; they produced writing in many different forms and published both whole-group and individual magazines; they sent articles, many of which were published, to the district's newsletter; they read and wrote and grew and changed. But, to Ross, the year was painful. His relationships with students fell apart; his classroom felt like a battlefield.

It is probably common for teachers to have occasional bad years. Most teachers, however, forget about them as soon as possible. In Ross's case, his bad year coincided with his participation in the research project. I was in his classroom three or four days a week for an entire school year to document what went on, the writing I did a constant reminder that the 1981–82 school year was, as he put it, "the worst I've had in twenty."

Of course, in the beginning, neither one of us knew that I was collecting data on "a bad year," nor did either of us ever think that what had gone awry could not be set straight. We were both conscious of "good days," of days when students worked well and produced good writing. But, in the end, Ross's estimation of the year was "failure." And, as a researcher, I found myself face to face with what failure meant to Ross, to me, and to the approach to writing we both believed in.

An Innocent Beginning

The night before school started, Ross said, "No matter what else you do on the first day of classes, Sondra, be sure to attend the opening meeting of my team." In Shoreham, he explained, middle school students are assigned to teams that stay together for sixth, seventh, and eighth grades. Each year, on the first day of school, the forty to fifty students on Ross's team meet with him and the other teachers on the team for a class that "sets the tone for the whole year."

The next day at 8:42 A.M., I walked down the halls of the middle school toward the wing that houses Team I. As I neared Ross's room, I was greeted by the steady beat of the Beatles singing, "You say it's your birthday. We're gonna have a good time ..." and as I entered, I saw Ross up front, moving in time to the music. I said hello to the math/science, music, phys. ed, and woodshop teachers who were also gathering near the front of the room, then chose a seat off to the side and watched as nervous and giggly eighth graders filed into the three rows of chairs, all facing front.

After everyone was seated, Ross turned down the music (which had switched to a soundtrack of the Rolling Stones followed by some Simon and Garfunkel) and began to read:

It's the first day.
In they come—
Some pausing hesitantly
At the door ...

I recognized the poem as one Ross had written in the 1980 summer institute, now obviously a part of the ritual he used to introduce himself to his students. When he finished reading about the "crisp clothing," the "clean-cover notebooks," and the other symbols that accompany the first day of school, he talked about the importance of this "first class." It was a time when the students would hear about their teachers and possibly sense some of the promise of the year.

As the teachers spoke about their lives, their interests, and their histories in the district, the students seemed interested, alert. When Ross's turn came, he began by reading two more poems. "Opportunity" by Berton Braley was a "poem my mother used to read to me," he said, adding that Braley's notion that "the best work" had yet to be done was as true today for these students as it was in 1884 when Braley wrote the poem. After reciting Frost's "The Road Not Taken," he commented, "It makes me wonder what roads you will travel down this year." Then Ross talked about his home in Wading River, his cats and new kitten, and a recent change in his life. For the first time during a school year, Theo, his son from his former marriage, was going to be living with him and his wife Diane. A seventh grader, Theo was on Team II in a different wing of the middle school. Ross then brought the morning meeting to a close by adding what really mattered to him and the other teachers. "Team spirit," he said. "Doing things together. It's tough to live on an island by yourself." And as students began to file out of the room, Ross turned the music back on.

Later that day, I returned to Ross's room for his first English class of the year. Immediately, I noticed that there was no longer any front of the room. Ross had rearranged the tables and chairs into a large open square. Pulling my chair alongside a student, I surveyed the room. Overhead more than a hundred posters on popular culture or environmental issues with puzzling, humorous, or artistic messages rustled in the air. Outside, beyond a small parking lot, chickens from the school farm pecked in the dirt. Inside the room, laminated signs describing aspects of the writing process lined one long row of free-standing cabinets. Behind the cabinets, Ross's vast array of media equipment was barely visible. Slide projectors, tape decks, splicers, record players, viewing screens, extension cords, tapes, records, earphones, microphones, all were stored on shelves and tables until Ross needed them for class activities.

My attention was drawn back to the center of the room as I heard Ross ask everyone to take out some paper. He explained, "We're going to write continuously for ten minutes. There are two rules: don't stop and don't worry." To the cries of "I don't know what to write" and the queries of "Write about anything?" he said, "That's right, anything at all," then put down his head and began. Craig asked in a surprised voice, "Mr. Burkhardt, are you writing too?" Ross answered, "Of course, if I'm a writer in this class, then I think it's only fair that I write the assignments too. Now, let's get going."

After ten minutes, Ross broke the silence by saying, "You might want to finish up the thought you are having," and a minute later added, "What I'd like us to do now is share what we've written. I'll go first." Ross read about his excitement on the first day of school, his impressions of his students, how silly he felt when he confused Chris's name with Craig's. Then when no one volunteered to read, he called on several students. "Barbara, would you start us off?" he asked. "Sam, would you read?"

Slowly, the students began to read what they had written. Diana's piece struck a chord with everyone: no one, it seemed, welcomed the sound of the alarm clock after several months of summer vacation. Other students, too, wrote about the summer. Becky described the poetry workshop she attended in August; Bill described the trip he took with his family. Jill mentioned the renovations that had taken place in the middle school since she'd been away. A seasoned middle schooler, she thought it disconcerting to find rooms and walls where she didn't expect them.

Thanking the twelve students who read, Ross moved on, picking up the point Craig raised earlier. "You know, if I give you an assignment, it's important for me to do it too. That way I understand what I'm asking you to do, and you get to see how I see the assignment. For next week, we'll all be doing poetry recitations. At that time, you will each come up front here, stand in front of a microphone, and recite a poem you have learned from memory." Explaining how he wanted it done, Ross then demonstrated how a poetry recitation can go wrong. After giving examples of "mumblers," or kids who don't maintain eye contact with their audience, or kids who can't stand still, Ross explained that he would judge the students on three criteria: accuracy, expression, and poise. Passing around a handout with four poems on it, Ross continued, "This time around, I selected the poems for you to choose from. Later on in the year, you can go to the library and find your own poems. Of course," he said smiling, "if you decide to memorize a poem I have written, that would be all right too."

Kelley asked about one of the signs taped to one of Ross's file cabinets, which said, "KEEP ALL DRAFTS." Ross explained that students in his classes had writing folders in which they stored all of the writing they did, even rough drafts. "Want to see me go crazy?" he asked. "Crumple paper and throw it out." Then he explained, "In that paper may be the seed of the best writing you are going to do. That's why it's important to keep all drafts."

Talking about writing brought Ross to the subject of what the students would need for the year: a process journal, a social studies journal, a notebook for in-class writing, most of all "a writing implement." "If you're going to learn to write," Ross said, "then you must have a writing implement with you at all times. That's rule number one." Pointing to a large and rather ominous poster of Darth Vader, he continued, "You think he's bad? Wait till you see what *I* do if you don't have a pen or pencil!"

Then Ross said, "Let's see if I've been paying attention since this morning." And, without looking at a list or missing a beat, he moved around the room and recited every student's name. Pleased when the students applauded, he said, "It looks like we're off to a good start. You look like a great bunch of kids. Thanks for today."

Teaching as Performing

To Ross, "the classroom is a stage and the year a play that unfolds each of its 180 acts on a day-by-day basis." He designed his room with its theatrical quality in mind and, occasionally, during the year, when students asked him if he would leave the room exactly as it was for next year's kids, he replied, "No, in June, I strike the set."

Students and visitors are generally struck by the dramatic appeal of Ross's room, but what soon takes center stage is the action occurring on the floor. Frequently, the action revolves around Ross and his writing. Often he can be found in the center of the room describing his writing and his writing process to his students. Sometimes he joins his students in the open square where they commonly sit and passes around different drafts of his work. On the fourth day of school, for example, Ross shared five drafts of his poem, "Fog Dog," with his students and read to them from his process journal, explaining how on the past Saturday morning, when he glimpsed a stray dog rolling in the morning mist, he "just had to write about it."

Occasionally, Ross composed in class in front of his students. When he did this he was conscious of setting himself up as a model for kids to follow. Believing strongly in "setting an example," Ross saw himself as "someone who can show the way and point out how things can or ought to be done."

Early in September, for example, while he was working on establishing the notion of studying the writing process, Ross decided to compose aloud, to "model" his writing process for students in order to help them discover what to look for in their own experience as writers.

He told the students that he was going to begin drafting a piece of writing in front of them and that he would ask them to observe everything he did. "For example," he said, "what decisions do I make while I'm writing? Take as many notes as you can."

Diana asked, "But how will we know what you are thinking?"

Ross responded, "Good question. I'll be composing out loud. What that means is that, as I'm writing, I'll say whatever goes through my mind."

Ross then pulled his chair into the middle of the square of tables and asked the kids to suggest a topic for him to write on. After discussing several possibilities, they agreed that Ross should compose a piece on the Muppets.

We watched as Ross got comfortable, blocked us out, and began writing. After twelve minutes, he stopped and asked the students to report their observations.

Becky: You write down ideas to describe what you are going to do before you begin.

Diana: You scratch your head a lot.

Lee: You really sit up straight.

[*Lots of kids murmured assent here.*]

Jeanine: Yeah, but you move in real close when you get involved.

Kristy: I notice that you reread a lot.

Kelley: You use the biggest vocabulary I ever heard.

[*Again a murmur of assent.*]

Kerri and Craig: Yeah, we couldn't write like that. It wouldn't sound like us.

[*At this point, Ross got up from his seat and moved to the board.*]

Ross: What you are talking about now is ownership [*writing the term on the board*].
   This is the vocabulary I've become comfortable with.

Sam: Yeah, those big words sound like you.

Ross: And I'd like your writing to sound like you.

After a bit more discussion, Ross concluded, "I hope observing me will give you a better understanding of one person's process. I also hope it will help you do a more complete job in your process journals for Friday."

Writing about his perception of the class, Ross thought that the students were particularly perceptive. "Kids say the darndest things—they focused on my hands and how they moved when I talked to myself. They commented on my posture—I wasn't hunched over like they profess to be. I moved towards the paper when I got excited about an idea, they said. ... In all," he wrote, "I think it was a valuable demonstration of one way to show process."

Yet as much as Ross loved to perform, loved an appreciative audience, and, as he put it, loved "putting on a show," he spent a great deal of time "offstage" agonizing over the best way to proceed. After the first week of school, he wrote of "the creeping doubts that gnaw at my insides. Am I doing the right thing?" he wondered. "Have I gone too fast? Do the kids understand process? How do I get kids more into writing and taking responsibility for their writing? How do I avoid the slapdash approach that I felt too many of my kids used too many times last year? Do I use grades and mark them down merely because their priorities are not congruent with mine?"

Once he began to question himself, Ross even began to wonder whether his own performances were really that effective:

> Am I too strong a writer to provide a good model for kids? I think I write well, and I have a facility with words, and I know how to do it. ... But my former principal used to caution me about being too forceful in a discussion, and I wonder if I am too strong as a writer, too together in my approach to be of value. Is this conceit, or is it real? I do not know. Can Toscanini instruct budding musicians?

Establishing Classroom Rules

Although Ross's doubts began to surface in his journal, in class, his performance remained polished—at least during the first half of the year. Seeing himself not only as performer but also as director, as "the educational leader in the classroom ... the driving force behind what happens," Ross made sure that his students were aware of what was expected of them and what mattered to him.

During the first few weeks of school, Ross established routines. Everyone would write, himself included; writing would be shared (by the third day of school, every student had already read something to the class); and everyone's writing would be respected. One thing Ross would not tolerate: noise when someone was sharing a piece of writing. "If I have a value, it's silence," he told his students one day. "If there's ever a time to be serious, it's when someone is reading his or her writing," he said on another. The first time he dismissed a student from the class because the student was being disruptive during a reading-aloud session, Ross told the class "to mark this moment indelibly in your memories so it won't happen again."

In fact, this moment was painful for Ross. It occurred in September on the twelfth day of school. That morning, Ross told the class that he would be teaching them how to do active listening and that I was going to take a break from taking notes to work with him. After he read his draft aloud, he asked me to reflect or to "say back" what I'd heard in it. While I responded to Ross, Lee and Karl began to fool around, leaning back in their chairs, not paying attention. When I finished speaking, Ross turned to them and said, "I'm disappointed when I'm trying to give you a model to look at and you don't listen. I don't consider my job a game, or school a game. I'm upset. Here are two people, not paying attention, being rude and disruptive. Is that accurate?" The boys nodded.

Ross continued, "Unfortunately, this takes me out of the piece I'm reading. I don't like to send people out of the classroom, but there's the door. Do you want to say anything?"

The boys looked away.

Ross, still upset, decided to make a point out of this incident. "I get to school at 6 A.M. I'm serious about what I do. If you people will focus on your job, your writing will improve. You can get an awful lot out of me and others in the room. There are twenty-three of you and only one of me. You know collectively far more than I do. If you fool around, it's a disservice to your neighbor, the class, and me. That's pretty straight out. You know the expectations. . . . You have no right to destroy someone else's education. It's wrong."

Ross paused to look at Lee and Karl. "When I make a heavy speech, it takes a while to get back to the happy mood we were in. I love to laugh and have a good time. I don't like to put up with tomfoolery or rudeness. When someone is talking, others should be listening. This is a priority." Ross then looked at Karl and noticed that he was tapping his pencil, looking at the ceiling, ignoring the lecture. Sternly, Ross ordered him to leave. "There's the door—use it." Karl sat still, seemingly uncomprehending.

Ross repeated his instruction: "There's the door. I'd just as soon not have you in here for the rest of the class." Slowly, Karl got up and left.

Ross turned back to the class to explain. "Now he's upset and I'm upset. Maybe he didn't do something so terribly wrong. But I have certain standards. You've got to listen. Nothing is more important than respect for others. . . . Now, does anyone want to say anything? I've got to listen too."

The class was quiet. Stunned, I thought. But since no one responded, Ross moved on. Soon we were back into class work, pairing up to read drafts to partners and to practice active listening. Sitting near Shruti and Becky, I observed as the two of them worked together. When they had finished, Shruti turned to me and asked quietly, "Where do you go when you're sent out of class?" I realized that I didn't know.

When the class ended, Ross caught me by the arm as I was on my way out the door. "Well, that's the speech," he said, in a tone that told me each year he expected to make this point one way or another. And, during his prep period, Ross wrote about the incident in his journal, explaining to himself and to me his own behavior:

> Karl violated something I feel is crucially important—that people listen when others read what they have written. Karl didn't—he did not think I was serious, perhaps, or he didn't care, or he was testing me, or something else— but at any rate, he was rudely inattentive.

I had several options, but I decided it was time to make the point about being attentive. I scolded him, then told the class that the most sacred moment in this class is when a person reads his/her writing, and that Karl's violation of that moment truly bothered me. Since the point is crucial—the writing groups won't work with inattentive participants—I decided to emphasize it.

After he left, I explained to the class why I was upset, because I wanted them to know my feelings. I intend to talk to Karl later today and clarify for him what I did and why I did it.

Ross was aware of the point he wanted to make, and he used Karl's behavior as the opportunity. He knew he was making a choice at that moment, and, in fact, he states that most of his behavior in class is as deliberate as his choice to send Karl out of the room:

The things I do in class are deliberate. I am aware of walking away from kids with soft voices, going to the opposite side of the room so they will have to raise their volume levels to reach me. I am aware of focusing in on a single kid and carrying on a dialogue with just that one kid, ignoring (apparently) the rest of the kids, to make them want to listen more carefully, to place them in the role of eavesdropper on a private conversation, so as to get them to listen effectively. I am aware of the design of the room, the posters mentioned in my poem, "The First Day," the open circles of chairs, the furniture ready for class before they come in, so they find a sense of order and planning. I am aware of always changing where I sit so no one place becomes the "source" of teacher information, and I am aware that I subtly try to get them to change their seats so they will have different "points of view" as far as the room and their classmates go.

As he wrote, Ross began to articulate the set of beliefs that guide his behavior in the classroom. While rules and discipline are important to him, what he primarily strives to create is "an open, informal, happy, trusting, sharing atmosphere, a place where it is all right to argue back, to laugh, and to have a good time." "I want the students to look forward to coming to class," he wrote, "and so I do many of the things I do—I 'put on a show' as it were, to make them like me. I want them to like me, because I feel that if they do, they will approach their tasks in my class with real commitment and interest."

Commemorating Classroom Events

One of the ways Ross reaches out to kids in an effort to bring laughter into the classroom is to write poems that "raise humdrum reality to exalted status." In these poems, Ross writes about particular students or shared classroom experiences; as he puts it, he tries "to take anything that occurs and weave it into tapestry for the kids." Ross explains the "recycling nature" of the way he approaches teaching by the phrase, "Everything is grist for the mill." He writes:

Whatever happens seems to wind up in some heroic ode and thus becomes enshrined in word patterns as an event in the school year, and one event leads on to another, just as "way leads on to way." I try to connect and recycle experiences. The image of grist being fed into the mill for refining and recreating, for tying together and connecting, seems quite appropriate. The mill most likely seems to be my pen, which attempts to commemorate whatever happens.

In September, Ross wrote poems to commemorate a Team I pie-eating contest and the successful completion of the first two weeks of school. In October, he wrote about a day trip he took with the kids in his advisory group and about the Halloween night Variety Show. In November, homework and deadlines began to be the central issues of the class, so Ross wrote about those. And, in January, when the eighth-grade curriculum was given over to a social studies simulation game called Radicals and Tories, he wrote a poem to commemorate the arguments made both by students who wanted to stay loyal to England and those who wanted to secede.

The poem that appealed to me most was the parody Ross wrote of John Masefield's "Sea Fever." Masefield's poem was among those the students could select for their first recitation. Many came to know it well since they either recited it from memory or heard their classmates recite it in front of the room. Ross's version brought smiles to many of their faces:

C Fever
With apologies to John Masefield

My grade goes down to the C's again, to the lowly C's and the D's,
And all I ask is memory and an end to knocking knees.
And the first line of the first verse and my knees still shaking,
And the second line and it's getting worse, and my voice now breaking.

My grade goes down to the C's again, for the call to recite a poem
Is a clear call and a fearful call that sets my mouth afoam;
And the clenched hands and the blank stare while I'm up here dying,
And the missed word and the blown line and the fear of crying.

My grade goes down to the C's again, where the grades are below C-level,
To the bozo's way and the mumbler's way—recitations are work of the Devil!
And all I ask is a straight face from a laughing fellow Grover,
And a quiet room and polite applause when the long task's over.

Ross believes that writing which commemorates classroom events also "legitimizes" those events and enshrines them as memories. Memories are important to Ross. He is always delighted when former students return to reminisce over a class trip or a multimedia show he worked on with them. And he sees his teaching over the years as a vehicle for "creating memories for kids."

When I asked him why this mattered to him, he said, "Because I want to validate kids and what they do. Because kids need memories. Because I am still a kid in many ways. Because I try to think of how I would have liked it were I still a kid, and then try to do it that way if it seems to fit. Because I want to leave 'footprints on the sands of time,' and affecting positively the lives of kids is one way to do that."

Writing All the Time

Writing has always been important to Ross. Long before he took the summer institute, he composed poems for members of his family, created skits and shows with his social studies students, and wrote letters and memos and parodies of school events. It was not, however, until after the summer institute in 1980 that Ross realized his love of writing could become the cornerstone of his approach to teaching. It took the summer institute to teach him "the joy of creating and sharing with a group." And when he thought back to his experience of the institute, he wrote:

> I remember the days when I read my stuff to the group and how my heart would race. I was alive, risking, wondering if they'd like it. It felt good to risk, to know that my senses were alert, searching. In writing a couple of pieces, I discovered that I could do more than poetry. And I liked that. I have fancied myself a creative person and this approach gave natural harness to my unbounded and undisciplined energy and focused my writing so that pieces began to emerge. I also had the opportunity to be the historian of the summer group, and my enjoyment of lampooning events via satirical writing was real and, for doing something I have always done, I got the rewards of an appreciative audience.

Ross's experience in the summer changed him so dramatically that he "shudders" when he thinks of how he used to teach writing: "On a regular basis students would have to write essays that conformed to the Writing Standards a group of us prepared in 1974. These standards called for neat pieces, in ink, corrected and proofed, and done as finished copies. And they were due two days after they had been assigned." Recalling a paper written by a gifted student, he remarked, "I gave her a B+ (you see, it was still early in the year). Her transgressions were by the way of spelling errors, punctuation, etc. I gave little or no thought to the content coming from the brilliant girl's mind; all I wanted was for it to be mechanically correct." Ross remembered the result: "Sandra fell into the trap; she started writing safe stuff that met the Standards of Writing so that she would not have to recopy the pieces (as kids who had many errors had to)." He concluded, "My way of teaching writing then was to give only fleeting interest or attention to content and focus primarily on the appearance and mechanics of the paper."

Reflecting on what he called "the abysmal state of my English lessons," Ross explained why the Writing Project was so important to him.

> It got me in touch with a way to go about teaching writing that was meaningful to me. I learned about audience, purpose, and topic—remember, I had had a freshman composition course in the fall of 1958, and after that, absolutely no instruction in English save for a fireside seminar in poetry that met once a week in the prof's home in the spring of my senior year at Dartmouth (1962). As a geography major, I had absolutely no training in teaching writing or literature or any aspect of English. I was an arid desert, parched and seeking the liquid (this is getting too deep)—I was empty—I had no vested interest or background in any approach to English—I was a sponge

absorbing whatever Sondra and Richard said—and what they said made sense based on my experience, my perceptions, and my view of the world. I wanted to do better at teaching English, and they gave me the tools to do that job.

More Doubts

The Writing Project provided Ross with "a philosophy, methods, a structure, a complete and holistic approach," but it could not guarantee success. Ross would have to find his own personal synthesis, melding the method he had taken so to heart with his own bent in teaching. The year I observed his classroom, his concerns centered upon the issue of control.

In November, for example, Ross wanted to run "a free-form series of classes." The students had a number of different tasks to work on: finding poems for their fourth recitations, making copies of the poems so Ross could approve them, meeting in writing groups for feedback on the pieces they had chosen to publish in their class magazine, editing their pieces for publication, or completing the novels they had selected for the next round of "booktalks" (a middle school program in which all the teachers and students in the school sign up to read novels, then meet together in small groups to discuss them). "There will be a lot of confusion and some tension on my part," Ross wrote as he planned these classes, and admitted, "When kids are working individually I always feel nervous—even after all these years I feel, what if they aren't doing what they are supposed to be doing?"

Later that week, Ross was annoyed at himself for "yelling at kids." "Two days in a row now," he wrote, "I had to speak sharply to the group, surely a sign of some pressure or tension I am feeling."

A month later, a similar situation arose. The students were working on drafts of articles to be sent to the district newsletter. Since they needed to be in their writing groups, Ross allowed them to leave the room and meet in various parts of the hallway, sitting on the floor, leaning up against the lockers. But as soon as he went out to check on how they were doing, he brought them right back to the room and began, once again, to scold them. "You have not met my expectations," he said. "Several of you were bunched together in the corridor, others were just wandering around."

Basically, it seemed to Ross, the students were just "wasting time." Ross was upset, however, with himself as well as the students. Thinking over what had happened and his reaction to it, he wrote, "I think I was mad at myself for not having structured the task more clearly for them—but I was also mad because I did not have control over the situation. I am still uncomfortable with that—letting kids go and not knowing."

The more Ross examined what he was doing with his students, the more uncertain he became. Always looking for the "teachable" moment, he was worried on the one hand about "intervening too soon" and on the other about "waiting too long." In November, he made a list of what he called a nagging series of questions:

Is Paul's piece too long? Should I let Lee get away with his copying since it's gone this far? Is Kara's piece too short? At what point is it appropriate to intervene in the "creation" of a piece so that I teach the child how to create/shape his/her own meaning rather than become dependent on me for help?

Later the same month, he wrote:

Will the kids' writing be good? Are they producing something "worthwhile" or just "filler"? How do you get kids to really care about what they write?

And in December:

I had the sense that writing groups were perfunctory, shallow and not really helpful. Kids on draft two were done in 5 minutes. I need to work on the skill of having them respond constructively ... But how does one do this, and at the expense of what?

At the same time, Ross began to worry whether his own easygoing attitude was giving some students the wrong message.

Since I do not grade stuff, kids this year and last do rushed, sloppy work and "get away with it." I have a vague feeling of unease about it, one that I cannot articulate yet. I know something is wrong, but exactly what, I do not know, and what to do about it I know not either ... In this writing process approach, I do not want to thwart kids, but some kids thus take advantage of my apparent unconcern or laxness and do minimal work. How do I get quality work without "thwarting" (I am sure there is a better word) kids and turning them off to writing?

In particular, Ross was thinking about Kenny, a student whose punctuation problems included "using one big run-on sentence for most of his pieces." Ross wanted to "up the ante" with Kenny, "get him to stop rushing through his work and put in the punctuation if he is capable of it." "I feel I do him no favors," Ross wrote, "if I allow him to deliberately take the easy way out and not meet acceptable standards." Yet Ross was confused. Kenny rarely showed any interest in writing; in fact, he rarely wrote at all. To focus attention on punctuation before Kenny found any use whatsoever for writing seemed premature. Not sure of what to do, Ross did nothing. Several days later, Kenny handed in the following poem:

He is the cause
of all my trobles
He is the cause
of all my problems
He is the cause
of all my fightes
He is the cause of all my grife
He is everything
I hate to be
Him!!! Him!!

Although the poem, like Kenny's other pieces of writing, still lacked punctuation, Ross was stunned. For the first time, Kenny had turned to writing to deal with a situation that was bothering him. From Kenny's process journal, Ross discovered that "Him" referred to Kenny's mother's boyfriend. And while this episode did not solve Ross's dilemma or Kenny's punctuation problem, Ross saw a fundamental imbalance in the situation. "It struck me as somewhat bizarre that I was overly concerned about his ability to punctuate when he had this incredible home situation that he was trying to deal with through his writing. I wrote a response in which I expressed concern and appreciation for his having told me."

Given the personal nature of what Kenny had written, Ross felt that his response was appropriate. Yet privately, he continued to remain concerned not only over Kenny's punctuation but over many other classroom issues as well. In fact, as the year wore on, Ross became acutely aware of the discrepancy between his offstage agonizing and his onstage performance. In a moment of openness and vulnerability, he wrote about how he saw himself:

> I feel not unlike Eisenhower planning D–Day—every step a carefully mea-
> sured pace toward the goal of better writing and much off-stage wringing of
> hands as I ponder which step of the many possible to take and why that one
> is "better" than another. . . . How interesting—the hand-wringing and agonizing
> indecision on my part and the apparently smooth appearance as seen by the
> kids. . . . This two-faced situation with me aware of both and the kids only
> aware of one. . . . Here is a drama being played out, unbeknownst to them, me
> trying to make the right decision, trying to think of what is best to do . . .
> and here they are blithely unaware of how difficult it is for me, how I worry
> about it so.

Resistance Begins to Surface

It was not until midyear that Ross's worries seemed to indicate more than a teacher's normal concern, not until then that I began to wonder if something more than the normal upheavals of classroom life was going on. It began to seem as if, no matter which class or group of kids he was teaching—those in his English classes or in social studies—very few students wanted to accept his plans or follow his directions.

By this time of year, in fact, Ross expected his students to be volunteering eagerly, reading their writing aloud, sharing their ideas and observations about their writing processes as last year's had done. Yet whenever he asked his students to read or to discuss their writing, they seemed to resent either the questions he asked or the way he asked them. A few dutiful students would always acquiesce, but the group as a whole seemed unwilling to give Ross what he wanted.

In February, for example, Ross planned to have the students write a "thank you letter" to someone who was important to them during their middle school years. Thinking that the letter would be an occasion for students to reflect on their experiences of the middle school, he talked about the difference between perfunctory and impelled writing. He explained that so often we all say "hello" or "thank you" and don't really mean it. This assignment, he hoped, would give students "an opportunity to acknowledge someone significant in their lives." Ross then gave students several minutes to jot down possible candidates, people who meant something to them or who had helped them in some way over the past few years. When he asked for volunteers to read the lists they had come up with, nine boys in a row flatly refused.

Later the same week, Ross again raised the issue of investment in writing. With prompting, many of his students admitted that writing a letter to someone they cared about was more important to them than the writing they often did for class. Yet as soon as Ross asked whether they would be willing to put the same kind of investment into their in-class writing, they balked. They heard his request as asking them to reveal more of themselves than they wanted to. They refused to expose what they were feeling and thinking to the whole class. They refused, as they put it, "to spill [their] guts on paper." Again, a stalemate.

Soon Ross began to see hostility in much of his students' behavior. Caught in a downward spiral, he began to interpret everything students did—even small actions that in an otherwise good year he might not have noticed—as signs of defiance. When Barbara, for example, came to class a few minutes late, then took a seat off by herself, outside the square, Ross was furious. "I'm tired of this," he said. "It's February, not the first day of school. When I say sit in the square, I shouldn't have to remind anyone to do it." In case she missed the point, he made it even clearer, "I'm talking to you, Barbara." A few minutes later, Frank turned his back to the whole group. When Ross said, "I don't like how you are sitting," Frank shifted slightly in his chair, only to block Bill's view of the class. Annoyed, Ross moved Frank's seat to the other side of the room.

As cooperation between Ross and the students deteriorated, as the easy give-and-take of classroom life turned into a tug-of-war, Ross noticed that his work and his attitude were deteriorating as well. Unable to meet all the deadlines he had set for himself, shocked at his inability to get things done, he felt more disturbed all the time:

> I feel badly that I'm not living up to my image of myself—by this I mean the image that I have of myself as a superman, capable of doing twenty things at once. I keep piling on tasks and responsibilities until the legs creak, and then I feel badly because I am overloaded. I have only myself to blame.

Ross's solution, however, was not to reduce his workload or to take on fewer tasks—it was to write. He used the time given over to writing in one of our Tuesday afternoon study groups to write a poem about the "tense, depressed state" he was in.

Impelled Poem

I have not penned a poem these many weeks.
Think not my muse has wandered off and died;
Rather, pressures heavy from without
Blocked rhythms seeking exit from inside.

A tense uneasy feeling—unrelaxed
Anxiety clenching gut and limb—
Now pervades my being, braced and taut.
Horizons once seen clearly have grown dim.
I live in fear of not achieving goals
I've taken on. Why am I afraid?
In my head I know there's nothing wrong
With missing several steps in the parade,
But in my heart, the pain does not subside
And give me rest. My need is real:
To stop and shape ideas more frequently
And capture how, poetically, I feel.

Ross felt that writing the poem "served the purpose of allowing me to feel better because I was honest with myself and the pain I feel on occasion." The next day, he brought it to class and explained what led him to write it: "Yesterday I did the first draft of a poem in Sondra's class. We meet in here. I was sitting where Lee is sitting now and I just wrote down this line: 'I haven't penned a poem these many weeks.' I liked that line and, you know, it's the truth. I'm feeling a lot of pressure now, you kids probably know that. I was feeling bad, and I wanted to deal with it, to capture it. That's what I did, and it led me to have a real investment in this poem."

Trying hard to find an opening, a way to reach his students, Ross continued to devise assignments that he hoped would be meaningful to them as well as to him. One such assignment, the "Gift of Writing," was fashioned after a very positive and real use of writing in Ross's life. In this assignment, Ross asked the students to create a piece of writing for someone else—for someone it would give them pleasure to write for. It could be a friend, a family member, someone in the school community. Like many of the poems Ross wrote for the kids, this piece of writing could be thought of as a "gift," as something "you do for that person, to make him or her happy." The piece did not have to be about that person, but it should relate to that person in some way. Ross's goal was "to have the kids write a piece in which they have a real investment, knowing ahead of time that it is going to someone and is about something real (even though it can be a story or a fable)." But Ross's students, while willing to do the assignment, nonetheless found a way to thwart his intentions.

Ross's plan was to have students do a first draft, bring it to writing groups for response, and then do a revision before giving the piece to the person it was written for. The students, aware of the importance Ross placed on writing groups, questioned whether groups were appropriate for this assignment. After all, they said, if the writing was for someone not in the class, why should anyone in the class see it? What if the writing were "too personal"? Besides, they argued, the person it was written for might understand it, but that didn't necessarily mean that Ross or a writing group would. It seemed to them that Ross was violating their sense of privacy. If they really owned their own writing, why should Ross dictate who should read it?

Ross once again found himself on the horns of a dilemma. He believed in the students' ownership of their writing, and he believed in the usefulness of writing groups for response and feedback. Both were important, yet what we taught him in the summer institute did not tell him which was more important. How was he to decide? Afraid that, if he gave in, he would be "setting a precedent that every 'real' piece of writing" didn't have to be shared, he was equally concerned that if he insisted that all students go to writing groups, they might not write with the investment he hoped this assignment would generate. He put it this way:

> My conflict is simple—that I do not want to compromise the model (it calls for sharing) and that I do not want to set a precedent that every "real" piece can't be shared. I guess the greater good is in question—is it better not to have a writing group and allow kids to write freely, or is it better to do a writing group and not get as good a piece of writing?

Ross, perplexed by the dilemma, asked my opinion. I, in turn, asked him what his purpose was when he gave this assignment and whether or not he felt students had the right "not to share." Although, given the dynamics of Ross's classroom, this was a tricky issue, I thought that he had more to gain by respecting the students' requests than by setting hard and fast rules.

By the time we finished talking, Ross decided that he would treat the students' objections seriously and honor their request. But since he had given the assignment for homework, the only way he could inform them of his decision was to write them a letter and deliver it to them before school ended. In the letter, Ross summarized the issue, then said, "This evening, when you work on your piece and do your process entry, you should know that not sharing the piece is your option." He then recorded what happened in his journal:

> I delivered the letter during lunch. I felt a lot better when Diana smiled, looked relieved, and said, "Thanks."
> Kristy and I just talked about it, and she let me know that she does not see it as a key issue for her—and now that I've removed the constraint of having to share, hopefully kids will be able to do some "real" writing tonight.
> I feel good about the letter. Rereading it, I see it as saying what I want it to say.

Yet as Ross wrote, he once again began to wonder about the students and their hostility:

> I wonder if part of this is the whole issue of these kids. I'm not sure. At one point I was afraid that pressing too hard on this issue might alienate the kids, might turn them from me or from writing, that their anger might harden into semi-permanent hostile attitudes. I do hope the issue has been diffused— and as Scarlett might say, tomorrow is another day.

In fact, Ross realized that he was feeling better about classes and kids once he began planning his own gift of writing. Having "stumbled across two students kissing in the hallway one afternoon," Ross decided to write a piece called "The Phenomenon of the 8th Grade Goodby," dedicated to the "Kiss-em-Goodby Guys and Gals." He was delighted with his plan, "a warm parody of the situation as seen by a teacher checking out the scene," and realized how long it had been since he was "inspired by student actions." "Grist for the mill," he noted, "the reappearance of the phrase helps. I haven't done a poem about kids on the team for a long time (since before Xmas)."

Resistance Comes to a Head

During the month of March, Ross compared his teaching to a "roller coaster—with abrupt highs and lows." One evening after a particularly difficult day, he wrote of the pain of receiving "one kick in the teeth after another." Much of his concern stemmed from difficulties with the multimedia show he was working on with his students.

A master at media shows, Ross loves making complex soundtracks, organizing slides, overseeing a host of complicated media decisions. In fact, multimedia shows are Ross's specialty. He is known throughout the district for the dramatic quality of his work, and, in addition to the show he usually creates with his class on a social studies issue, he often produces several others each year for friends, for college reunions, for conference presentations, and for the middle school's graduation party for eighth graders. This year, however, he was experiencing tremendous difficulty with his class. Students were not following his directions; work was not getting done.

Why wouldn't his students do it? he wondered. Was the task too large? Was "Survival," the theme he had chosen to complement the conference theme of the New York State Social Studies Conference, too abstract? The students had spent several months, in social studies as well as in their English classes, viewing shows Ross had done on other subjects, making notes and interviewing people on the issue of survival, drafting pieces on war, on poverty, on famine, and on pollution, organizing the writing into the various sections of the show, designing a logo. Hours and hours had gone into planning, rehearsing, and drafting, and yet, when everything should have been coming together, it was falling apart. "Maybe I lost the vision for this show," Ross wrote. And, on another day, "I better get it done soon or it will continue to grow like an albatross."

Yet every time Ross assigned students to work in groups, to make decisions about content or sequence, they made little or no progress. They fooled around, especially during rehearsals. Many were even unwilling to stand in front of a microphone and read what they had written. Ross found himself yelling more and more, and as time passed, making more and more of the decisions himself.

After school one day, Ross returned to his room to find that wires to one of his tape recorders had been cut, mike jacks were missing from three sets of earphones and a number of earphones were missing as well. "It sickens me," he wrote, "to think that there are kids who wantonly destroy stuff in my room. I guess I'll have to tell them that."

That evening, Ross and I spent some time talking. As he sorted through his reactions, he realized that he had a lot to tell his students. He was, as he wrote later, "sick to [his] stomach with their lethargy and lassitude." He felt as if his students were "ponderous bags of sand" which he was "dragging through the mud." Their hostility had been getting to him for some time. This latest violation was intolerable.

But as angry as Ross was, he knew that blaming his students would do no good. Their defensiveness, he felt, would only become more entrenched. What was needed, he thought, was reconciliation, a fresh start. While he knew he would have to address the issue of vandalism, he wanted to keep it separate from the issue of failure that was gnawing at his insides and sapping his strength. Privately, in fact, Ross believed that the attack on his equipment was just another symbol of his "failure to succeed with these kids," and it was his sense of failure that he wanted to address as soon as possible.

The next day, in the midst of a particularly trying rehearsal during which students once again subtly resisted his directions, Ross stopped everything and gathered the students together on the floor. "I know something is wrong," he said. "Classes aren't working and I feel responsible." The kids were quiet and could hear in his shaky voice, as I could, that Ross was upset. "I've been feeling very badly. I don't think I've been doing a good job as a teacher and I want to. I care very much about you and I need you to tell me what I have done wrong."

The kids, sensing Ross's pain, were not sure how to answer. Kerri broke the silence by admitting that the kids were wrong, too. They also played a part in what was going on. Kenny asked Ross what he really wanted from them. He answered quietly, "Respect, cooperation, and a willingness to try." Shruti spoke next. "Mr. B.," she said, "I don't want to be mean, but maybe you're too personal, maybe you care too much."

Sam responded immediately, "Is that bad?" But no one wanted to answer. It seemed as if there was more to say but no one willing to say it. Finally, Chris admitted that some people might not want to talk in such a large group. Ross, taking Chris's comment as a suggestion, asked, "Would it be better if you wrote about it?" As students murmured assent, he continued, "Please, if you care to, write to me about what has happened, your feelings, what I should do to improve. I can't force you to write, but I would appreciate it, and it would help."

Many students took Ross up on his invitation. Most wanted to reassure him. "What have you done wrong?" they asked. "Nothing! Absolutely nothing!" "You're a great teacher!" "I think it's terrific that you care so much about your students."

Yet others seemed to agree that underlying all the activity of classroom life, something wasn't working. Tina wrote, "I think maybe you're doing something wrong and we are too. I'm not sure what, but I know there's something wrong." Kerri admitted, "Sometimes I feel we don't live up to your expectations and then we feel, or I do, that we let you down." Bob and Marc suggested in a letter they wrote together that Ross "should take things a little lighter, be a bit more understanding and try not to be so serious all the time." Bill advised Ross not to be "so hard on yourself and try not to do so many things at once." But mainly Bill blamed Ross's problems on the students. "Some of the kids act like jerks and are totally irisponsible. I know if I were a teacher and worked with kides all year it would depress me too if they set fire to the bathroom and destroyed AV equipment." Kara had a similar perception. She wrote, "I can see why you get so mad in school often. I would too if I were you. The kids (some of them) are very rude, unrespectable and deliberately try to do things to try your patientce."

Becky was the only student to discuss directly the resistance to the social studies show and to bring up other issues related to the way Ross was teaching English:

> Mr. Burkhardt,
>
> I think one of the main problems is about the show. We (some of us) don't feel that the show is ours anymore. You do everything (well, almost everything). It's sort of like you are taking over.
> I feel like our show isn't any different from all the other shows. The info is different but the pattern is the same. It's like we use the same plans that you used 10 years ago.
> It reminds me of an assembly line. Us being the workers and you being the boss, passing the show down toward the finish line. And all it seems like we are doing is following orders!
> I also think that what Shruti said is half true but not all true. "Personal" isn't the right word. I think you pry into other people's business too much. You seem to think that honesty means sharing all of our personal problems and concerns with you. Well, that's being nosey, not honest!
> I feel that the 2 problems I mentioned are very important.
>
> > Becky

Ross responded by typing lengthy letters to all of the students who wrote to him. In his responses, he sincerely thanked the students for the support they offered him and then went on to explain in more detail the thinking behind his behavior in class. His response to Becky was typical:

> Dear Becky,
>
> I appreciate the ideas you raised in your letter and the fact that you took time to write me. You raised two significant ideas—that the show is not "yours" anymore, and that I "pry into other people's business" too much. I'd like to reflect on both ideas.
> As far as the show being "yours" or "mine," what I am trying to get to is how to make the show "ours." I cannot do it alone, and I believe that you and the other kids cannot do it alone. Thus, it is a mutual effort. The presentation that Diana and Darlene made is part of an attempt to have kids take responsibility for the show. And one thing that is missing is that as a group you need a way to participate in the decision making process. I am going to try something in social studies tomorrow that gets at that—please let me know what you think of it. Hopefully kids will be able to take part in the important deci-

sions and will thus feel that the show is "theirs." I thank you for pointing this out and thus moving me in this direction.

As for being personal, perhaps I did not explain myself well enough. I do not believe that honesty in writing means sharing all your personal problems and concerns, nor is it my intention to pry into your personal life. You should share those things you feel comfortable sharing. Honesty to me means that you say what you are feeling in your writing—as you did in your letter to me. It was "invested," not perfunctory, because you stopped to take the time to think about what you wanted to say, and you wrote ideas that were important to you. But then, you do this so often that I am not surprised at it. I do find that many kids write about things that are distant from their experience—men of Mars, kidnappings, etc. I think that people write best when they write about what they know. That leads to invested writing—writing in which the author has some voice, some commitment, some interest. When you wrote the letter to me, Becky, you were trying to communicate ideas and feelings— you wanted me to understand—you wanted me to know what you were thinking—and in that, your writing was invested, not perfunctory. It was honest, not dishonest. It was real, not unreal.

I apologize to you if I have been prying into your business too much. If you sense that I am doing this again, it would be helpful to me for you to say so to me. What I perceive as a simple assignment or exercise may be seen much differently by someone else, and unless you and others share your honest reactions with me, I cannot know how you feel.

Thanks again for the letter, Becky. It was helpful—it gave me things to think about. As you know, I have great respect for you as a person. Thus, what you write means a lot to me.

RB

Reflecting on Failure

After this series of letters, Ross and I openly acknowledged to each other that something was wrong. Up until March, we had both managed to act as if the resistance to sharing writing, the anger at the social studies show, and the lack of participation by most of the students in his classes were the minor mishaps that could accompany any school year. Now, however, we both had to face the fact that resistance to him and his teaching had become the issue he faced each time he went to class.

By March, then, Ross found himself taking an even harder look at his own teaching. Brief encounters with former students, even casual school events, became occasions for him to examine himself and what he was doing. One Friday night, for example, Ross "did [his] role as announcer for the Teachers' Association basketball game." Joking around and "renewing friendships with former students" lifted his spirits. Upon leaving, he found himself "exiting the high school in a delightful mood, one I have not felt often this year." Yet immediately his mood became reason to doubt:

> Were past years different? Or was I harried then as I feel now? I do not
> think so—perhaps I am letting things get to me too much, and what I need is

more distance from the problems. I have not done a "1st Annual Team I 8th Grade. . . ." activity in a while (since Christmas), nor have I written a poem for kids in a while—and this may be because of my ambivalent feeling about the kids and what is happening.

Ambivalence brought Ross to think about the students in his advisory and how each had managed to disappoint him:

> It is easy to be distracted when Todd demands energy, or Bill screws up constantly, or Eric lies his way through life. And I do not feel the close relationships with other kids I have known. I was hoping it would develop with Becky, but it has not—she does not seem to want to be close to me. Kara whispers asides during group time, Kelley is mute, Paul is nice but shallow, Jane is frightened, and Jeanne is the only one who seems on a friendly, even keel, and I feel I am trying too hard when I talk with her—I would like to be friends in a casual way but it does not seem to happen. And with kids in the other advisories, the relationships are not there either.

A performer needs applause. As Ross wrote, he began to realize that he missed "feeling appreciated," something he had come to count on over his many years in the classroom:

> I remember 1977 and Gretchen and feeling appreciated. I remember 1978 and Sue and feeling appreciated. I remember 1980 and Cindy and Kathy and feeling appreciated. And even last year, I remember Matt and feeling appreciated. This year Jill comes closest, but if there are others, they do not show it. And it bothers me.

Later in the month, I felt the need to talk to Ross. Since the early winter, I had felt distant from him, and I began to wonder if what was going on in class was also occurring between us. I had noticed as well that our lack of a strong working relationship had the effect of making it more difficult for me to be fully involved in his classroom. I attended his classes regularly, I took notes, I had even come to know several of his students quite well, but I did not feel that he and I were in any sense working together. If it were possible to do something about this, I wanted to, and so I approached Ross one night and asked to have a talk with him.

I suspected that it would be difficult for both of us to talk about what was going on. Ross was painfully aware that at the same time events were taking a turn for the worse in his classroom, his wife Diane and I were working well as a team in another wing of the middle school. And while I wanted to be of help to Ross, I was concerned that he would hear whatever I said as criticism. I decided that the simplest approach would be to raise questions, to see if the questions themselves might open a new avenue of inquiry, or to see if, by questioning, we might discover some answers together. I hoped that if nothing else occurred, Ross might at least take solace in the fact that someone else was sharing his burden.

I began by saying that I, too, had felt uneasy in class and strangely cut off, both from Ross and many of the students. I wondered if my presence in the room every day was making it more difficult for him. Perhaps I was contributing to what was going on. Did he think there was a way to turn things around? Could I be of any help? Ross listened, responded, even seemed pleased that I had thought so much about his class and taken the time to talk with him, but my questions did not lead to the collaborative inquiry I had envisioned. Rather, they seemed only to be another occasion for Ross to rehash the events of the fall and early winter:

> Last night Sondra raised some questions with me about our relationship and about my teaching. She felt there had been a distance growing between us and that some of what had happened in my class—her lessened enjoyment at being there—was due in part to that. I sensed something, but did not and do not attribute it to a poor relationship with her. Rather, since November I have felt differently about the kids—I do not fully understand why. The months of September and October went well, and I remember the Variety Show (Oct. 31) and the fun my advisory had with that. And then, some time between then and Christmas, something changed. I do not know what it was, but I know a change occurred. I remember the hassle I felt putting together the Xmas activity and the Christmas carolling, and realizing that I had mis-judged the kids I was working with. They were not as close to me as I thought, perhaps, or something. I am still not sure what it was, but I do know that by Christmas, things were different, and I could feel and sense the difference.

Yet, in reflecting on our relationship, Ross began once again to think about himself. It wasn't a relationship with me that he missed but rather his own sense of self:

> Sondra also talked about our working together. But, I guess, more than anything else, I'm just disappointed in myself, because I started off so well and am not living up to my image of myself. Maybe that is it. It is so hard to know.

Throughout March, Ross wrestled with whether or not he could turn things around:

> And then the question—is it too late to salvage anything? No—it is not too late. In one way I have to—there it is, the tightening of the stomach even as I write this. I was very up when I started this, but even thinking about the deteriorated state of my relationships with kids makes me feel bad, and that feeds on itself. It is hard to get enthusiastic and excited when you do not really know what is going to happen and you are worried, as I am.

No matter how Ross tried, he seemed unable to extricate himself from the doubts that seemed now to overshadow all of his encounters with students. Even after an extended spring break in April due to an unexpected and heavy snowfall, Ross was flooded with misgivings the minute he returned to school. Having begun the first class after vacation by having the class do some free writing, he used the time to capture the moment-by-moment anguish he was experiencing just being back in the room with his students:

Back in school, doing free writing—getting the kids back into the groove and me as well—when we last met we had a blizzard and we got 1½ days off—Now I sit here somewhat flushed, hot, wondering what they are thinking, feeling the same "anguish" or whatever—feeling rejected or "distant"—but does it really make a difference? I'm not sure—I know that I feel distant from these kids—I experience their "disinterest" in me as a person—and that they are not really "with" me—or, some are, and some aren't—I guess I'm experiencing a kind of fear and anxiety at wanting to be liked but recognizing I've not done a decent job—or would it matter? Didn't I feel the same thing last year with Julie and a bunch of other kids? How do I get them to care? Do I get stricter? Do I demand more? Be less pleasant? I'm confused—directionless—it is the absence of feelings—no, the sense of "bad" vibes that bothers me. I want to be liked—it is important to me—why?

For a moment, he was brought back to the classroom by an interruption from a student, which he then recorded:

Kerri—"I'm sorry"—me—"Why are you sorry?"—Kerri—"For laughing"—me—"Have you written 'I'm stuck'? Try it." She did something, because now she's not laughing but writing instead—

But immediately, he was pulled back by the press of his emotions:

I have no desire, no energy—I feel myself slipping back—a basket case of sorts—it feels good to write my doubts and fears—It's painful to feel insecure, uneasy, doubting—especially after lots of years of good feelings—

until, finally, he asked the real question underneath all his pain:

but was I really that good? I don't know—I have my doubts.

The Show Must Go On

No matter how deeply his students' hostility hurt him, Ross was too responsible to walk away and tend to his wounds. Time for that would come in June, at the end of school. For now, though, he had to find a way to make it to the end. Occasionally, he thought of himself as "a crippled WWII bomber flying back to the base after an attack. If I jerry rig this and watch out for that and make this adjustment here," he wrote, "I can keep the damn thing in the air until I get to the runway—June 25th."

As one end-of-the-year activity, Ross planned to involve his students in a magazine publishing project. Based on themes they had chosen to explore, each of their magazines would have at least five separate pieces of writing in it, using different forms or written from different points of view. Class time would be set aside for writing, meeting in writing groups, revising, and editing. At the end of several weeks of work, students would send their final versions off to the district office for duplicating.

In and around the edges of the magazine project, Ross also decided to make time for several other activities. One week in May, he turned his classes over to Ron Overton, a visiting poet from the New York State Poets in the Schools program, and let Ron instruct his students in ways to read and write poetry. Another week, he encouraged his students to read several young adult novels in order to talk with the writers visiting the middle school for "Authors' Week." Several weeks later, he had to devote class time to the new districtwide writing assessment test.

Structured time, clear tasks, and outside influences seemed, somehow, to clear the air. Ross and his students began to establish a new, more harmonious rhythm. Gone were the wild crescendos of March and April. With May, the classroom became quiet and more steady. Ross noticed the change. "I see little things," he wrote, "smiles, acceptance, and I feel the mood shifting as the kids approach the end of the year. Certainly the past few days I have not been down in the dumps, and certainly the kids have basically been good to me and we have not had arguments nor have I felt distant."

But it was May, and no decision had yet been made on the social studies multimedia show. Ross had "put it on a back burner ... shelved it to get some room to breathe and to think." Finally, he could avoid it no longer.

On May 19, he raised the issue in class, wondering whether the students wanted to abandon the whole idea. Several students argued passionately to go ahead. "We put in a lot of work," they said. "If we don't finish, the work will be wasted." The majority felt that "there's not enough time," "we've lost interest," and "it would be better to move on to something else."

Ross's feelings remained as mixed as those of the kids. One day, he was all for it:

> I am going ahead with the show—and will finish it next week, most likely, after much decision making and activity. But we will get it done.

Two days later, he doubted whether he could face all the work:

> Yesterday, I found that I did not want to approach the subject of the show. I think I do not have the energy and the patience to go through with building it up again. I know there is a group who wants to complete it, and then there is a group that does not want to. I still am on the fence. The possibility of dividing the kids into two groups seems the best solution for all, but that may not work—I know that whatever I do, I feel unhappy about the choices in front of me. To complete it with all kids means dealing with a large negative group. To abandon it means disappointing/ripping off many kids. To split and go two ways with it means frustration for me in terms of keeping up, splitting into groups (as though the kids could be more subdivided), and of feeling the pressure of two preparations rather than one.

Four days later, he made his decision. The show, he realized, was "a dead horse," and, with all the other work he had to complete (a media show for his Dartmouth College twentieth reunion, another for the eighth-grade graduation celebration, the magazines, and the planning for next year's New York State Middle School Conference), he decided to "bag the show." Having "put the issue to rest," in his own mind at least, he reported, "It feels somewhat better to have decided that—it was a long time in letting go."

Once he let go, Ross was able to move on to other things. In social studies, he taught a unit on immigration and began to feel comfortable again:

> My social studies classes went well these past couple of days. I felt like a teacher again, teaching structured content lessons, doing some old familiar stuff that got kids interested. I liked it. I got in touch with my old self as a teacher—a nice feeling to have as the year winds to a close.

But Ross's sense of self was fragile and easily shattered. After a difficult day administering the districtwide writing test, during which students fooled around and did not take the work seriously, Ross wrote angrily of the students' "resistance, hostility, apathy, unproductiveness." He continued, "They made me realize again how little influence I have over them, how weak I am in my control, and how badly I feel about the poor job I have done. It seems that no matter what I do, they resist, they back off, they are sullen, they don't understand, they procrastinate, they do this, they do that." "Normally," he reflected, "I keep this kind of shit bottled up inside me, but I need to put it down somewhere or I will be poisoned by it."

And, even on good days, on days when things were going "smoothly," Ross noted, "I miss the warm give-and-take that I remember from years past with other groups."

The students, too, were aware that the year did not live up to their expectations. In her end-of-the-year evaluation, Kristy wrote, "The writting I did was O.K. I guess. But I expected this year to be better. Everyone last year said it would be great."

Becky had a similar perception: "At the beginning of the year I was really excited about being in your class but since around Jan. I don't know how I feel. I do know my interest in Eng/S.S. has gone down drasticly."

Even those students who felt they had learned something spoke of their anger or their disappointment. Diana, for example, admitted that several of the pieces she did not submit for her magazine were "very deep and personal," and that she would "always cherish them." In fact, she wrote, "Just thinking about some of this stuff gave me new insight on how I really feel." But she was leaving eighth grade still angry about the issue of sharing: "I think it is unfair of you to have us write personal stuff and then expect us to share it with the class. You might like to do this, but I sure as hell don't."

Shruti felt that Ross's class was "a pretty good one because it teaches kids about writing and its process," but, like Diana, she too was upset about the sharing issue. "If kids write something and don't want to share it, they shouldn't have to," she wrote, explaining, "Sometimes you share your writing because you *want* to, but you see sometimes we don't want to."

Jeanine had a good year and thanked Ross for the role he played in it. "You really helped me with writing. This year was differant for me because I *really* learned something. I like the way you trusted people and believed in them. But," she continued, "there is something I want to ask. Your very dissapointed in our class aren't you? I never wanted to dissapoint you but, I'm part of the class so I'm also partly responsible for it."

Kenny's reversal was perhaps the biggest surprise. He confessed to a change of heart in the matter of writing. "In Sept. I told you I hate to write but I guess I was wrong, I do really like to write. Now I feel more confedent with my writing." But Kenny, too, couldn't end the year without commenting on what had occurred: "I think you shouldn't get as close (to the people in your class) as you where this year because in every class you have their is always some one trying to give you hell."

Giving Ross hell. The words stuck. Ross felt that Kenny was right. The students had given him hell all year. They tried his patience, exhausted his will, defeated his spirit. And, by the end of the year, they had won. On the last day of school, unlike so many years past, Ross organized no final, culminating class, wrote no poem to commemorate the occasion, staged no play to perform in—perhaps the most telling sign of defeat.

On July 4, after school was over, Ross wrote one final account of the year, recording what went on and searching once again for the clues to understand it.

> It is somewhat symbolic that I should be typing this final entry to my 1981–82 school year teaching journal on Independence Day. I feel so liberated from the bad feelings and sense of incompleteness and unconnectedness to kids that I experienced from December on. Even now after my retellings to Sondra, Di, friends, staff members, etc., I still do not fully understand what went wrong and why I did not enjoy the year. I do know that in the period after November 11 up to Christmas, things went wrong and stayed wrong in terms of how I felt about the kids, my teaching, etc. . . . Someone said that many teachers might like to have the "failure" of my year, in which I success- fully ran a middle school conference; made several conference presentations in NYC, Chicago, Boston; did a good job on Radicals and Tories; got every kid to publish a magazine with a theme and the minimum number of pieces; kept a fine "daily" journal of my teaching experiences; gave the kids some val- uable writing experiences; did the Dartmouth slide show and the 8th grade slide show; did a great two acts in the Variety Show; organized a successful advisory trip in the fall; got my students' writing published in the District Newsletter on a regular basis; did 23 social studies journal entries with kids and got them to do a lot of thinking and writing as a result; organized the Pie Eating Contest, the Turkey Trot, the Apple Dunk, and the Christmas celebra- tion; did some good writing and published my own booklet; participated suc- cessfully in the Study Group (most of the time) and produced (at this writing) a good draft of a paper that may have some merit. There were probably other things I did that were good—helping staff members do slide shows, helping individual students—and many people might look at this list of accomplish- ments and feel good.
>
> But I am ambivalent. There is a warm therapeutic value to enumerating my accomplishments here, and the list does appear impressive—clearly, I did not sit on my hands this year. But if the central job I am trying to do is to relate to and teach kids, I can state clearly that I did not engender in them the kind of spirit I was shooting for, nor did I experience with them the kinds

of joys I have known in the past. Simply put, they were not my cup of tea, and I was unable to motivate them to respond as I have been able to motivate other classes to respond. I remarked to Sondra that this was the first time in seventeen years or so that I did not do some kind of closing exercise—the last class lessons of the past were ignored, and instead we dispersed to play softball that last Wednesday afternoon.

Teacher and Researcher

A bad year. Failure. How did it happen? What did it mean? These were the kinds of questions I knew I would have to face if I were to make sense out of the time I spent in Ross's classroom. Yet, at the same time, I knew that there would never be a simple or a complete explanation. Classrooms are complex. Immersing myself in them made me even more aware of the hundreds of fleeting interactions that give rise to the learning and living that occur there. Perhaps, I thought, if I retraced not only the road I had taken, but the one Ross took as well. . . .

There were very few clues in the beginning. I was excited by what I saw in Ross's classroom—so much activity and all of it related in one way or another to writing—and Ross was excited that I was there. He saw my presence as "affirmation that what I was doing counted for something." "It was flattering," he wrote, "to think that my work was of interest to Sondra, and so I enjoyed having her in the room. I had a sense of pride about it."

As the year went on, though, my excitement diminished. At times, I found it difficult to face the hostility and pain so close to the surface in Ross's room. But initially, the only clue I had that Ross, too, was no longer excited about what was going on in his room was that he did less writing than usual. He explained, "Something went wrong in November/December—I am not sure what. I do know that I stopped writing pieces—a sign that I was hurting inside. When I feel good, my mind bubbles and I compose lots of pieces. When I feel badly, I do not compose because I do not want to deal with negative stuff. And perhaps that is it—that there was a lot of negative stuff that got to me."

Whatever it was that got to Ross, neither he nor I found a way to come to grips with it directly as the school year wore on. For Ross, the press of students was often too great; the demands of teaching, too heavy. And slowly, I became accustomed to life in his classroom and the routine we seemed to have established. Ross planned, made decisions, and taught. I came in, took notes, and left. Frequently, because I was staying in Ross's home and also studying how his wife Diane was teaching writing, our dinner conversations were filled with classroom talk. But, after dinner, Ross would go off to a chorus rehearsal, spend some time with his son Theo, return to school to work on one of his media shows, or retire upstairs with a book. He seemed most comfortable communicating with me via his journal, typing long entries every morning before school started and leaving Xerox copies for me in my mailbox in the middle school. And once he had written down what he was thinking, he seemed ready to move on.

In fact, I had only one indication through the whole year that Ross might have preferred to forget everything, including the research project. At the end of June, at a time when I was collecting mounds of student writing, Ross returned all the data—all the drafts of student writing he had stored all year—to his students. Before I had copied them or asked permission to keep them, he just nonchalantly handed back all the writing folders and process journals. And many of the students, perhaps not surprisingly in the light of what had happened that year, threw their writing out.

That afternoon, when Ross mentioned in passing that he had returned the students' writing, I turned pale. Soon we were out behind the school, searching through the dumpster, trying to identify familiar folders. Of course, some students had saved their folders and the next day in class I was able to retrieve them. But, in addition to the knowledge that many students had discarded their year's work without much thought, it was disconcerting to discover that Ross in a moment's distraction had also forgotten about the study.

Once the year ended and Ross had a chance to think about it, other issues came to light. Several months into a new semester, Ross wrote that his "pride" probably kept him from seeing what was really happening and that it probably kept me at a distance as well. More than a year after I had left his classroom, he admitted that other issues were also working on him. In retrospect, he realized that he had begun to compare himself to Diane and had begun to feel like the "extra-added attraction compared with the main event":

> I remember feeling a subtle competition with Di. Di was the central focus of the study—Sondra was in both of her English classes and sometimes in her social studies class each day compared with only 1 visit to 1 English course of mine. Also, since Di was a year "ahead" of me in implementing the National Writing Project approach, I felt that she did a "better" job than I in teaching the kids writing. And I felt that Sondra knew this, and that that was why she was going to Di's room as often as she did, two and sometimes three times daily. And so I felt envious of Di and the attention she was getting. What further complicated the issue was that my year went bad. The issues are muddy, but it is true that I experienced incredible pain, frustration, and disappointment in my relationships with my students at a time when Di was flying high and entering into a real partnership with Sondra.
>
> I also felt bad for Sondra because she was spending a lot of time and energy in observing in my room and the good feelings and lessons that I so often generate were just not coming forth. I felt I was short-changing Sondra with a poor performance.

It was true that I often experienced myself as a spectator at a performance in Ross's room. That I might have felt "short-changed" was not. Although initially what happened in his room was distasteful to me—the sort of thing I preferred to ignore—it began to dawn on me that figuring out what went wrong in his classroom would be as important to this project as detailing the successes other teachers had.

Neither Ross nor I was prepared for the pain, the anguish, the raw emotions that surfaced as a result of failure. We were even less aware that the issue of failure would force each of us to come to grips with teaching in a way that nothing else ever had. For Ross, it raised some hard questions.

First, for many months after school ended, he found himself asking a set of inner-directed questions that put the blame solely on himself: "How did I screw up with so many kids? Where did I go wrong?"

Several months later, he began to widen his horizon, wondering about the profession as a whole and whether anything he did in class was worth studying and sharing with a wider audience:

> Who am I trying to kid? What do I do that people will want to read about? What I am doing is not that great or not that worthwhile writing about.

Then, months later as he continued to scrutinize himself, his teaching, and his writing, he had a sudden insight. A pattern in his behavior was beginning to emerge, a pattern it is likely he might never have seen had he always received applause:

> In my journal and in each of my papers (those I have drafted thus far), the overwhelming emphasis is on me—myself—I! I have an ego problem. "The Teacher as Writer." The title alone puts undue emphasis on me and I find it increasingly embarrassing to write about myself. I guess I need Sondra to tell me, "It's okay, Ross, you have my permission to write about yourself, and it's fine." Because I am not so sure it is fine.
>
> None of this is to say that there weren't important and valuable things going on in my class. On the contrary—in the face of all the adversity, the writing program continued to function during the entire year, and in the end, I know that I accomplished some of my goals. What's wrong is that I now feel self-conscious about the overstress on "I." . . . Am I really, fundamentally, interested in blowing my own horn? Or at least making myself look good?

Ross was beginning to come face-to-face with a central issue. How much of his writing, his thinking, even his teaching, was self-involved, exclusionary? How often was his performance so polished that students were put off, unable to catch even a glimpse of themselves in it? And when Ross did share the stage, how often did students leave it feeling as if their performances were merely dry runs, poor imitations of the real thing?

In the years that followed, Ross worked to resolve the issues that came to light as a result of his participation in the research project. As time passed, I saw that he had a heightened awareness of issues of control, of managing group work, of setting clear limits and boundaries, of recognizing when to perform and when to share the stage. His teaching, I realized, had begun to change as a result of the careful scrutiny we both gave it.

Yet, in those years, as Ross regained his footing in the classroom, I continued to write about the year he lost it. Occasionally, when I showed him my drafts, I wondered whether he wouldn't have wished that I rewrite history, soften a description, rework a particular incident. Yet, throughout all of our meetings, Ross was remarkably consistent, saying—and meaning—that if there were something in his struggle that might be of value to other teachers, then I should tell his story as I was doing, no holds barred. Several years later, I am still struck by his willingness to allow me to use his story to serve others.

In the end, Ross's story served me. Through my experience in his classroom, I came face-to-face with an unsettling paradox. Ross as much as any other teacher in the study took the principles of the writing process approach to heart. His class was a model of process teaching: his students wrote frequently, practiced active listening, met in writing groups, kept process journals, revised, edited, published, and on and on. And, much to my chagrin and disappointment, things didn't work.

Could it be, I found myself asking, that my own belief in the process approach was misguided? Was there something else underlying the approach that I had yet to see or to articulate? Could Ross have shown me my own failure to see beyond the confines of method?

After twenty years of teaching, Ross found himself struggling to work out the kinks in his teaching. After ten years of studying the writing process, I began to look for what lay beyond it.

Chapter 5

Len Schutzman
Twelfth Grade

"Teaching writing allows for a kind of growth in the classroom I have rarely experienced before," Len Schutzman wrote in his journal at the end of the year I joined his class. "Teaching writing allowed me to grow and the students each to grow and the class. ..."

Growth—human growth—is what Len cares about. As a teacher, he seemed to me more attached to teaching itself than to any particular subject. Although his high school teaching license is in social studies, he was teaching English the year I observed his class; when he joined the Writing Project in 1980, he was on leave from the high school and teaching third grade. A student of psychology in graduate school, he once created and taught a course in child development for high school students, has led workshops on parenting, and shares his observations of his own small children with the teenagers he teaches. In literature, in his own journals, in conversation, Len studies the process of growth. Teaching writing is exciting to him because writing, as he sees it, both fosters growth and makes it visible.

In 1981, when I visited his class, Len had an unusual opportunity to observe his students' growth. That year he taught only one class, one period a day. An administrative internship occupied the rest of his teaching day but that, although demanding and time-consuming in its own way, did not add names to his roster. "What a luxury," he wrote later, "to focus my attention on only twenty-four students."

His reduced teaching load gave Len a chance to become a full participant in the work of the class—not only to start pieces with his students and write with them in class, as many teachers do, but also, as few do, to complete them. That year Len, along with his students, wrote constantly, piece after piece, one cycle of writing and revising leading into another. Every so often, when he felt everyone was temporarily "written out," he would give the class a breather and discuss literature for a while without writing. But "writing was what I wanted them to do, and I wanted them to do a lot of it," he had decided, so, for most of the year, Len's students wrote—memory pieces, poems, essays, stories, accounts of their writing processes—and Len wrote with them. Len's folder of work in progress was filed along with students' folders in the drawer set aside for that purpose; at the end of the year his "senior essay" appeared with theirs in the class anthology.

For each new piece, Len joined a different writing group and stayed with it through the complete cycle of drafting and revising until his piece, along with those of the students, was finished. He observed the same deadlines he set for students, though he had the same trouble meeting them his students did. He agonized along with them: "I'm overwhelmed by my story; don't know how I'm going to finish it by Tuesday." "This one just goes on and on ... I need to talk to somebody about it." If he found he couldn't, after all, "finish by Tuesday," he and his students would talk about the deadline and decide together whether or not to extend it.

Working so closely with his students, Len felt more able than he might otherwise have been to raise questions, to encourage his students to explore issues they found difficult to write about, and to invite them to take risks. For writing, he knew, could be a risky undertaking.

A Personal Activity

"Writing is a deeply personal activity," Len told his students early in the year. Writing, he wrote in his journal, "allows the writer to look inside and to express that knowledge and refine it and enjoy the expression of it. It allows for an openness of exchange and a truthfulness ..." By the same token, however, writing, in Len's view, can be "threatening" to students.

Len discussed this problem openly and often with the students in his senior class. "You have to be willing to take risks in writing," he told them. "You have to leave yourself open. You have to be willing to share, at least to some extent and with some people, if you want to write well." When a student hesitated one day, stumbling over an emotionally loaded word in a story, Len told her, smiling, "You have to be brave in this class."

Len himself set an example of bravery. "He always plunges in first," said Terri, and Kim added, "He says, 'I'll read.'" Describing his own work in a students' writing group, Len wrote:

> I remember a story I was trying to write with Teresa and Terri and

Katherine and Kim. It was about an experience I had with my father-in-law lighting Christmas candles several years ago. I got stuck in the piece and had to write a poem to get out of it and then finished the story. During those meetings with my group the student-teacher distinction was virtually absent from my classes yet I was probably never a more effective teacher. We sat and discussed my story and theirs and made real suggestions about the work and where to go. I talked of my past in a comfortable and not too revealing way.

What I think happened there was that the students saw me as a writer as well as a teacher. They saw me struggling over meaning and getting frustrated with the process. They experienced my joy with me when I finally broke through and discovered the poem I had to write before I could write any story. They were so proud of me when I finally finished. . . .

Reflecting on the experience, he added, "I didn't have the answers in a book . . . I didn't hide behind my chalk and my knowledge . . . I was real and trusting . . . I hoped that seeing me go through all those emotions would be like a virulent virus and I believe it was."

Len hoped his example would prove contagious. He wanted his students to learn to look closely at themselves, as he did; to be able to build on their strengths, become aware of their weaknesses, and change if they wanted to change. He wanted them to listen to and provide support for one another, both as writers and as people, through this last year of high school, a year he saw as one of sorting out past and future. He wanted them to use writing, as he did, in the service of growth.

Len's emphasis on personal growth in the classroom raised questions for me. Always aware that, as he had told his students, "writing is a personal activity," Len listened for emotional undercurrents in his classroom, discussed them, held them up to the light, and examined them with his students. His manner of doing this, and especially the language he used, sometimes made me uneasy.

Len's vocabulary reflects his grounding in psychology: he sees students through the lens of that discipline and uses its language to describe them. In class and in his journal, he spoke of students as "adolescents": "conflicted," "defending against conflict," "rejecting" old identities, "resisting" assignments; of situations as "threatening" or "non-threatening." My own background is in literature. I read fiction more often than nonfiction and take nineteenth-century novels to the beach. I found Len's vocabulary unsettling at first. I had to get used to it, as if I were observing someone teaching in a foreign language, a language I had studied but not made my own.

Yet if differences between Len and me raised one set of questions, then similarities raised others. For though we differed in the words we used to describe what we did, Len and I used many of the same strategies in the classroom. And although I thought I understood, from my own experience, why Len was doing what he was doing—what its connection was to teaching writing— I wasn't sure I could explain it to someone else. I remembered the gibes of unsympathetic visitors to my own classroom. "What is this?" the teacher down the hall or the supervisor for basic skills would grumble, as he or she watched me teach active listening or lead my students through the "Guidelines for Com-posing," "a writing class or group therapy?" I knew the difference myself but was not always sure I could explain it to skeptics. And now, in Len's classroom, I was once again made uncomfortably aware of possible questions about my own way of teaching.

Why, I wondered, was I so sure that learning active listening (a skill developed by psychotherapists) would help my students learn to write? Why did I, like Len, put so much faith in small-group work? How could Len and I, using such different words to describe our concerns, be so completely in agreement as to what, in the long run, mattered most? If Len discussed his students' writing processes but hardly ever their writing itself, what exactly did he do that enabled his students to write?

I didn't expect to find final answers to these questions, but I knew that observing Len's class would help me look at them more closely than I had before.

Teacher and Researcher

It took me a while to find a way into Len's class. In other classrooms, I had studied walls and bulletin boards for clues to a teacher's concerns, but in Len's room that year such clues were missing.

Because Len was teaching only one group of seniors, he had no classroom of his own. He met his students in a room used the rest of the time by another teacher, its blackboard often covered by the other teacher's instructions to his students ("3–5 paragraphs ... 3–5 sentences in each paragraph ... Final draft: ink script and margins"), its chairs arranged to suit the other teacher's teaching style. I could find few clues in the arrangement of that room or on its walls to Len's own values, style, or priorities in teaching.

Nor could I piece together a view of Len from events taking place around the edges of the classroom: those casual encounters between students and teacher at change-of-period and throughout the school day that often round out the picture an observer puts together during class. Once Len's teaching period was finished, the other teacher returned to his classroom, and Len disappeared— to a meeting or to the tiny office in the basement of C-wing that was his base of operations for the internship. I seldom saw him outside of class.

Len felt as frustrated as I did by the stop-and-start nature of our early encounters. The research project was important to him, and he wanted to give it his full attention. He had participated in the summer institute two years running, had, in his own words, "loved writing, felt great doing it and wanted to do it more and more," and had, since his first summer in the Project, taught writing enthusiastically. He wanted to concentrate on writing and teaching writing and studying the teaching of writing, but he couldn't—at least at first. A conflict in scheduling prevented him from attending study-group meetings more than oc-casionally in the fall, and then, when he was finally free to join us, he felt that he "always seemed to be catching up." "I never really caught on to what everyone else was doing," he wrote sadly, "and my journal never seemed as important to me as it did to the rest of the group."

In fact, Len's teaching journal, another potential source of information about his classroom, seldom told me what I wanted to know. To start with, there wasn't much of it. Len tended to see this journal, unlike the one in which he recorded his children's growth or the writing he did with his students, as writing for the study group—"an assignment," as he put it—for others, not for himself; he got to it late and last if he got to it at all. I usually had to guess at his reasons for doing things because he seldom wrote them down. "I'm sure you wanted to just strangle me at times," he wrote later, and he was right; I did.

But meanwhile I was going to class, and it was in class, I gradually began to realize, that Len revealed, explained, and discussed not only his theories about writing but also his theories about teaching, learning, and human growth. What many teachers wrote in their journals, Len talked over with his students: how he saw them, what he was worried about, what he read between the lines. As I came to know Len, I saw that I had been looking in the wrong places for information, that Len, more than most teachers, brought his thoughts about teaching to class. If I wanted to know what he was thinking, I had only to sit with his students and listen.

So I came to class, and listened—to Len and, more and more, to the students themselves. As it turned out, in the end, it was through students, and in particular through four students in one writing group, that I came to know Len's class most intimately. In the sections that follow, I will refer often to these four students: Teresa, Terri, Kim, and Katherine. In January, following Len's example, I joined their writing group, meaning to stay awhile and then move on. I never did move on. I brought my own writing to class instead and became a working, if not always present, member of the group. When Terri was asked in June to describe her writing group, she began, "My writing group, consisting of Kim, Katherine, Teresa, and Nancy. . . ."

I came to see Len's class not only through Len's eyes but also through the eyes of these four students. I spoke, of course, to other students, but, as a member of their writing group, I felt a special closeness to Teresa, Terri, Katherine, and Kim. I talked with them about what they thought was going on in class and read them what I was writing about them. And it was through listening to and observing these four students that I came to understand, among other things, what Len meant when he spoke of writing as "allowing for growth."

Case Studies

Early in October, Len visited New York University with a group of teachers from Shoreham-Wading River. He came back excited. Lil Brannon, the director of NYU's Writing Center, was preparing college students to work as peer tutors. As part of their training, she was asking them to study one another's writing processes. Len thought a similar assignment might solve a problem in his own English 12 class.

Len's seniors, for the most part, were wary of writing. Students who liked to write most often chose composition or journalism courses to fulfill the English requirement in senior year; those who didn't were assigned to English 12. English 12, Len's students informed me, was a "general" English course. It wasn't supposed to require a lot of writing.

Kim hoped she would be analyzing literature most of the year. Cindy wanted to work on vocabulary and grammar. Terri just wanted to get the English requirement out of the way with as little trouble as possible. Teachers considered Len's students "average" to "lower end of the scale"—in academic performance, at least, and often in interest in English as well. Most had missed the wave of writing activity that had swept through the lower grades just after their class passed on. Few had studied their own writing processes or met in writing groups; few thought of themselves as writers or had pleasant memories of writing in school. Nearly all, Len thought, were "uptight about their writing and their ability to reveal themselves in writing."

Yet English 12, in Len's hands, and over the protests of some of his students, became a writing class. By late October, when the case study sequence started, Len and his students had already taken three pieces of writing through drafts, revisions, and meetings of writing groups, stopping along the way to write process notes on what was happening to them as they wrote. But despite all the writing, Len wasn't satisfied with the mood of the class. "The electricity wasn't there—we just couldn't take off—we were waiting at a crowded runway, engines idling but the line was long."

Some students, he thought, were beginning to enjoy writing, and others were at least willing to work on it, but "what they all didn't want to do was look deeply at what was going on inside themselves when they were writing. How did they feel about the process they were engaged in?" He decided to try to bring their perceptions into the open through case studies.

Toward the end of October, Len announced to his students that they would be embarking on a major research and writing project that would extend, alongside other writing assignments, over the next several months: a two-part case study "designed to get each student-writer to understand in an intensive way the writing of another student-writer."

"I thought that one way to get them to look at their own process was to look at somebody else's," he wrote later.

> If they could really see what someone else went through when writing maybe they would reflect on themselves. ... Looking at someone else is often a look at yourself. ... So I felt that if I forced or rather structured the assignment so that students would look at students they would discover one another and then discover themselves. In discovering their process they would see the bonds with other people and begin to break down resistance. Their defensiveness would diminish as the portrait was revealed. A mirror is hard to refute.

Everyone would all be involved in the same looking or discovery or process and just the bond that that would create would help to unify the class. . . .

Len's students were skeptical, at first, about the value of such a project. Writing constantly in class and for homework was bad enough, many felt; Len's asking them to write about each other's writing on top of that was adding insult to injury. "Is this supposed to help me with my writing?" Teresa asked. "If so, I don't see how."

Len, characteristically, tackled the issue head-on. For the first part of the case study, he asked his students to look at their own behavior and history as writers, to examine their attitudes toward writing, and to try to explain to themselves and each other how they had come by these attitudes. Rather than defend writing to those who were uncomfortable with it, Len asked them to become students of their own discomfort—to examine and come to terms with it.

As a first step in generating material to be examined in the case study, Len asked each student to look back on the writing he or she had done so far for class and try to describe his or her own writing processes.

"What is the writing process like for you?" Len asked his students one day, looking around the open square of tables. "How do you get from nothing to a finished piece?" The students, Len, and I all wrote for about ten minutes; at the end of the alotted time, Len and I and a number of students found it hard to stop.

Cindy was surprised that she had so much to say. "I thought I only had about a paragraph to write about this, but I wrote a page and a half and I'm still not finished."

Others, too, found they knew more about themselves as writers than they thought they did. Jeff noticed that his process was changing:

> Usually when I write a story, I spend most of my time thinking of an idea and organizing and sorting ideas in my head . . .
> Then an idea finally hits me and I start writing. It usually takes three or four pieces of paper to get started. I usually don't revise I try to get it right the first time. Lately I'm trying to approach my writing technique differently. I just start writing without trying to do it right the first time and then I go back and cut, chop and splice the pieces.

In well-formed sentences neatly written in a careful script, Kim described an orderly writing process; then scrawled at the end, "I'm tired of writing like this. I wish we could maybe read a novel or a play."

At the end of the session, Len instructed the students to write "Draft #1" on whatever they'd written and to "*save everything*. You are collecting data for your partner's case study of what kind of writer you are."

In order to focus students' attention on the process of revision, Len asked them to revise their process pieces and then to describe and analyze the changes they had made. Kim "tried to make everything clearer . . . let the story flow," "omitted sentences not important," and changed the ending. Jeff's first draft was "a rough jumble of ideas," from which he drew an outline that gave him "a good, solid base from which to build my paper."

Teresa wrote:

> I changed my second paragraph greatly, feeling in my first draft I was not exploring how my emotions effect my stories I added more insight to myself.
> It is in my second draft that I specifically state "a short story deals mainly with my feelings."
> Through this change I accomplished a greater understanding of the meaning behind my stories.

Len next asked students to meet in pairs to discuss their revision processes. "What questions are you going to ask your partner?" he asked the class. "What will help you understand his or her process better?" "What is the hardest part of writing for you?" students suggested. "Do you like to write about true life experiences or to make up stories?" "How do you feel about writing?" Armed with these questions, students began to meet in pairs, interviewing one another and writing up the interviews.

"Approach [Part I] as you would in writing a biography," Len directed each student-researcher in his assignment sheet:

> What information is interesting and relevant to understanding this person as a writer?
> Basically divide your inquiry into three parts:
> A. General Background—age, family, history, interests.
> B. Past School Experience—feelings about school, writing, English classes, reading.
> C. Writing Today—attitudes about writing, competence as perceived by the subject, difficulties, process.
> These are only suggested guidelines. You may certainly vary the order or even the topics you will discuss in your paper. The reader should, however, understand who this person is and what s/he thinks about school and writing.

The room hummed with talk and laughter during interview sessions as students shared old school memories ("My kindergarten teacher used to bring a whiskey flask to class ... She said it was cough medicine") or relived past injustices ("It was grammar, grammar, grammar all the time ... You'd write a whole story and the teacher would say, 'Terri, where's the semicolon?' ").

As students took notes on one another's memories of writing, Len commented on the process of studying a process. Studying the way you write, Len told the class, is like analyzing a golf swing on film: you learn from looking carefully at (for instance) movements of arm and wrist, describing them, thinking about them, and making generalizations based on observation to help you decide what to do next. In golf, you might decide, "I need to follow through on my swing"; in writing, "I need to think about something for a long time before I write," or "I need to concentrate on editing."

The first phase of the case-study project ended with the writing up of the interviews. Case-study subjects were honest in replying to their interviewers' questions, and interviewers were equally honest in recording their subjects' misgivings about writing.

Terri reported on Kim:

> Kim is athletic. She enjoys running a lot. She has been a member of the track team for four years straight. One of her biggest interests is reading. She reads in her spare time and "even when mom and dad think I'm studying." ...
>
> Kim dislikes all english courses, "I never have liked it." ... She finds writing boring. "There are *rare* moments when I like to write, then I could write forever." She likes writing when she finds a subject interesting to her.
>
> Kim feels that she is not imaganitive thus hindering her writing. She finds it difficult to get her ideas on paper. She does not like people to read her writing "except for my writing group, I feel very comfortable with them." She enjoys journal and diary type writing where she can express her feelings "and people won't see it."

Kim wrote about Terri:

> Terri has never really liked school but she says she enjoys Boces [a work-study program]. At Boces she is studying to become a nurse. She takes courses in anatomy psycology and introductory biology.
>
> This year English is Terri's only class in the High School. She spends most of her time in Central Suffolk Hospital taking specilized courses.
>
> Terri has always enjoyed writing ... in a journal, [where] she feels she can include anything personal without anyone looking through it ... Terri doesn't read very much but when she does, she finds it hard to put the book down ... Terri has always felt indifferent about her English classes.

Teresa described Katherine:

> Out of a family of 7 children, Katherine is the third child to begin preparing for college. Having lived all seventeen years of her life on Long Island she is looking forward to attending a college off the island and being independant. Looking forward to being independant does not mean that Katherine is looking forward to ecsape from family life. In fact Katherine has a rather close family. An interest Katherine shares with her family is reading. For as long as Katherine can remember she has enjoyed a good book ...
>
> It is writing that Katherine tends to dislike. She doesn't mind writing when her ideas are flowing easily but when she gets caught on a phase she really must force herself to complete the assignment.

And Katherine wrote about Teresa:

> Teresa's interests are piano, guitar, singing and walking ... she would like to pursue teaching music or science ... This year Teresa is very against writing. She has so much writing to do she claims. She feels that she's putting in the most time she ever put into writing, trying to be a "good student." But the rewards for all this hard work isn't immediate and Teresa feels discouraged. She hates writing now. She doesn't even enjoy writing letters.

Part I of each case study included a brief, general account of its subject's writing process:

—Teresa's writing process is quite consistent. Once she has a topic to write on, she brainstorms ideas and descriptive words related to her topic. Sometimes she feels like she should write an outline. This is used as a reminder, so she doesn't leave anything out. The story is always completely clear in her head, before transfering it onto paper. . . .

—Kim sits in a quiet room to gather her thoughts and ideas. During this time, she also writes whatever comes into her mind. That is her first draft. This is read over and words are changed "to make it flow." This is when she does most of her editing.

Once revisions are made she proofreads it again, this time for grammatical errors. "I try to get all this done on my final copy." Many times her final copy is no more than another copy of her second draft.

—Katherine's difficulties lie in sentence structure, verb tenses and making the plots flow.

"Case studies," Len wrote once, "unveil the writing process." In Part I of the case-study project, he asked his students to learn from one another's accounts of their processes; in Part II, he asked them to analyze evidence of the processes themselves. He described the task on a new assignment sheet:

For this part of the case study you are to concentrate on how your subject writes. You should do this by using one specific piece of writing for which the author has saved all the drafts and the process entries. You need to explain the process, the changes, the stumbling blocks, the intended meaning and the author's feelings about the piece overall and throughout the process. . . .
Specifically you need to do the following:
1. Pick one section of the piece that has been revised and appears in the final draft and analyze the changes it has gone through. List all the changes that have occurred and why you believe the author changed them.
2. Analyze the entire piece. What was the main idea or theme the author had in mind in writing this piece? Has that idea been conveyed? Where was it brought out most strongly and where is it weak?
3. How do others, the writing group, help the author to discover what s/he wants to say and to say it more clearly? What kinds of responses to the piece were helpful and what kinds weren't? (This needs to be done in the writing group so try to build in some time for it.)

One day, I brought in a set of photocopies of published writers' manuscripts. Len used them in class to provide his students with practice in analyzing texts in progress. Students listed and speculated about changes in pieces by Sinclair Lewis, Kay Boyle, Thoreau, and others. Discussing drafts of the poem, "A Bracelet," by Robert Graves, they guessed at reasons for the poet's changes: "Is 'split' a typo? Did he mean 'spilt'? If it isn't, what does it mean?" "Maybe it could have to do with stars and moon all over the place?"

They continued to speculate, encouraged by Len, who listened, redirecting students who spoke only to him ("Not just me—everybody") and throwing in occasional questions himself. "Why?" . . . "What's the point?" . . . "Guess" . . . "Throw some ideas out" . . . "Take a chance." When someone asked, "Is it an imaginary bracelet or a real one?" Len stopped to comment, *"Good* question";

when Joanne asked what "busy" could mean in the phrase, "for her busy wrist," Len beamed and said, "Thank you, Joanne." When a clamor for certainties built up, with students turning to Len in confusion, Len refused to resolve the conflict: "You want me to *give* you the answer? Look it up in my book? *I* don't have the answer!" And they went back to debating.

As they studied the revisions of published writers, Len and his students were also generating their own texts to revise and study. Late in November, they started new pieces. They began, as they usually began new pieces in Len's class, by writing their way through the "Guidelines for Composing," stopping at the end of the period to write process notes. As they developed pieces started from ideas discovered in class, while working through the "Guidelines," or found later, at home, by some other method, each student kept careful track of his or her case study subject's progress.

Mary: I don't have a topic yet.

John [*writing "Does not have topic."*]: How are you going to get one?

Mary: Usually, I start daydreaming—but I don't think you should put that down; it's embarrassing. . . .

Students studied one another's drafts, interviewed one another, and discussed the workings of their writing groups. Eventually, each wrote a detailed report on his or her subject's writing process for the piece. Many of these reports included observations about the subject's writing process in general.

Katherine described Teresa's writing process and the contributions her group made to it:

> Teresa has the skill to be able to write a story without being interupted by the corrections of grammar and spelling. She writes her first draft without corrections so many of the changes in her second draft are grammatical. . . . Many of the misspelled words Teresa knew how to spell correctly but in her train of thought just wrote down the first thing that came to her mind. The changes of "definetly" to "definitely" and "hatered" to "hatred" are just a few examples of this. . . .
> Her writing group includes Terri, Kim, Katherine and most importantly *herself.* Many times her ears are hearing the piece for the first time also. She is often the first to correct a sentence that is badly worded . . . She has ideas in her head that aren't put into her story on paper but are assumed by her. We ask her questions about the things she assumed and get her to realize that it wasn't included . . . Frequently the other members of the writing group don't have to say anything because their expressions tell Teresa that something was confusing. She would recognize it and self correct . . . In an untitled story Teresa writes about an old man who has fallen onto the tracks of an oncoming train. She writes "Beginning to panic he groped with his one good arm." The audience at this point in the story doesn't know of the oncoming train and wonders why the man is beginning to panic. [When she read the story] not a word had to be said because Teresa understood that it was unclear by [our] puzzled looks. . . .

Terri analyzed an essay of Kim's in great detail, drew from her analysis a conclusion about the direction Kim's writing was taking, and strongly recommended another course.

> [Kim's] latest piece of literature, presently untitled, has to do with college applications and picking the "right" college. The changes in this piece are quite drastic at times (in fact, she set out to write a story about Thanksgiving, but changed topics because "I found college on my mind more and more. I didn't even realize that I was writing about it at first").
>
> The first draft begins very general, "College is a big part of *everyone's* life . . . ," as does her final draft, becoming a little more specific, "Many *seniors* (as opposed to "everyone") are now going through the process of finding a college. . . ."
>
> One then observes Kims personal feelings on this subject reflected in her first draft. This change is not subtle and changes like night to day at the third sentence of the first paragraph. "Now *I'm* just finishing up *my* applications . . ." This personal line of thought is continued until the end. It increases in intensity and personality and somewhat breaks away from the main theme, "Being on my own [in college] I think will change a lot of my habits without my mother breathing down my back about homework, what I do at night, who I go out with, and what I eat."
>
> None of these feelings, however are included in the final product. The final copy is somewhat more low-key, matter-of-fact, and textbook like. It appears that no feelings or chances are taken. Kim seems to not want to express any of her own personal opinions, views, or feelings. These all appear to come out in the first few drafts but get cut out by the final draft . . .
>
> The writing group . . . attempts to help and encourage Kim to leave her personal opinions and feelings in the final copy. However, she physically agrees, but appears to mentally edit them out. "I started my story and then drifted off into my own story about college. I didn't want to do that! I wanted it to be an impersonal story. Very general." I feel that where as it may not "hurt" the story (one whom hasn't read the first few drafts would not even realize it's absence), if these genuine feelings were not omitted, the audience could relate to it more readily and obtain it's true value and message.
>
> Kim is a talented personal writer. However she witholds too much. She appears to concerned about the audience's reaction. Hopefully Kim will in time learn to loosen up and relax her writing somewhat. I feel it would enhance her writing.

About Terri's study of Kim, Len wrote me later, "WOW so true and she knew it and Kim knew it and any reader would. . . ." And about Katherine's of Teresa:

> What a great analysis this is—so powerful and insightful—Isn't Katherine great. . . . She says Teresa has *the skill* to write without being interrupted by editing concerns. I wish more teachers understood that. . . . Katherine has understood the writing process and has gained respect for another writer and, I am sure, although unstated here, understood herself better. What more could a teacher want.

Opening Up the Teaching Process

Len wanted his students to understand the writing process—and themselves, one another, and the workings of the class. He wanted the outer layers of his teaching to be transparent. He often called his students' attention to what he was doing in the classroom and explained why he was doing it. In his daily practice, he removed the mystery from teaching by showing students, again and again, the scaffolding beneath the edifice he built.

The day after starting a new piece with the "Guidelines for Composing," for instance, Len and his students discussed what had happened the day before.

"How many of you feel that the topic you came up with yesterday is something you can write about?" Len asked. A few hands went up. "How many have no idea what you are going to write about?" Many hands.

"I feel I'm not in touch with you about what you are doing with this writing," Len continued. "Let's look at the process writing you did at the end of the period and talk about where you are now." He called on Katherine.

Katherine: I wrote a lot, but it's not very interesting. It isn't what I want to write more about.

Marie: What I wrote was *boring.*

Jeff: No one would be interested in what I wrote except me.

[*Kim started to say that what she wrote wasn't interesting enough to continue, but stopped, sounding uncertain.*]

Len [*looking around the class*]: Can anyone ask Kim a question that will help her think about it?

Students: Wasn't there anything on the list that was just a *little* interesting? Was there something you could make into a story?

Kim: Well, yes, there *were* some interesting things on the list, but they were too personal to write about for class. I wouldn't want anyone to see what I wrote. . . .

Jeff: When you write, it's like a part of yourself. . . . When you read it, it's like opening yourself up, inviting people to take a pot shot at it. [*Murmurs of assent around the room.*]

Len [*nodding*]: We all have these problems. But you're going to write best about what you know best—so what can we do about this?

Katherine: Kim could disguise the personal parts of her writing—write it as if it happened to someone else.

Len: You're in her writing group; would that fool *you?* [*Katherine smiled and shook her head.*]

Jeff: You can write something like, "I went to the beach"—that's personal but okay; other things you wouldn't want to share.

Len: Yes, I could write about highjumping, for instance; that's something I know about from personal experience, but it isn't a private kind of personal. . . . But I don't think that's the kind of "personal" Kim meant. . . . Some things that are personal I may never want to tell anybody; others I'm willing to talk about with some people. I'm willing to take risks in a writing group because others are willing to take risks too. . . .

Joe: I can't decide whether to write about something I know about or write a story.

Len: There are lots of people who haven't decided what to write about—that's okay.

Joanne [*a dental hygiene student*]: I had a lot of ideas, but when I sat down to write, my mind went blank. I had so much to say about teeth. . . . [*A few students laughed.*] Talking about it is embarrassing.

Len: I get the feeling in the group that we're getting to a point where we're willing to trust one another. ... I think that laughter was sympathetic.

Others [*comparing their experiences to Joanne's*]: I just sat and stared at the page for forty-five minutes. It got me mad. ... I couldn't settle on one topic. ...

Len: Know what that's called?

Students: Writer's block.

Len: Or getting stuck. It happens to everyone, even if you've written a lot before. ... I wrote eleven pages; don't think I'm going to use any of them. But I knew I had to write them first.

Cindy [*repeating a question from the "Guidelines" recorded in a process note*]: "What is missing? You're asking me? The whole thing is missing. Time to think is missing. A TOPIC IS MISSING. And I'm getting pissed so I will stop writing right now so I can think of a topic. I still can not think of a topic." I spend a lot of time 'running ideas through my head, so I can find something I can enjoy writing about and not want to just rush through. ...

Len: So you need to be interested in your topic?

Cindy: Yeah, I don't like to write it if I think it's going to be blah and dull. ... [*reading*] "It has to have a lot of parts to it, so I can keep on writing ... I need a lot of time to think about it ... I want the reader to want to finish it, too. ..."

Len: Sounds like there might be a conflict between writing what you want and ...

Cindy: ... what someone will want to read. Yeah, I want the reader to be interested, but it has to be something *I'm* interested in first—something I can just keep on writing and writing about ... that I'll be willing to put more work into. ... If I'm not interested then I just don't want to be bothered with it, and I just do it in an hour or two just to have something to hand in. ...

Len: Cindy, thank you for thinking deeply about writing. Katherine, when Cindy was reading, what did I just do?

Katherine: You asked questions to get her to talk more.

Jeff: You left some sentences open, so she finished them.

Len: I used Cindy's writing to demonstrate a model of responding to someone's writing. That's called "modeling": I've been modeling a way of responding. One of the goals of this course is for you to be able to listen very carefully and respond to another person's writing. We'll be practicing that a lot in class and in your groups.

As students gathered their books at the end of class, Len told them, "I have a good feeling about what has happened today. Everyone was serious. ... There was a good feeling in the room ... laughter too ... the best class so far." And, to the last student lingering at the door, "I really thought that was a great class."

Len often stopped the class to offer an observation about students' behavior or to let students into the thinking behind his own decisions.

"What's happening here?" he would ask in the middle of a class. "Why are we having so much trouble with this question?" "I feel you're resisting this assignment," or "I need to know where you are on this," or "I have a good feeling about what happened today," or "I'm going to be less careful than my instinct is telling me. I'm going to trust you [to work in groups] now instead of next week."

Reflecting, in his journal, on the thinking behind a particular assignment, he wrote, "Those are the reasons I remember and I don't think there were others and I especially don't think I had some hidden reasons I kept from the students."

Len invited his students behind the scenes of his teaching. He offered them techniques to practice and questions to ponder and hoped that they would learn, in his class, to teach one another. As I watched him immerse himself fully in the work of one writing group at a time, trusting the other groups to get on without him, I thought that I might understand his teaching best not by observing it directly but rather by joining a group of students with whom he had worked. I wanted to see if I could find in the students' work traces of the teacher's influence. The group I joined was one Len told me he had been sorry to leave.

A Writing Group

Like others in English 12, Kim, Katherine, Teresa, and Terri were wary of writing—school writing at least—when they entered Len's class. In their case-study interviews, Kim and Terri said they liked writing in journals, for themselves, but only, as Terri wrote about Kim, "where people won't see it." Teresa wrote that Katherine "tends to dislike" writing; when words flow, she "doesn't mind" it. And Teresa herself had come to "hate" it—"even writing letters." Yet together they wrote, encouraged one another to write about what mattered to each, and developed a group style that supported each one's individual struggle.

Part of the strength of the group, we all agreed, came from long association. Theirs was the only group in the class that stayed together all year. Other students switched groups, at Len's suggestion or their own, but Katherine, Kim, Terri, and Teresa chose to stay together. "We know each other's ways of working," said Terri in May. "For instance, Teresa sometimes drops characters in a story— she just forgets about them—but we know to watch for that. We remind her to pick them up again." "They came to know each others habits, quirks, and style," Len wrote. "They absorbed each other."

Kim was the most painfully shy about reading her work out loud, and Teresa the most sharply self-critical, but all understood shyness and self-doubt. They calmed each other. When one prefaced her reading with a ritual disclaimer ("It's dumb," or "I just dashed this off in ten minutes last night—it's no good"), the others would wait patiently for her embarrassment to subside, then gently encourage her to go on. When Teresa, who often read at breakneck speed and interrupted herself constantly with second thoughts and self-corrections, sometimes so dissatisfied with what she was reading she could hardly go on, stopped abruptly one day and said, "You don't want to hear this," the others assured her calmly that they did. During one of these tortured readings, Terri complained that Teresa was "so hard to listen to" and asked her to stop for a while, but Katherine said, "No—let her—," and the others listened, patiently, as Teresa thrashed her way through her draft. Once, when I was reading a piece of my own to Teresa, I stopped, hesitated, and said I thought it might be too long to read out loud.

But Teresa, sensitive from her own experience to self-consciousness in others, reassured me. "Are you afraid I'll be bored?" she asked. "It's okay—I won't be."

Once discussion of a piece got under way, separate voices blended in a murmur of encouragement and helpful questioning. Nods and a chorus of "yeahs" and "uh-huh's" punctuated discussion; questions moved it along. "What's going to happen next?" "Is it from your point of view?" "So you're going to have an accident in it?" "What could you do with the next part?" Teresa often thought out loud about her plans for a piece; Terri often remained silent for a while, then contributed a brief, focusing question. When Teresa said she had "a lot on my mind to write about," Terri said, "Such as?" When Teresa ended a tangled sentence with, "*You* know . . . ," Terri said, "I *don't* know," and pressed Teresa to make her meaning clear.

"It was important to me to hear other people retell my story," Teresa said later. "Before this I thought of writing groups unclearly. I thought you were expected to point out grammar and say if it was good or bad. But when I heard my story retold, I got exactly what my audience received."

As revision proceeded, members of the group often tried to protect one another from the premature and harsh judgments each tended to make of her own work. When Teresa scrawled "THAT'S UNINTERESTING" over one of her drafts, the others asked her why she thought so and suggested she look at it again. "Why didn't you like that sentence?" they would ask each other. "How come you crossed out this part in the middle?" Kim, who often said of her own work, "It's dumb," "This is no good," etc., gently questioned similar statements from Teresa. Teresa, quick to call her own work "garbage," was equally quick to sense self-doubt in others and challenge it. Most of their questions and comments were intended to help a writer recognize what was good in what she already had and then to help her carry it forward. "What's going to happen next?" Katherine or Kim or Teresa or Terri would ask and then sit back to listen as the reader expanded on what was there.

If I was impressed by the generally supportive tone of this group, its members were less so. When I read my accounts of their work to them, they reminded me that they weren't always productive. "We don't always have our writing." "We goof off a lot." "We talk about other stuff besides writing." I knew that and told them so. But their nonproductive moments, too, seemed to me to be part of the fabric they wove together.

Paying close attention to ancedotes and jokes and questions and the feelings that lay behind them, they were able to read one another's writing sensitively and provide support to one another as writers. Terri, reading Kim's case-study account of her revisions of a piece, was surprised at what Kim had seen. "*I* knew why I made those changes, but I didn't think anyone else would." Kim, in turn, was impressed by Terri's description of a pattern in her revising that Kim herself hadn't noticed. "I didn't realize I was doing all that [editing out]," she said, "but when Terri wrote about it I could see it was true." And Teresa told Katherine, "You understand my process better than I do!"

By the time May came, and with it the senior essay, the group had a history. They knew each other's ways of working and allowed for them. They were ready to help each other choose topics, write, rewrite, and struggle through their essays—pieces Len saw as serving several purposes.

Seniors, in Len's view, are faced with a major developmental task: to work their way through the series of events that mark the passage from high school to college or jobs in the outside world, from childhood to adulthood. He refers to these events, from applying to college to the senior trip and graduation, as "rites of passage." In his own "senior essay," Len explained his view of seniors as both "rejecting the school and trying to form a new identity" and "trying to hold on to what they know and are familiar with." He compared seniors in high school to his year-old son, who would throw his bottle to the floor, wait for his parents to pick it up, hold on to it a while, then throw it down again. "He holds on and then lets go and holds on and lets go and works out a whole series of complex relationships through this game."

Discussing this essay with the seniors he was writing about, Len admitted that, as a teacher, he planned to "seize upon the dynamics of senioritis and use its power to produce better writing." The senior essay, he wrote, could offer his students "a place where these issues can be explored and the tension released through exploration," a chance to look back on their lives so far, to examine and to reflect on them before taking the next steps forward. The writing of senior essays, he hoped, would become one more "rite of passage." A last major piece of work, taken through drafts and revisions and writing group meetings over a period of six weeks, it "says to the class that graduation is hard, it takes a long time, it works its way through your being slowly and in mysterious ways and here is one more ceremony for you to participate in before the final march." And Katherine, Kim, Terri, and Teresa participated in it, each in her own way.

Katherine had started out a fluent and prolific writer, especially of fiction. Once, after a prewriting exercise, when Len asked the class to look at what they had written and "see if there's a story in it," Katherine murmured to her group in a smiling undertone, "How could there *not* be a story?" In the middle of the year, however, she suffered what Len described (in his own senior essay) as a classic case of "senioritis." She lost interest in school, missed assignments, dried up as a writer. Her group waited. They knew that Katherine's writing came, when it came, "all in a clump." They were tolerant of her dry spell. From time to time, they teased her about it, gently, but for the most part they just sat it out with her, waiting patiently for her words to flow again. They never seemed to doubt that Katherine's words *would* flow again. They only wondered how long it would take and what they could do to help. And when the dam broke at last, and Katherine wrote and extensively revised an eighteen-page fairy tale for her senior essay, her group rejoiced with her.

"A long, long time ago, in a land far, far away . . ." Katherine read, and Kim, Terri, Teresa, and I gave ourselves over to the magic of her storytelling. We listened raptly as, installment after installment, Katherine's tale unfolded:

Leezel had many dolls: rooms full of ballerinas suspended on their toes, china dolls with billowing satin dresses, dolls with shoes carved from shark teeth, dolls with coats made of panther fur, dolls with skin as white as freshly whipped cream, dolls with diamond and ruby rings to fit their petite fingers, dolls with boots made from seahorse skin, dolls with hair so fine that it was impossible to separate one strand from the rest and every other kind of beautiful doll you could imagine. All the dolls were very elegant. All of them except one. . . .

"How did you *think* of all that?" Kim asked when Katherine's story of mystery and magical transformation was finally finished. "How did you work out all the connections: Leezel's 'purple' eyes—the boy looking for a girl called 'Amethyst'— Did you know from the beginning how it was going to end?" They relished details, point by point, and agreed the story was "*so* good"—"great"—"fantastic."

Terri, though a helpful responder in the group, seldom brought in her own writing to share. She would often start work on a piece just before it was due, leaving no time for group work or revision, and hand it in at the last minute, having read only a sentence or two to the group. Sometimes she would "talk" a piece in the group but not get around to writing it down, or write down only part of it. She wrote, for instance, several pieces about the hospital where she spent most of her time, including a scathing account, written as a dialogue, of the way nurses she considered insensitive talked about their patients, but she didn't feel satisfied with any of them. She felt she had more to say about the hopsital, but as the year went on, less desire to say it—in writing at least. "I've exhausted that subject; it's burnt out."

As the senior essay approached, Terri felt increasingly "stuck." Len, describing his goals for this extended project, had said, "I don't care what you write about, but it has to be something you *want* to write about." Terri didn't want to write about anything. There was something on her mind, but she felt it was "too personal" for a senior essay; when she tried to write about anything else, however, she couldn't get off the ground. She tried another hospital story but was bored by it. She tried what she called a "still life" but abandoned it:

It was a chilly New England day. The foliage was at it's height of colors. The wind was carelessly flowing with gusts of harsh whips at times. All aspects were illuminated by the sinking red fireball sun.

She tried again:

It was a brisk New England day. The wind was flowing carelessly and aimlessly, with exhilarating gusts at unexpected times. The sun, just past it's peak, attempting to counter-act the chill with its warmth, brilliantly accented and illuminated the ripened foliage.

Finally, in desperation, Terri sat down to write about the subject she couldn't avoid: the pregnancy of a friend, another teenager, whose main support Terri had been through the past five tension-filled months. Her friend's baby had just been born when Terri began to write. She decided to tell the story as honestly as she could but to cast it as fiction and, in the spirit of an assignment completed earlier in the year, to tell it in the first person, from the point of view of her friend.

"The entire ordeal was finally all coming to an end," she wrote, "or was it just beginning. . . . I cried and cried and cried when I found out I was pregnant . . . 'This can't be real,' I thought, 'God this can't be happening to me!!? . . .' " As the story unfolds, the pregnant girl becomes increasingly distraught and leans heavily on "Sheri," her supportive friend. She confides her "uncertainties and fears":

> Thousands of hours were spent between Sheri and I discussing and even fighting about my loss of self esteem and respect. Everytime I'd get down on myself Sheri would try calmly to get me out of it. . . . It was hard on Sheri and I knew it. It was causing her to have problems at school, her job and even her private life. . . .

Once she got started, Terri wrote twenty-one pages of this story within three days. "I didn't realize how upset I was until I started writing," she told me. "I thought I could take it all—be strong—but by the end of her pregnancy I couldn't concentrate on anything else, and when I started writing it all just came out. I didn't mean to put my own feelings in—only hers—but I noticed after I finished that I'd given the friend in the story a name like mine, 'Sheri,' and some of my feelings too."

Terri did not bring this piece to her group, nor did she publish it with the other senior essays. After school was over, she added to it, revised it, and edited and typed it, but during school Len and I were the only people she allowed to read it. Although Len had intended to publish everything written for this assignment, he accepted Terri's decision not to share this particular piece of work because it was "so personal and so current"—and because Terri was telling another person's story as well as her own—but allowed her to submit it anyway as her senior essay, because (as he told her), "This is what you need to write right now."

Kim, at the end of the year, remained caught between her desire to write about what mattered to her and her equally strong wish to protect her privacy. At one point, she had written—but not shared with her group—an interior monologue based on a family argument; at another, one that started out as a report on child abuse but became a first-person, emotion-filled, but entirely fictional account of an abused child, deliberately revised to sound "real." "I cut out all the parts that sounded boring and statistical," she told me. She enjoyed writing an essay on *Hamlet*—"putting the pieces together"—and was relieved whenever the class left personal writing for a while to discuss literature. As the year went on, she became more willing to bring personal writing to her group but was still in doubt about how much of herself to commit to paper.

For her senior essay, she decided to write about running, a subject close to her heart. She planned to go back to a piece about a track meet she had written in October and "put the feelings in." "It had no point of view," she told her group, "nothing of myself in it."

With the encouragement of the group, she explored ways she might handle the subject: interior monologue? a story? a poem? She tried several approaches and finally, she reported, wrote a piece—but didn't bring it in. "It wasn't any good ... The excitement was there, in my mind, but I couldn't get it into the piece." Instead, she submitted as her senior essay a collection of poems, some of which seem to touch, again, on the issue of revealing or not revealing self:

She

As she looks into the mirror she sees a
girl thats so confused.
A girl thats full of mystery and plays
the game she plays too well.
She knows what she is doing but
can't tell herself why she's here.
She wonders what others think of
her, as she does just as she wants.
Sometimes she can be figured out and
she lets a piece of herself out.
She is hidden in a cage opening the
lock to the door while at the same time
closing another door behind her. ...

Len, in his journal, described Kim as "hiding behind the vagueness of the poems" and concluded, "They are good some of them anyway but it was not what she really needed to write in this class."

In her last piece of writing for the class, a fragment written for an in-class exercise, Kim returned to running. She appears in the piece in "faded lavender sweats and a white tee," running through the woods, under a bright moon.

And Teresa, that year, discovered that, as she put it later, "you can learn who you are at the tip of a plastic ball point pen."

Teresa's previous school career had been, as Len described it, "one of good starts, poor middles and poorer ends." She came to senior year leaving behind a trail of unfinished work, erratic performance, and teachers left bewildered (as she said they kept telling her) by her failure to live up to her "potential." Her interest in reading and writing, once keen, was at a low ebb; even her spelling had fallen into disrepair.

Before senior year began, however, she had decided, as Katherine reported in her case study, to become "a good student." She determined to and did complete not only assigned work but also much that was not assigned. She wrote stories, essays, memoirs, poems; revised more and more extensively. Where she had once composed only rough and final drafts, she began to work through approximately five drafts per piece. She let her writing group show her how much of what was in her head was not getting onto paper, found two friends in another class who were able to help her edit, and talked with Len (who had chosen her as the subject of his own case study) for hours about her intentions and achievements in writing.

In a process piece written early in the year, Teresa explained that her stories

> are one of the ways I deal with my enviorment. My stories are derived from some event that has occured in my enviorment, They are a statment. concerning only my feelings about what has or is happining. When I am getting ready to write, I pull out the strongest emotion I feel from an event that has aroused my interest. I then decide upon the best story to amplify my emotion.

Writing about other writers' stories, as she chose to do several times during the year, Teresa kept her attention on what Katherine described as "the hidden undertones" of a work. For her senior essay, she analyzed stories and novels by Kurt Vonnegut, concentrating on Vonnegut's ability to write fiction that leads readers to think about their lives. About the story " 'Tomorrow and tomorrow and tomorrow,' " in which people's lives are prolonged by a drug that keeps them from aging, she wrote:

> Vonnegut is hoping his audience, by reading this story, will think not only of death as bad. Perhaps his reader will aquire a wider perspective. Seeing things clearly eventually helps a person come to terms with anything.

Writing about Vonnegut, Teresa was keeping a promise to herself. She had begun a similar piece the year before, in another class, but left it unfinished, like so much of her work in previous years; this year, she finished what she had started. But though she was still fascinated by Vonnegut, Teresa was not satisfied with the piece she had written about him. Her own best work, she thought (and her group agreed), had been done during a late-February burst of creativity, when she first discovered what she later called the "power" of writing. At that time she had written, among other things, a short poem, which she revised and then followed with a detailed (and unassigned) study of her revisions. The analysis, modeled on ones she had made during the case-study unit, covered six pages.

First Draft

Tradition

The river panacking
let itself loos
it raced across the surface
of tender emotion
until at last it cut and wore out
a path into the stone
that attempted to guide it
and at last it
broke free.

Final Draft

Tradition

The river
    broke loose
it raced across the surface
    of tender emotion
until at last it cut and carved
   a path into the rock that attempted
    to lead
and when the time came
   the freshly melted snow broke loose
   from the confinement
of the narrow stone gourge

Process

. . . . The river is of course life, perhaps my life. I like that it breaks loose and races across tender emotion . . . The river my thoughts . . . my being cuts and carves it way through rock. Rock my father, also other obsticles in life, and they can lead a person. Sometimes things in life do lead people thats why the river does not carve a straigh path although there is no line in this poem describing the path of the river. for me it is curved because some things influence me and others don't. That is why the river attempts. It does not nececarly suceed . . .

Changes and Reasons

    let itself loose—broke loose
let itself does not imply a fight
broke loose shows it took effort
    cut and wore—cut and carved
Wore . . . well you wear away something from continual friction. That is not at all what this river is doing. It is experiencing new things it definitly carves . . .
    lead its way—lead
its way was not needed. It may have made the poem more clear but it to me was too many words. They were just excess
    I just right now while writing about the changes and reasons decided to cut out "for the age of the river to end." Parents don't die when a kid starts thinking independantly
    The River Panaking—The River
Panaking, the river is not panicking it is growing. . . .

Awed by where her writing had taken her, she added, at the end of her detailed analysis:

    I'm surprised that I wrote all this stuff. I generally do not like my own poetry but writing all the process stuff out really gave me alote of insight. It is like this poem was in me and then I analyzed it and learned alote about myself. I am very interested and amazed in this event.

I like this poem. The whole world could not understand it or dislike it, but I understand exactly what it says. I am amazed at how much this poem represents growth. How fascinating that poetry could do that. What a discovery. Wow. writing can be a very discovering experience. wow. I'm so shocked I wish there was someone here I could talk with. I love it.

An Alternative Class

While Terri, Teresa, Katherine, and Kim were working on their senior essays, Len was working with Joanne, Leon, and Cindy on his own. Outside of class, however, in what had once been a free period for him, he was guiding another group of students through a different version of the senior "rite of passage."

In February, at the request of Norman Bussiere, the high school principal, Len created a special class for four students from his regular class who were failing the course. These four, Andy, Louis, John, and David, had been the hard-core nonwriters of the class the previous term. They had missed assignments, refused to work in writing groups, cut class. Unless they changed their ways, they would not graduate in June. All had been in special skills classes in previous years; the regular class "never was nonthreatening enough for them," Len thought. He agreed to offer them the extra support a class of four would make possible. He consulted them about plans for the class and reported in his journal, "It seems they all want to do some sort of writing about stuff they really know about." What most of them knew about, Len discovered, was auto mechanics.

So the alternative English class became a class in car repair. The students taught Len what they knew about pistons and crank shafts; Len taught them, as far as he could, the patience necessary to record their knowledge in writing. Some days, the students brought machine parts to class and sat around a table piled high with greasy valves, explaining their uses to Len. "Mr. Schutzman is going to know a lot about auto mechanics," said Andy.

Len was impressed by the extent of their knowledge. He reported in his journal:

> Andy and John are working on this book about rebuilding engines and they are doing an excellent job. Andy really can't write at all in terms of his skills but on this subject he is organized and the material is well thought out. He must really know how to rebuild engines.

The manual, *Rebuilding an Engine,* took most of the term to complete. When it was finished, Andy and John illustrated it with detailed diagrams and drawings of auto parts, and someone's girlfriend typed it. It ran to seventeen pages. An excerpt from chapter 4, "Micing," gives the flavor of the whole:

> When you are micing you look for worn parts, out of roundness, and tapper. The tools needed for this job are a set of micromitors, bore and stroke mic. Select the right size mic to mic the lobs on the cam. Mic them in two spots, one from the highest point to the lowest point and one from side to side.

Mic up all the lobs on the cam and write them all down on paper; look up in the manufacturer's specs and find your motor; then find the specs on the cam lobs. Once you find them match them up with the ones you took. . . .

Next you have to mic the block. On the block, you mic the bores, where the pistons go. You check for bad scratches, tapper and out of roundness. First start with the tapper, take the bore mic and put it into the cylinder. Start at the bottom and work your way up to the top. Watch the difference as you come to the top and write it down on paper. Once you do all the cylinders, look up your motor in the book and find out how much tapper you are allowed. Then you measure for the out of roundness, for this you have to mic it two times for each cylinder, once vertical and once horizontal. Then subtract both numbers from each other. . . . If the block falls within the specs then all you will have to do is hone out the glaze. If it does not fall with in the specs, then you will have to bore out the block, which isn't cheap. That is all that has to be miced.

While John and Andy were writing their manual, Louis was working on a related piece, "How to Do a Valve Job," and David, who was about to enlist in the Navy, was writing about his experiences with the Navy recruitment process.

Len wanted John, Andy, Louis, and David each to find what others had found: a subject on which he, not the teacher, was the authority. When John, Andy, and Louis found their subject in car engines, and David found his in Navy recruitment procedures, Len was delighted. The students were too. While they were writing their manuals, they came to class every day, wrote regularly, and discussed, informally, the problems of writing. Some began to talk to Len about other things as well.

Looking back on this class, Len was impressed by what he and Andy, Louis, John, and David had accomplished together. At the end of the fall term, as he wrote later, he remembered

being really bitter and defensive (it's their fault if they can't make it) and finally decided to do something convinced they would fail anyway. They didn't. They worked and succeeded. They grew and learned and so did I. They wrote their tails off . . . It was wonderful to see them graduate.

The Academic Voice

As Len's seniors neared graduation, many of those preparing for college began to ask questions about "academic" writing. Should they be doing more of it? Should they be learning the forms for college term papers? Len worried too.

When he assigned "academic" (as opposed to "personal") writing, Len questioned the standard forms many of his students were trying to follow. In a batch of essays about *Hamlet,* for instance, he noted "these horrible introductory and concluding paragraphs that were just part of a form they had learned and really served no substantive function" and described an awkwardness arising from "confusion about how to express their opinions. A lot of the kids didn't use 'I' but 'this writer' which is absurd."

In a discussion of George Orwell's "Shooting an Elephant," Len improvised a third-person essay on imperialism in Burma, based on information from Orwell's essay ("The British colonized Burma in ... During this period some British officers felt ..."), and asked students to compare it with Orwell's first-person original. "What does it mean to write as 'I'?" he asked them. Nearly everyone agreed that Orwell's essay was more "interesting," "forceful," "dramatic," "believable"; that "it makes it seem as if it's happening to you." But, said Jeff, "if you handed it in to Mr. X [a social studies teacher], he'd say 'You used "I"' and give it an *F*." Len, a social studies teacher himself, admitted ruefully that that might be so. "We used to teach them not to use 'I,'" he told me later and, reflecting in his journal on voiceless academic writing, added:

> I think about the article we just read for [a course in cognitive psychology] and how dead it was and unreadable and then I think about all the teaching it took to get those people to write such trash. No one would write that way if they could help it ...

Len gave his students opportunities to practice "academic" writing but, in all but a very few assignments, gave them other choices too. In January, for instance, at the end of a unit on fairy tales, he asked them to write literary analyses of the tales—or fairy tales of their own. He called a major piece of work "the senior essay" but left the choice of mode as well as subject entirely up to his students, most of whom, in fact, wrote stories, poems, or memory pieces rather than formal essays. He asked those students who were preparing for college to think about "keeping yourself in your writing" and explored the subject in class: "How can you write about academic subjects and still own your writing?"

In his journal, he asked himself the same question:

> I know for myself that it is a very different proposition to write a paper for a course than it is to write a story. I don't really have my hands on all the dynamics but I know I adopt this academic voice when I write papers and I expect to have it done after the first go round or so. I would never subject a creative piece of mine to that process and I know my other writing, the academic voice, would be much improved if I would allow my feelings to express themselves in it, but somehow I am unable to do that.

From time to time during the year, Len wrestled with this issue. At the end of June, he sighed and admitted he had not yet resolved it. Next year, he hoped, he would make more progress with it—especially if he taught social studies again.

Reflecting on Growth

At the end of the year, Len invited his students to comment, in serious and playful ways, on the class and on what they had learned from it. He composed a final exam that, as he put it, went "in and out of seriousness," calling for responses ranging from written evaluations of writing groups to cartoons. Most students responded thoughtfully and honestly. About writing groups, Tom wrote:

> In the beginning of the year our writing group really didn't know what it was doing. It was as if we were lost. But as the year went on we began to understand what it was that we were supposed to do. As we got better and better in our roles in the writing group (ex Reader, Listener) it began to function more and more smoothly.
>
> As one person read the other people in the group would listen and then respond. I feel as the year went on we helped each others writing out immensely. We each knew each others writing style and what to look for.
>
> One area in which I would have liked our group to improve in is reading the story out loud. I don't think that we got over the fear of reading it out loud to others ...

Others, too, wrote about their groups. Terri:

> ... The questions were asked with genuine interest—not just to speak and keep things rolling. Most of the time, we functioned as we should, or were expected to. But other times, we did nothing but talk and waste time, which could have been improved.

Katherine:

> If I read a piece of writing [from my group] without knowing who wrote it I think that after looking carefully at it I would be able to determine whose it was because everyone had their own style. Also just by the topic of the paper I think I could guess. ...

Kim:

> Our writing group functioned great! We made each other not only read their piece but also talk about its process—feelings toward piece—mistakes and asked many questions to make the reader think about the particular piece. I think our group has become more open with each other now we each could read anything to our group w/o being hesitant ...

Looking back on the year, Kim wrote:

> I really don't think my process has changed much over the year—generally its the same. ... Most of the time, my first draft looks just like my final draft, maybe with some structural and spelling corrections.

but added:

> In the beginning of the year, I dreaded reading my writing to anyone but myself. Now I feel very comfortable with my writing group and believe it or not, I don't mind writing and reading pieces to the class ...

Terri wrote:

> In the past, I wrote to do the assignment. I didn't care what I handed in, whether I liked it or not. ... Now I write for myself—to get things clear. ... The most difficult piece I wrote this year was my senior essay. It was a piece that dealt with a very sensitive and private time in my life. It was very hard

to put into words, in a proper sequence, without "letting it all out." It was also hard because it was on a subject that I never totally came to grips with, and when I started writing it, I finally came to grip.

Teresa, who once expressed herself primarily through music, spoke of the "harmony" of writing. "Writing is a new adventure for me," she wrote. Her paper ended with a cartoon of Len, captioned, "Thank you for being brave."

On the last day of class, Len read aloud from his own evaluation of students' work, a postscript tacked onto his piece on teaching seniors and included in the just-published collection of senior essays. (To protect students from embarrassment, he disguised the identities of those he mentioned.)

> I sit here with all the senior essays ready to go to the Xerox machine for copying and I have yet to put my own piece into final form for the magazine. Looking at the stack of writing fills me with pride. I feel a real sense of accomplishment as a teacher for having set up a framework to enable these seniors to produce this work. More importantly I am proud of what the students have written. The quality and commitment evident in their writing surpassed my expectations. Many of the seniors held on to this assignment as a way to close out their year with me and even their high school careers. There was a lot of "I did it" when the papers were handed in and a lot of pride from me when I read and graded them.
>
> For the record one student did not do the assignment, just deciding it was beyond him after several starts. Another student produced a long, very personal piece, that will not appear in the magazine at his insistence. Despite all the efforts at building a trusting relationship this year, this particular piece is too close to share in a published form. There were two pieces handed in that I was very disappointed in but the remainder really did represent the best each student was capable of producing now. Some work dazzled me and I, at least, will keep the magazine on my shelf to thumb through in the years ahead.

He thanked the students for a good year and told them, "I felt very relaxed with this class. I trusted you."

And, reflecting in his journal, he wrote that this had been "a special class ... We did break through some barriers. The honesty was there not all the time or from all the students but in moments fleeting and brave and we all grew from those moments."

A Language of Teaching

I had always assumed, without thinking about it much, that to teach English well a teacher would have to be steeped in literature. I knew, of course, that a background in literature would not in itself guarantee success in teaching English, but I thought it to be a necessary prerequisite—a starting point, without which there was no point in trying. Watching Len, I began to question that assumption.

Len was interested in literature, as he freely admitted, mainly for the insights it provided into human psychology. When he read *Hamlet* with his seniors, he lectured on the Oedipus complex; when he taught fairy tales, he concentrated on Freudian interpretation. Like his students, I sometimes balked as he led the class beneath the surface of a text. Where, I wondered, was the magic of language? Did Len appreciate or even notice the rhythms of English prose and poetry, the images that move a reader in mysterious ways?

Yet as Len's students wrote and read and gained in confidence through the year, I was forced to ask myself how much it mattered. Not much, apparently— or not, at least, as much as I had thought it did. When Kim lost her shyness about reading her work, or Terri turned personal experience into fiction, or Katherine wove enchantment in a fairy tale, or Teresa studied her writing process and was "amazed" at what she had discovered, each had become, in her own way, a writer. Len had, as he described it, "set up a framework"; within it, students had discovered, on their own, the power of language.

When Teresa returned to the high school after graduation, in the throes of a rough transition to college, she told Len that she had been afraid to come to see him because she knew that as soon as she started to talk to him she would begin to cry. "She knew she would cry," Len wrote,

> because she could envision the kind of discussion we would have. Part of that is just me but part of it is the context in which Teresa knew me. As her writing teacher she saw me as an honest and open human being ready to listen to what she had to say and willing to give her the space in which to say it.

Len's definition of a writing teacher had little to do with expertise in literature or even writing. He spoke of what he did in terms of "listening" and "giving space." In teaching, as in reading literature or talking with students, he looked, as always, beneath the surface: not to words but to the human connections that make learning possible.

Watching Len, I was led to think about how much of the technique or art of teaching lies beneath the surface of the subjects we teach. Len's students, I thought, could have learned anything in his class; as it was, they had learned to write. And though, in my own classes, I knew, I would continue to speak the language of literature, as Len would speak the language of psychology, I had come to see that beneath the different vocabularies we used lay a language we shared: a language of tone and gesture, of use of time and space, of a way of looking at students—a language not limited to the teaching of English.

Chapter 6

Bill Silver
Fourth and
Fifth Grades

"Intellectual questions ... always interest me," Bill Silver wrote in his journal as our project began: "How kids learn to write, cognitive limitations on what they write, how similar/different upper elementary children are to adults learning to write, what forms/genres/experiences are most appropriate ... how 'intelligence' (whatever that is) affects the content and form of children's writing ..."

He was interested, too, he wrote, in theories about learning in math and science, in cognitive psychology, and in "tying together pieces of theories and models and making connections." The making of such connections, he thought, would be "a major force in keeping me interested in the project."

The study group, he hoped, would "support" his writing program; besides that, he added, participating in the study "will force me to look critically at what I'm doing. ... I teach better when I'm introspective about the process."

Thinking about thinking—his students' and his own—is what keeps Bill interested, both in teaching and in his fourth- and fifth-grade interage classroom. A scientist by training, he has always been concerned with how knowledge is structured, how it is acquired, how it is tested and proved. "I was one of those weird chemistry majors who took philosophy of science," he told me once. "I've always been interested in theory—how it's developed, how you research it."

When Bill entered college, he was planning to become a chemist. A political science course attracted him, however, and then a series of humanities and education courses until, although he retained his interest in chemistry, he had changed his mind about what he wanted to do with it. When he became a teacher, he chose to teach not in high school or college, where he would have taught chemistry alone, but rather in elementary school, where he teaches not only science but also math, writing, reading, social studies, and a host of academic and social skills he describes as "ways of looking at the world (conceptual frameworks, if you like, and models) that can be applied in various circumstances to many kinds of subject matter."

Models of the way people think are of particular interest to Bill. While he respects the value of "inductive" thinking, his own mind works, he says, "deductively," through "charts and matrices through which I organize the world." When he wants to understand something, he observes it, generates a hypothesis about it, and tests the hypothesis. While he could understand, intellectually, the value of the ethnographic approach we researchers were using in our study, he couldn't imagine using it himself: just sitting around, as we seemed to be doing, observing, taking notes, sifting through our observations, waiting for patterns to emerge. He watched us with an amused tolerance, sometimes shaking his head over us. "I'll be damned if I understand how you can observe anything without having a hypothesis first."

The parts of his own research for the study that he found most congenial were those he could start with a prediction about what would happen. "Then either it did or it didn't, and you could look at why." A study group assignment to write a case study designed along ethnographic lines went against his grain.

> I've found it draining and superfluous often, not worth the time I put into it. Could be a difference in learning style or something, but that inductive, look at one closely and then apply is hard for me. And the purely descriptive-type stuff is not useful for me, either—I tend to dismiss it too quickly, perhaps, but I *need* to look for patterns, predictions, theories—things that help me explain and control what goes on.

In the classroom, Bill observes the behavior of his students (and his own behavior), asks himself questions about it, spins theories to answer the questions, and invents tests for the theories. It matters to him that a theory be testable, "not just a set of beliefs"; he wants to understand, not just guess at, why things happen.

Watching Bill watch his students, it seemed to me sometimes that he had turned his classroom into a laboratory for the study and development of children's thinking. And as time went on, his interest in the nature of learning began to emerge for me as a central theme—a thread that tied together what I had at first seen as unrelated aspects of his teaching.

Teacher and Researcher

"Teachers (or classrooms) are like islands in a way," Bill wrote in his teaching journal toward the end of our project's first year,

> tenuously connected by the means for communication, but often not using them well or often. . . . Early in the year the ferry service to my particular is- land was quite good, coming several times a week. . . . But like most ferries, wintertime reduced the schedule, and I've felt some of that familiar isolation.

Bill's "island" image, which I came upon in his journal two years after he had written it, rang true to me. I knew all too well what he meant. James Carter, the first researcher in Bill's classroom, had found himself spread too thin, trying to cover four classes in two different schools; midway through the first year of our study, he had begun to cut back on his visits to Bill's room. After the second year, he had left Shoreham to return to his own high school teaching job, and I had taken over as researcher for fourth and fifth grade. That year was a busy one, however, and, by the time I read Bill's journal, I too had become a ferry making irregular and infrequent visits to the island of his classroom.

Trying to pick up where Jamie had left off, I felt bewildered and often frustrated. I had fragments rather than wholes from which to piece together a picture: Jamie's notes, Bill's journals, writing from students from several different classes, tape recordings of classroom sessions, my own notes on the students and classes I had begun to observe myself. Visiting Bill's class only a few days a month, I knew I could not hope to know Bill and his students as I knew teachers and students in the high school, whose classes I had attended three or four days a week for a year. And if even the high school classes still held mysteries for me, Bill's class, which I had joined so late, seemed practically impenetrable.

Coming to elementary school from the relative calm of the high school where, for the most part, students sat quietly in their seats during class, wrote for long stretches of time, and generally maintained a pace I could understand, if not always follow, I found it hard, at first, to keep up with Bill and his fourth and fifth graders. In Bill's classroom, as far as I could see, no one sat still for more than a minute or two, and no one was quiet for long.

I was stunned at first by the seeming confusion generated by nine- and ten-year-olds at work. One student might be sitting at a table writing a story; at the same table, two others might be composing a play out loud while a third looked up from a math sheet now and then to throw out ideas. Various individuals, groups, and pairs might be perched on top of the file cabinets, or sprawled on the rug in the open area used for class meetings, or propped up on the window sills. As Bill himself observed ruefully in his journal, after watching his students at work, "Body positions . . . funny—only 2 kids in the class in 'good penmanship' position—both arms fully on table, feet on ground etc. Everyone else all over the place."

Half a dozen kids might be in transit from one place to another: going to or from their lockers, the water fountain, the wastebasket, or to special lessons or meetings or appointments, stopping to talk to their friends on the way. Others might be in their seats but calling back and forth between tables. Yet, somehow, most would be writing, I could see that: some oblivious to the noise and commotion around them, others apparently comfortable in the midst of it. But I couldn't see how. I myself could hardly take notes.

Bill's class intrigued me. The information Jamie had gathered, in fieldnotes, interview notes, and folders of students' writing, looked worth exploring; Bill's journal, rich with questions and speculations, attracted me, and the fourth and fifth graders I talked to from time to time seemed full of life. Surely there must be a way to put all this together, find patterns in it, make sense of it?

I began to move around the room, as Bill did, to try to follow students as they wrote and talked about writing. I asked kids questions. And gradually, as I began to get used to the ebb and flow of classroom life in fourth and fifth grades, I began to see what Bill was after: a rhythm suiting nine- and ten-year-olds, not adults; a setting open enough so that each student could find a way of working comfortably within it, as most did. Every so often a kid protested: "There's too much noise in here! I can't think," but, for the most part, members of the class agreed that they didn't want talk and movement banned from writing time. For most, the sociability and freedom of movement contributed to their feeling at ease with writing; they agreed, from time to time, to try to keep the noise level down, but hardly anyone wanted to write in silence. They agreed, instead, on common-sense rules for writing times: do whatever you want or need to do, as long as it doesn't keep you (or anyone else) from getting the work done.

In this setting, Bill's students wrote stories or composed plays together or drew pictures or discussed one another's writing, following a curriculum Bill says he puts together in

> bits and pieces, questions about questions, intuitively feeling my way through activities and sequences of activities, refining and changing within a vague outline of assumptions and beliefs about writing, writers and 4th and 5th graders.

It is these "beliefs and assumptions" that Bill tests, while acting on them as he teaches. It was the process of his inquiry that intrigued me as I sat in his classroom.

The report that follows, therefore, is composed not of a chronological account of a single class and teacher working through a particular year, but rather of scenes and impressions clustering around the theme of inquiry that, while present in all the classes we observed, is particularly strong in Bill's. It begins with an incident that raised a question and follows Bill as he attempts to answer that question and others to which it gave rise.

A Question of Purpose

In December of his fifth-grade year, Chris, a fluent and inventive writer of made-up stories, ran out of ideas. "I really want to write a story but I really can't get ideas," he wrote in his journal.

> I always write about kids with unusual names because I like writing with funny characters ... but right now I have 5 beginings and I should be done with two drafts of one or two things ... I need to find more ways of finding Ideas I want to write a funny Interesting and Detailed story but I really don't have any Ideas for one. ...

Bill wrote back:

> Chris—You're really stuck! I'm sorry ...
> Don't worry too much about deadlines, but I do want something before Christmas.
> I also think you should try something different—a report, news article, memory story—something that deals with a topic you know about. Just getting a piece written should help you out. And writing from your own experience (things that happened to you or that you know about) is sometimes easier than "making things up."

Chris responded by writing an eyewitness account of pigs being born on his grandparents' farm in Iowa.

> I jumped out of the Hayloft and into the barn to watch the babies being born from a sow. The sow squealed loudly as it rolled back and forth. Suddenly I saw something pink coming out of the sow. Blood dripped out rapidly. I could tell what it was, it was a snout of an infant pig.
> I looked happily at my sisters and my cousin. The mother squeled again and dripped more blood. The little head slipped out suddenly. The little pig fell out of the mother sow.
> I clicked my camera to get the picture of the new baby piglet. The small piglet was pink and had a small thin mask over its mouth so it could'nt breathe. My uncle cut it's mask so it could breathe. The umbilical cord was still attached as the baby pig gave a squeal that I hardly heard. ...

He described, moment by moment, the births of five more piglets and on the third page ended,

> I walked out of the barn and across the feild. As I got into the truck I realized that I never had seen anything being born before.

Bill was enchanted by this story: by its detail, its freshness, its truth. He brought it to the study group where the rest of us—teachers and researchers—shared his delight. Chris, however, was not impressed.

It wasn't, he said, one of his better pieces. He had no desire to write another piece from personal experience. The carefully observed and precisely recorded details of the pig story, which had so excited members of our study group, didn't interest him. He returned, in his next few pieces, to the freedom of invention, presenting ordinary life shot through with magic: in one story, a giant Rubik's cube turned reality inside out; in another, the king of an imaginary kingdom appeared to a boy bored by everyday life. His last story of the year did, in fact, include a pig, but not an ordinary Iowa farm pig: this pig, Slime, snorted and grunted in front of a TV set in a Manhattan apartment where, in the company of other members of a (human) family, he watched Mr. Rogers cut up a squash.

> Hortence sat next to Slime with a bread knife in her hand. She was very influenced by the Mr. Rogers special when he dissected the squash. She wanted to do the same thing, but they didn't have any squash, so she used Slime. His heart, brain, intestines, everything from his body was on the floor. There were bloodstains all over the wall to wall carpet. She was caught by Isabelle.
> "Look what you did to the rug," she yelled. "It's stained!" . . .

The story got wilder and wilder, culminating in a series of macabre murders and suicides. "I was going to make it a fantasy," Chris commented, "but I changed it to a comedy." He added that he had made some further changes because "grown-ups didn't like the part where Hortence dissected her parents."

Chris's first "pig" story and his own lack of enthusiasm for it sparked off a series of questions in Bill's journal. What do fourth and fifth graders see as "good" writing? Bill wanted to know. Are the qualities adults look for in kids' writing—truth, freshness, a personal voice—not important to kids? Or less important to them than other qualities? If so, what are those other qualities? As Bill put it himself, "Are kids' criteria for good writing different from adults' criteria for good kids' writing?"

We discussed the matter, at length, in the study group. We agreed that we adults frequently preferred children's "personal experience" writing to their fantasy writing, which often seemed to us shallow or derivative. When fourth and fifth graders wrote about personal experiences, then, were they responding to subtle pressures from us? We wondered if our adult preferences were blinding us to children's own purposes in writing. What were fourth and fifth graders after? Could we find out? We encouraged Bill in his attempt to answer these questions—for us and for himself.

At the beginning of the study, Bill had mentioned his interest in similarities and differences between adults and upper elementary school children. He knew, for a start, that kids and adults often said similar things in discussions of their writing processes. At the end of one such discussion with his students, he told them about a writing workshop he had recently led, commenting, "A lot of the things you guys said—about some of you having trouble getting started, some of you knowing right away what you were going to write about, some of you having a hard time because there was time pressure—those are all things the adults mentioned in the workshop. It's interesting to hear the same things whether people are fifty years old or nine years old." But if kids' writing processes seemed in some ways to resemble those of adults, their attitudes toward their written products, he was beginning to think, might turn out to be different. He decided, as a first step, to bring his question to the students themselves.

Toward the end of several weeks of intense writing, he asked his students to review their stories, memory pieces, reports, and poems and to respond, in writing, to the questions, "What was your best piece of writing?" and "Why did you like it?" Their answers raised new questions.

Sue wrote, "Rich kid was one of my best pieces because It was long." Matt liked "Guess" because "it's very long and typed." Jeffrey liked " 'Mystery at Cove Beach' ... because it is probably the longest story I have written this whole entire year."

Was length, then, a deciding factor in kids' evaluations of their own work? He read on.

Andria liked " 'St. Patrick's Day Parade' ... because I think that was my longest story and I'm pretty sure that it was the one I did the most revision on and the most work on." Shannon liked "My Valentine Sweetheart" because "I put alot of time into it and really thought about it." Scott liked his murder story because "when I got up in the story nothing stoped me I just felt I could go on fore ever and ever becous I just keped coming on with all the Idears and for some reason it just fit in ... I really enjoyed it." Jon liked "Liserds of Oz" and "Return to the Liserds of Oz" because "thay were fun to write and fun to read."

So the quality of the writing experience, too, could be important.

A few liked "true-to-life" stories. Darren liked his piece about his best friend because "I talked about him and me and the things we did together and how we met." Valerie liked "Goose and Grandpa" because "I think its funny that my Grandpa had a problem but the problem disapeared."

But most, like Chris, preferred their "made-up" stories. Deane liked his war story "because it had alot of action and it was probbley my most Detailed peise of writing I ever wrote." Jeff liked " 'Sasha's Day' ... becos I put my self in my dog's point of view and I think I did a very good job of writing how my dog thinks things happen." And Erika was pleased by her four-page "No Good Very Bad Day" story because, as she told me, "it's absolutely all made up—not one word of truth in it."

Literal truth, then, which often delights adults when they find it in children's writing, seemed irrelevant to Bill's students' purposes. If anything, they wanted to avoid it—or at least transform it into something more interesting. If this were so, Bill wondered, were his own writing assignments (memory chains and student biographies, for instance) preventing his students from writing what they wanted to write? To begin to answer this question, Bill asked himself first, "What sorts of things do kids write about when left to their own devices?"

When they chose pieces from free writing, class exercises, and journals to revise and/or publish in class anthologies, he noticed, most kids chose fantasy-adventure stories, mysteries, etc., often featuring detectives, magicians, or aliens from Mars. Andria's story, "Adventure at the Circus," was typical of this kind of writing:

> Beep beep beep beep. We interupt this program to being you a special news bulletin, 2 strange creatures from outer space are invading the circus. ...

Were the proportions of "real" to "made up" any different, Bill wondered, in what students chose *not* to publish? What, for instance, were they writing in their journals?

At the beginning of the year, he had described journals as

1. A place to practice writing privately—no corrections by parents or me.
2. A place to communicate privately to me—no need to show it to anyone else—I never will.
3. A place for me to communicate privately to each student.

Now he studied the pages of his students' journals to see if he could find patterns in what they were writing about. He reported:

> Some kids write nothing but stories, some never [write stories]. In the "all story" category, most popular are the serial stories ("to be continued"). Many kids do this—the stories tend to be vacuous and below their regular writing in quality (e.g., Matt, Chrissie). Other patterns: What I did over the weekend, reports on sporting events (my soccer team won ...), games, puzzles and pictures (95% girls), one-shot stories, and personal concerns (infrequent, usually at my prodding). Jenny did sectioned pages, laid out with puzzles, poems, places for me to write, etc.—unusual. Almost everyone asks me a page of questions or two at some point, and almost everyone spends a couple of entries writing how they didn't know what to write. Finally, the past two years have seen numerous memory chains.

If students seemed content with what they were writing, should he just leave them alone? Bill wondered. Or should he intervene from time to time—assign new forms, push kids to explore new possibilities? Wanting them to try memory chains, limericks, biography, experiments with metaphor and description as well as fiction, he sometimes led his students through directed writing exercises; when he did, however, he worried that he was interfering with the students' own purposes in writing. What is most useful for a fourth or fifth grader to write? he asked himself. "Are 'good' Pac-Man stories better than ... poor memory stories?" Should he continue to insist that kids try new forms, at least occasionally, or should he just stand back and let them write whatever they wanted to write? In study group, we discussed the issue and asked each other: How much of teaching is recognizing the right moment to make a suggestion? How much is biding one's time or "getting out of the way"?

"Getting out of the way," Bill wrote in his journal,

> that was a simple phrase, made sense, had lots of surface validity—but it really is much more complicated. ...
> There are degrees of getting out of the way in teaching writing—it's not like standing in the road and either you're hit or you're not. Aside from the

basic considerations of class organization and structure, each kid is different and each piece of writing is different. . . .

So then the question is, how do you decide? What do you look for? What general guidelines are followed? Take Matt and Jon, for example. They would write D. & D. mazes, codes, whatever they're doing, for days on end. But if I say they can't, they find other things to write about. Which is better? The D. & D. writing is purposeful, they feel committed, they have an audience, it's useful—but I oppose it. Is that wrong?

Again he consulted the kids. "What kinds of writing would you like to do for the next four or five weeks?" he asked them in February after a short school vacation. He suggested that they write about their choices for about ten minutes. In his journal, he reported:

> They drove me crazy—I don't think anyone wrote for more than 3 or 4 minutes, they were talking, came over and interrupted me—just awful. I was really annoyed, and when I collected them they didn't look like much, either. I figured it was wasted time. But when I got to look at them later, they were really interesting. A total of 16 kids (of 19) said they wanted to continue writing and sharing or publishing stories (13 mentioned revision and publishing!), and 8 wanted to do more freewriting in class . . .

Bill was impressed by some of the reasons students gave for wanting to write freely and choose their own topics. He copied or inserted several students' responses into his teaching journal:

> Writing is something I really like to do . . . I especially like to make stories because I can imagine things up that could never possibly happen. (Tricia)

> I would like to do free writing again because I throt it was fun and we got to write anything we wanted to write like things that don't make seince or just Keep writing numbers or Letters or even the alfubet. When I throw about it, it Berout back Memores and as I wous riting I just cept on thinking of more and more things I like writing adventer misterys the best. (Deane)

> I like writing because you can open your mined and you can create whatever you really like. In September when we started writing, I was relly nervess about being yelled at because I didn't write so good. But now I'm not scared. I now think I write good. I can write pretty good stories. I like to write about U.F.O.'s and magic powers . . . (Mike)

Bill commented, in his journal:

> The kids seem incredibly eager to write. But to write about what they want to. I feel like I'm holding them back, trying to teach them (show them?) models or types of responses when what they really need is to write themselves out a bit first. . . . My wanting them to become more or less comfortable with memory chains, memory stories, etc. may be misplaced—it's the old "let's do this individual activity as a whole group" syndrome. . . . I really think that in the long run the "best" writing comes from themselves—their topics, ideas and forms—not from provisions I make. . . .

Yet he noted that the kids, in addition to requesting more free writing, had made about 10 other suggestions, all of which mentioned different *forms* of writing—cartoons/comics, plays, picture story books, whole-class stories, poetry—certainly food for thought.

The inquiry in our study group took on a new dimension. We'd been talking about students' choices of topic; now we turned our attention to their choices of form. Which came first in students' minds, Bill wondered, form or content? Was form another factor determining what kids thought of as "good" writing—or, at any rate, what they liked to write? Did kids first decide to write "a play" and then decide what the play was to be about, or did they think of plot or situation first, and then decide that what they had might take the form of (for instance) a play? Was choosing a form and exploring its possibilities as important to kids as finding a subject? Once again, Bill consulted his students.

One day in class, Jeff read the beginning of a story that was going to be, he said, "a so-called true story." It was to begin, he announced, with "kind of an introduction, like the 'Tanglewood Porch' section in 'The Gorgon's Head.'" He read the first few lines aloud: "'I don't know why or when this happened, cause I heard it from my mom, who heard it from Mrs. Duffrin, who heard it from Mrs. Katz, who heard it from who knows who. . . .'"

A few literal-minded kids were puzzled. "If you heard it from your mother and Mrs. Duffrin, then it *must* be true. . . ." Jeff explained patiently, "I didn't *really* hear it from my mother. . . ."

Bill: So what you have in mind is a structure for the story—a frame sort of thing. This is the beginning, and then you'll tell the story, and then there'll be an end . . . but you're stuck on what the story should be.

Jeff: Yeah, yeah, yeah.

Bill: An interesting problem. What does the story have to be like? Can it be a fantasy?

Jeff: It has to be sort of like a little bit realistic. You know, like that story about this guy who takes this kid in the car and then drives off—like that—It has to be not so fake—not like they flew into this dragon cave and . . .

Other kids [*chiming in*]: It's got to be half fairy tale and half real . . . Something that could be true, but it's not. . . . Something that could really happen, but it didn't. . . . [*They explore, for a while, the boundaries of the possible in a "so-called true story."*]

Bill: You know what's interesting, Jeff, is how much you know about what the story has to be like, but you don't have the story yet. That's really interesting.

Jeff created a frame, then looked for a story to put in it. Other students did the same. Amy planned to write a story about a magic tea saucer, talking animals, and a king, queen, and princess; when she actually wrote it, she started, like Jeff, with an introduction similar to the ones in *Tanglewood Tales*:

Shoreham Attic—before the story
    It was a warm summers eve. My grandchildren and I were in the attic, when Janice came across a beautiful white silk cape and a lovely silk dress.
    "What's this?" asked Janice. "It's very pretty."

"Oh just an exciting memory" I replied.
"What memory?" asked Susie.
"Tell us" exclaimed Nancy.
"Okay—okay" I told them. . . .

At the end of the story, she returned to the attic:

Shoreham Attic—after the story
   Nancy asked "Is that it?"
   "Yes" I chuckled.
   "Is that true?" beamed Janice.
   "Yes" I said again.
   "Tomorrow can you tell us another story?" asked Susie.
   "Yes" I exclaimed since you were so good.
   "Good" they all yelled together.
   "Well then let's go down stairs and get ready for bed."

Other students borrowed formulas from TV series or movies or adventure stories or whatever, then filled them out with characters and plots of their own invention. Maryellen ended a chapter of a story based on something that had happened to her: "I thought Jennifer was the worst, but then came

MELISA!"

She told me she wanted to end every chapter on a note of suspense, "You know, the way they do it in the Hardy Boys books."

Bill calls these choices "stylistic." Fourth and fifth graders, he says, are fascinated by patterns, structures, forms—even TV formulas. They like to know how things work. For many kids this age, part of the pleasure of reading comes from being able to recognize repeating patterns: that's how chapters *always* end in Hardy Boys books; that's how fairy tales *always* begin. And part of the pleasure of writing, for many, comes from being able to use these recognizable patterns in their own stories.

The seemingly interminable serial stories, for instance—the ones that try the patience of adults (as Bill once put it, in a moment of exasperation, "Tune in next week for the next boring installment")—are exciting to kids. Look, they seem to be saying, I can do it too! I can write a story that's *just like* one you've read before—but not really just like it, because I've added something of mine, too. In discussions of their writing processes, they are proud to acknowledge their sources: in one, students mentioned TV shows, games, comic books, novels. "Sometimes I get an idea from a movie," said Chrissy, "or from my brother— he has these great ideas—but then I change it around a lot, so there's my imagination in it, too."

And Bill responded, "So by changing it around the ideas become yours . . . even if you borrow ideas from other people, or books . . . Yeah, when you're writing, it *does* become yours."

Jeffrey, an expert on the first three *Rocky* movies, explained the mixture of formula and invention he was aiming for in a movie script he had started in

August, before school opened. He called it *Rocky IV*. *Rocky IV* became Jeffrey's big project for the year; from September through May, he added to the script, revised it, discussed it with friends, typed and retyped it, and eventually, published it in a class anthology.

He wanted to get the outline of the story down first, he told me, so he started with the dialogue for the main plot-moving scenes, leaving spaces between them for detailed descriptions of fights, training matches, etc. "I could go back and put those in later," he explained. In October, he added a new beginning, partly, he said, "because all the *Rocky* movies start with something really exciting happening."

> Rocky's doorbell rings in living room.
>
> *Rocky:* Can I help you
>
> *Police:* Yes. I can tell that you are Rocky Balboa from your fights. Anyway, you do have a brother in law named Paulie, don't you?
>
> *Rocky:* Yeah, what did he do this time?
>
> *Police:* Well, he was drunk, as usual, and well, today he was walking down the sidewalk and got hit by a car.
>
> *Rocky:* Is he alright?
>
> *Police:* Well, not exactly. He's, well, been killed. He died in the operating room of the Philadelphia hospital. ...

Once Jeffrey had sketched in the plot, he went back to explore characters' motivations, to add dialogue that dealt with feelings, and to cut out scenes and lines (a fight, a kiss) that "didn't add any meaning to the story." Once the structure was in place, he was free to invent.

Perhaps, Bill thought, kids' eagerness to study and imitate the forms of popular fiction and drama could be explained by "the idea that fourth- and fifth-grade kids are storytellers primarily." "The storyteller idea," he wrote,

> is compelling because it defines, I think, the writing goals of kids at this age and therefore, the parameters within which we as teachers can operate. That's not to say we can't introduce other skills, or genres, or modes of writing, or process discussions, but that all those are primarily teacher concerns and will be secondary to kids.

Bill and his students had engaged in an inquiry into the goals and purposes of fourth- and fifith-grade writers. When it was over—or at least temporarily put aside in favor of other inquiries—Bill didn't give up introducing the limericks, games, memory chains, and other writing activities he found valuable, but once he had introduced them, he left it to his students to decide whether or not they wanted to continue them. And he went on questioning the kids as he studied their writing and thinking processes and tried to decide how best to teach them.

Patterns and Strategies

"Central to my teaching," Bill explains, "is getting kids to look at how they do what they do and why. I try to teach kids to think: to be inquisitive, ask questions, make predictions, use evidence to find answers; to look for underlying patterns, distinctions, differences, similarities, underlying meanings; to structure knowledge for themselves. It's not a matter of teaching kids disjointed skills, now, so that later they can do the thinking."

In their journals, he called kids' attention to patterns in the ways they wrote:

Jeff—
You have lots of writing and lots of ideas in here! One thing I notice about your process is that you start a piece several times before you get into it, and you start it on a new page every time! I find that interesting—have you ever noticed?

In class, he asked students to compare one writer's process to another's, to catalog and classify: "Are you the kind of a writer who ... ?" "How many of you revise a piece? put it away to come back to later? throw it away if it's yucky?" At one point, Bill and his students prepared a chart in which they classified the writers in the class by type:

- Type A = (1st draft ... revise, 2nd draft ... edit).
- Type B = (1st draft/1st draft/1st draft).
- Type C = (junk/1st draft).

They planned to revise the chart later, in the light of further observations.

When a book of biographies of students in the class, written from interviews by other students and carefully revised, came back from the duplicating room, Bill's kids, as he described it, "gobbled them up." After the first excitement had subsided, Bill asked his students to turn their attention from striking details ("Matt loves baked ziti and broiled lamb chops. He doesn't like ratatouille") to underlying patterns in the collection as a whole. How could we classify these biographies? he asked. What different approaches to writing biography can we find in them?

A common pattern, they discovered, was what Bill called the "soup to nuts" biography:

Lisa was born on March 30, 1972 in St.James, N.Y. She has an older brother Thomas who is two years older than her and is now 11. Lisa and her family moved when she was 2 years old to Virginia. Then she moved to 3 Dawn Rd. Shoreham, N.Y. Then another brother was born, Jeffrey and he is now 5 yrs. old. ...

Two pages later, Kelly's biography of Lisa ended, "Lisa is looking forward to the end of the [current] school year."

After a brief introduction ("Jon was born on ...."), Shannon had divided her biography of Jon into sections: Jon and his family, Jon and School, Hobbies Jon has. Bill and his students agreed that this piece, too, belonged in the "soup to nuts" category.

In contrast, Peter's biography of Sean and Sean's of Peter seemed to be stories of specific incidents in their subjects' lives:

> When Sean was 9 his parents decided to take a trip to Vermont. Sean was excited. He packed almost everything. . . .
>
> One day when Peter was 3 he and his family went to Disneyworld. . . .

Biographies, Bill told his students, could be built around themes, like his own biography of Jen, which began,

> Being a middle child is not the easiest thing in the world. And Jennifer is a middle child. . . .

But most of those in the class book, Bill and his students agreed, could probably be described as "some things I know about" pieces, like Andria's of Scott:

> Scott is the oldest child in his family. He is 10 years old and his sister, Laura, is 8 years old. Scotts birthday is on June 29th. Scotts favorite food is pizza, his favorite sport is street hockey and he thinks he's good at it. Scott has one dog named Jenny and one hamster named fluffy. Scott doesn't have a favorite T.V. show. He was born at St. Charles Hospital in Port Jefferson. In his spare time he sets traps on his sister, plays monopoly with his mom or dad or has a race with mom on the rubiks cube. Scotts favorite subject in school is math . . .

In this category, one of the most interesting to students was the one Jen wrote of Bill himself:

> It seems like Mr. Silver's life is pretty interesting. It's pretty obvious that his favorite color is brown. In his life he has a lot of things that are brown for instance his car, kitchen, bathroom, curtains, pens, and clothes stuff like that. He was born in Brooklyn June 4 1951. His favorite show is Hill Street Blues. He likes snow especially shoveling his driveway. Mr. Silver was married on June 18 1972 Sunday midday. They had there first child a boy his name is Marc David Silver how Mr. and Mrs. Silver met was on the way home from school there school was in Manhattan so he had to take the subway from quens. Mrs. Silver did too and that is how they met. Mr. Silver's favorite sport is . . .

When Bill and his students read together, either their own work or the works of published authors, Bill looked for categories into which readers might organize their experiences. Although (as he reminded me once) he didn't forget "the whole, [which is] usually greater than the sum of [its] parts!" he was nevertheless fascinated by the parts: naming them, looking at them one by one, categorizing. "It has always made sense to me to look at literature by its component parts," he wrote: "character, setting, incident, plot, theme, crisis, resolution. . . ." Just about anything, Bill believes, can be classified.

In the same spirit, just about any activity, he believes, can be analyzed to reveal the thinking behind it. In math, in science, in social studies, in everything they study, Bill directs his students' attention to their own thinking processes.

Teaching math, he hurries past the answers ("What did you get?") to explore the problem-solving techniques behind them. "Even if you've got the answer," he will ask, "how did you get there?"

Discussing solutions to a math problem involving an unspecified number of ducks and cows with nine heads and twenty-six feet between them, he accepted charts, lists, guesses, and diagrams; when Francoise solved the problem by drawing a picure, he beamed. "That's the greatest way of doing this! I've seen adults in a math workshop do all kinds of crazy things with this problem— algebra, all kinds of things—but for a problem like this, the best way is just what Francoise did: to draw a picture."

Learning how to learn—how to recognize and apply problem-solving strategies, how to find and use help from other people, how to plan and organize a project so that it gets done—takes place in math and in science, in writing, social studies, trip planning, and whatever else is going on.

When I first saw the chart headed "Groups of Four" on the wall of Bill's classroom, I thought it was meant to provide directions for writing groups.

- Rule 1   You are responsible for your own work and behavior.
- Rule 2   You must be willing to help any group member who asks.
- Rule 3   You may ask for help from the teacher only when everybody in your group has the same question.

But no—it was designed to be used by students working on math problems. "It can't help but aid writing groups," however, Bill explained, "especially in conjunction with Magic Circle rules (e.g., active listening) and the skills needed there." His experience with Magic Circle, a structured group-discussion program, provided, he thought, a good example of how this worked. At one point during the year, he said, he had become impatient with the behavior of kids at Magic Circle time. They seemed to him to be mouthing platitudes, merely going through the motions of listening respectfully to one another, adopting the form rather than the substance of maturity in group discussion. But then a real issue came up, a social problem that needed to be dealt with, and the practice, he said, paid off. "The kids really listened to one another. They used all those skills. I was amazed."

"So much of what I do is interconnected and ongoing," he wrote in his journal.

> What's important to me in the curriculum in general is how the different components meld together and support each other, that is, how what is being done in one area reinforces skills necessary in another curricular area.

In 1981, after taking a math workshop in Oregon,[1] Bill was "amazed," he said, by parallels between the math and writing process approaches:

> One of the striking things in my visit to Oregon was the math problem solving people saying precisely the same things about atmosphere as Lucy Calkins did over the summer (almost the same words!) ... The discussion often turned to process, and the type of environment necessary for successful problem solving is so similar to that necessary for successful writing. The notion of workshops, trust, planning, consistency, sharing, *process*—I can't help but notice that 2 radically different curricular areas are seeing the same needs to get kids to participate fully.

So again and again, Bill turns kids' attention to process—how they solve problems, how they write, how they think. Late in the year, for instance, he watched from the sidelines as a student, following the formula set out by the Magic Circle manual,[2] led a discussion of "a person I feel safe with":

Brett: I feel safe with my father ... He takes me out to dinner ... I can talk about my problems with him.

Gina: I'm going to ask a stupid question: Where do you go out to dinner?

Bill [*after waiting for Brett to reply, "Friendly's and McDonald's"*]*:* That's interesting. That's the kind of question people used to ask at the beginning of the year: "What was the name of your dog?" But you notice, when Gina went to ask that question now, she felt embarrassed about it.

He pointed out that kids' questions had become less superficial and invited them to join him in finding examples of different kinds of questions they were asking or might ask.

Often Bill helps students make connections between processes used in one area of the curriculum and those used in another: "They may have been doing writing process work for three or four years," he explains, "but here's a social studies report—They don't write rough drafts, they don't share, they don't revise—unless you show them it's the same process. Part of my job is making those connections for kids, the 'remember what we did yesterday' kind of thing."

The programs Bill has chosen to teach—Man: A Course of Study,[3] (MACOS), the Oregon problem-solving curriculum in math, Junior Great Books, the writing process approach—all express what he sees as similar philosophies of learning. The 1979 Writing Project summer institute, like other courses Bill had taken, provided "a reaffirmation" of what he was doing before he participated in it.

---

[1] "Problem-Solving in Mathematics," developed by the Lane County Mathematics Project.

[2] Uvaldo Palomares and Geraldine Ball, "The Magic Circle" Human Development Program. LaMesa, CA: Human Development Training Institute, 1974.

[3] *Man: A Course of Study.* Cambridge, MA: Educational Development Center, 1968, 1969. Distributed by Curriculum Development Associates, Suite 414, 1211 Connecticut Ave., Washington, D.C. 20036.

He had been using Donald Murray's "Write to Communicate" program,[4] the first that, as he put it, "seemed to fit my feelings about how writing ought to be organized." The summer institute led to "further discovery" and, he thought, added "the feel of writing: the work it took, the effort, the problems when stuck, the difficulty finding topics—the empathy I had for my students that was missing before." At the end of that summer, Bill added a new writing program to those programs he was already using. And, like the others, it had to fight for time.

If articulating a curriculum philosophy is easy for Bill, working it out in terms of hours and minutes in the classroom is more difficult. "Linkages among curriculum areas" he once described as his "pet professional goal"—but how to find the time each area demands, let alone the time to make connections between one and another? Looking over his plan book ("a retrospective document that records what I actually did"), he wrote one day,

> I have 3 major foci in my room—writing, math and MACOS—and each
> one demands large blocks and quantities of time to do well. How I balance
> that and find links between them so as not to overwhelm the kids is not clear,
> but I know that time in class will be a scarce resource.

Sometimes one area suffers from neglect, sometimes another. Sometimes, as Bill himself admits, the writing program almost disappears, lost in a welter of science, math, and social studies activities, class trips and projects, and special events. But eventually, one way or another, Bill comes back to writing since, in investigating their writing processes with his students, he is studying their thinking, too.

Conferences

Conferences with his students are, for Bill, a way of taking a closer look at how nine- and ten-year-olds think. He learns, in conferences, what his students can do on their own; he finds out what he can do to help them. In a class in which so many different things were going on at the same time, conferences, Bill wrote,

> . . . became the glue that held the class together. The kids I knew best and
> liked best were, by and large, the ones I conferenced with the most. It was as
> if conferencing became the medium through which I really learned about
> their needs as *people,* and they came to understand my needs.

Bill's conferences are usually brief. Sometimes students come to visit him as he works at his desk, but more often he goes to them, moving rapidly around the room, stopping here to check a student's progress or there to set another off in a new direction. I found it hard to keep up with him as he traveled: by the time I arrived, notebook in hand, at the site of one conference, he was off

---

[4] Donald M. Murray and Burton Albert, Jr., *Write to Communicate: The Language Arts in Process.* Pleasantville, NY: Reader's Digest Services, 1973.

to another. I'd catch only a question: "Where do you want to go with this?" "What do you have to do to do what you have to do?" or the end of a sentence: "Umhmm ... OK," as he nodded and passed on to the next.

When he gave longer conferences, and especially when he taped them, I had better luck. One day Cathy and Irene brought in a piece they had written collaboratively with Fran. Each had written one section, then combined it with those of the others.

> Nervousness.
> We all get nervous.
> School.
>
> Its tests, its report cards, its papers.
> When we take tests we get pale ... and we start to
>   shake ... we get nervous.
>
> ...
>
> Meeting New People
>
> We've moved into a new neighborhood ...
> Strangers asking me questions ...
> "Are you new?"
> They are judging me.
>
> ...
>
> The Doctor
>
> ... Will he give me a shot with a big needle? Will he choke me with a tongue
> depresser? ... I'm nervous.

The writers had a problem, they told Bill. "Every now and then we write 'we,' then 'I.' We don't know whether to use 'we' for all of it or 'I' for all of it."

"Which way do you think it sounds best?" Bill asked, and then continued, "It's funny that you bring that up, because I didn't notice it at all. ... I guess when I was listening I was listening for—the school stuff and the doctor stuff, like the big needle ... things that we've all experienced. ... The moving into a new neighborhood—is that something you've all experienced?" His tone suggested (to me at least) that he doubted it, that he found the section on new neighborhoods less convincing than the others, but when Cathy and Irene said they liked it and wanted to keep it, he accepted their decision. "You seem happy with the content," he commented and moved on to other matters.

"How are you going to format this?" he asked. "How's it going to look? In some ways it's a cross between a free verse poem and a description, so I wonder ..."

Cathy agreed. "We were going to make it into a poem, but Fran doesn't know how to write poems, so we just made it like a monologue," she said, and Bill replied, "You're right: it *is* like a monologue—a group monologue. You know, there's a kind of poetry called free verse. ..."

At the end of the conference, Bill asked, "So where do you want to go with this?" Cathy and Irene answered that they were going to discuss the "I" and "we" question with Fran (eventually they settled on "we"), and experiment with the arrangement of lines on the page. Bill nodded and pointed out a few lines he especially liked before sending them off.

In his journal, Bill noted his observations of individual kids, in conference and in class. "What do I know about each writer in the class?" he asked himself and wrote:

> Cindy—has all the tools and intelligence to be a fine writer; is very good at working with (conferencing with) others, analyzing their stories and asking questions for clarification; can't seem to do that with her own writing, which remains relatively immature in themes and forms. Why???
>
> Tracy—... works hard at her pieces. Can't seem to improve the meaning much, though, or articulate exactly what she wants to say. Often she thinks something is perfectly clear when I can't understand it at all—another mystery.
>
> Joy—writes *lots* ... Stories are surprisingly short and undeveloped; puts more effort into other kinds of writing (reports, journals, etc.). I think she needs room, and time to develop.
>
> Eddie—Spends a lot of time *not* writing during class time. I get the feeling that he gets too much help at home; things really don't belong to him. He's also often in fog city, not listening to discussions or directions. ...

Such observations helped Bill plan his next set of conferences. With Joy, for instance, he planned to ask questions that might help her develop her stories: "Can you tell me more about ... ?" With Tracy, questions that might help her clarify her meaning: "I don't understand this part; can you explain it to me?" In an article he wrote about his roles in conferences,[5] he described himself as "prodder" for some kids, "reflector" for others, and "collaborator" for a few. Could fourth- and fifth-grade students, he wondered, play some of these roles for and with each other?

He had often invited kids to pair up to discuss one another's writing but, after one set of spontaneous conferences, expressed some doubts.

> How effective were those conferences? What sorts of things did they say to one another? Does it matter? Will it improve their piece of writing? Does just hearing it aloud give them a sense of what needs fixing/changing/elaborating? (For example, Mike told me his story was great and just needed editing, but he hadn't shared it. I asked him to; he read it to Chad who also announced that it was wonderful—lots of details, good sequence, focused in. Mike responded by saying, "I know a place that needs to be better. ... ")
>
> Should [I] give them specific criteria to look at, or just general guidelines?

He tried setting up writing groups with guide sheets but wasn't satisfied

---

[5] " 'Can you read my story?': Approaches to Conferencing with Children," *Elementary School Journal* 84 (September 1983):35–39.

with the results. He tried pairs with guide sheets, then, finally, informal conferences without guide sheets. "They seem to say the same things anyway, with or without the guidesheets," he observed. Were peer conferences working? he wondered. Once again, he asked the kids. What kinds of conferences, he asked (with him, with friends, with groups), had been the most helpful to them?

Kevin, who described himself as "a person who gets stuck a lot," and who "couldn't write endings," wrote that he liked conferences sometimes, "but only with friends Because they would give me endings."

Most, however, agreed with Emily, who complained that her friends "wouldn't give me ideas. Usually they would just say, 'I don't know,'" and Chrissie, who wrote:

> Conferences were semi useful. When I met with friends, they usually said "It's good" or "I like it as it is," and didn't help me. When I met with you, you helped me a little.

Jeff, too, preferred conferences with Bill,

> because you showed me what stuff to get rid of and what stuff to keep. I really thought it was fun because we got to talk about my writing. Conferences with friends never really worked so well because all my friends would do was fool around instead of talking about my writing.

And Cindy agreed: "You talked about my story a whole bunch and told me how to improve it."

Bill made a note to himself to work with students on conferencing skills. More modeling, he hoped, would help. But comments like Jeff's and Cindy's still worried him. "I am starting to feel like 'God,'" he wrote in the journal.

> Kids are using me for responses and ideas. ... If a kid gets suggestions from other kids, these must be verified with me first (before any revision takes place). I'm not sure if they see my suggestions as more valuable (constructive), or if I give more positive feedback, or I give more alternatives to try, or I'm the audience they're actually writing to (hardly my intent!)—

"Your writing is yours!" Bill wrote to his students, and added, "Do you really believe this?"

Yes, several students wrote back, but your ideas help, too. Andria wrote:

> On the Patrick story when I couldn't think of an ending and I kept writing down all different ones and none fit, you gave me alot of different ways to end it and also told me lots of ideas about how to find a good ending.

And Scott reassured him:

> The first time you helped me on my writing in a conference, I realy thout you were doing my writing but [now] I know I realy know I did it.

Pace

Toward the end of the year he spent writing action-packed adventure stories, Brett expressed a doubt about one chapter of his latest, "Secret Under the Sea." "It goes back and forth too fast," he told me. "First my parents—then the dolphins—then the barracuda."

Brett's problem is a common one for kids this age. Fourth and fifth graders move fast. They are often so anxious to get on to the next stories, math sheets, activities on the schedule that they leave the ones they are working on half-finished, or consider them done when Bill thinks them barely begun. Sometimes Bill sees his job as just slowing kids down: encouraging (or forcing) them to stay with projects long enough to explore their possibilities.

"Why are you in such a hurry?" he asked Rachel, who had come to him for editing help on a story she had just started writing. "You're not ready for editing yet. We've just talked for ten minutes about things you want to change." Rachel protested, "But I *like* the story," and Bill replied, "You can *like* it and still want to change it. You need to do some more work on this; then worry about editing."

When Larry reported about his story, "The Adventure to Gold Land," "I didn't like the first sentence, so I went to a different story," Bill asked him to hold on a minute. "When you came up with that title, you obviously had an idea. Now, if you don't like that idea, that's OK—you don't have to be married to your ideas—but if you think it's an OK idea, just because you don't like the first sentence, you don't throw it out. You say, 'Well, that sentence doesn't work for my idea.' Do you see the difference? Let me give you a strategy idea: If you write on every line the way you did here, from margin to margin, you have no room to make changes—and what you really need to do on a draft is leave yourself room to change things."

Maryellen told Bill she had written a poem, based on a story she had read in a magazine, about white lies.

Chyrstel clear
Shimmering with gold
Until they are fortold . . .

After reading the poem out loud, she began to count syllables. "I made it a haiku," she explained. "See? Three, five . . ." "Wait a minute," Bill said. "Before we even worry about the syllables, let me just ask about the meaning. . . ."

Kids often think they are ready to move on when Bill is fairly sure they aren't. He applies the brakes when he thinks it is necessary. Once I heard him call a book discussion group back to go over a story again until he was sure everyone had understood it; another time, he stopped discussion of a math problem to review the meaning of fractions. When he thinks some kids have questions but aren't going to ask them for fear of losing face, he asks the "dumb" questions himself: "Wait a minute; I'm not sure I understand."

Slow down . . . Wait a minute . . . Let's think about. . . . Bill's own calm seemed to me at times to anchor the class, to hold his volatile nine- and ten-year-olds to earth. In the midst of seeming chaos, he seldom raised his voice. He listened to questions and complaints and answered them seriously. He was careful not to laugh, or let others laugh, at even the most ludicrous of mistakes. Performing a science experiment, for instance, he frowned at kids who hooted at wild guesses. "Did anyone laugh?" he asked sternly. "Of course not. You're making predictions. It doesn't matter if it's right or not."

"Patience, patience!" he exhorted himself in his journal and made what he called "a conscious effort" to slow down himself, to stay even-tempered, to tame his own quick wit so that vulnerable fourth and fifth graders would not be hurt by it. He held in check the conceptualizing mind that tended to leap ahead of kids, broke down large chunks of material into manageable pieces ("We're going to do two things this afternoon: first . . . and then . . ." or "Step 1 . . . Step 2 . . ."), and softened the edges of the puns and tongue-in-cheek jokes with which he amused himself and those few kids who could follow them ("You want to wear freckles for your book presentation? Well, there might be a special glue you use to stick things on your face—or you might get the measles before next week—"). Quick to joke and pun, quick to grasp ideas, formulate theories, speculate widely, Bill schooled himself in his classroom to a willed patience— a slower pace.

Inquiry

One day in the middle of the year, as Bill's students were working on early drafts of pieces to be published in a class magazine, Bill gathered the whole class around him for a discussion of "how you wrote your piece."

"What were you thinking of while you were writing yesterday?" he asked. "What were you doing? What were you feeling? What was going on in your head while you were busy writing? What was going on in your fingers and toes?"

Bill's students, sitting, kneeling, or sprawled out comfortably on the big rug that defines the meeting area next to the blackboard, put away the last of the apples and potato chips from snack time ("It's OK to eat," said Bill, "so long as it doesn't crunch") and prepared to join Bill in an inquiry.

Scott said it had been "pretty easy" for him to start. "Jon read me his murder story about fifteen times. I thought, why don't *I* write a murder story too? I didn't copy off Jon's or anything; I just wrote a murder story. But I guess it was Jon that gave me the idea."

Bill: So you were thinking before you ever started writing. Anyone else notice you got ideas from other people?

Darren: I got my ideas from looking out into the road. I saw stuff and then I started writing about what I saw and then it reminded me of some more stuff that I started writing about.

Bill: So it was almost like a memory chain?

Darren: Yeah—sort of.

Chrissy: I started by writing ideas for stories. Then after that I wrote things like "This is dumb" and "I hate writing," and then I'd come up with another idea and then I'd write, "No, that doesn't work," and then I'd come up with another idea. Then I just dropped all the ideas and wrote about what I was going to do when I got home.

Bill: So writing down your ideas didn't help you. How did you finally settle on writing about what you were going to do when you got home?

Chrissy [*shrugging*]: I just decided.

Kim: On another page back here I had wrote all these titles. I looked at them to get ideas for my story.

Bill: Anyone else do that? [*After some discussion*] A couple of people said they had trouble finding topics. I found it *easy* to get started—I'd been thinking about the idea I wrote about for a while—but once I got going I discovered that I wasn't very clear about what I meant. The writing is very confused.

Another voice: Same with me!

Jeff: This is weird ... My process was to draw a lot of pictures and then write. I got one of my ideas from a picture.

Bill: That's not so weird. How many of the rest of you used pictures to help you get ideas?

After noting (and pointing out to Jeff) several raised hands, Bill proceeded to ask a different kind of question. Looking around the circle, he said, "*You* mentioned 'idea,' and *you* mentioned 'idea.' ... What do you mean when you say, 'I get ideas'? What is an 'idea'?"

The inquiry proceeded: "You might—like you think of something that happened or something funny that you did," said Danny, and Bill responded, "You think of an event—something that happened? So when you think of ideas you think of something that happened?"

Sue: I think of—like something I *want* to have happen.

Bill: So for you it's not something that happened but something you hope will happen?

And they were off on an inquiry into the multiple meanings of a word they had been using all morning.

Bill led his students, that morning, in a discussion that ranged back and forth from specific experiences to generalizations drawn from experience, from concrete to abstract, from practical to philosophical. Listening to his questions, I noticed how often a question about a specific instance ("How did I get my idea?") leads, for him, to a broader question ("How do people get ideas?") and often to a deeper or more philosophical one as well ("What is an 'idea,' anyway?").

The ordinary, seemingly simple words and concepts we use every day are the ones Bill finds interesting to study. He wants his students to examine the everyday—to look closely at events and question them as he does himself.

In his own journal, for example, he asked himself one day, "What is 'teaching'?"

> . . . is what I do with kids in writing really teaching? What do I mean by teaching? What do others think I mean by teaching (parents, administrators, kids, colleagues)? Talk about assumptions built into the word . . .

He examines with his students the words and concepts they use, not with vocabulary lists or guessing games, but with inquiry into meaning. The unfamiliar in language he deals with directly so that mere strangeness won't keep kids from using words they need: "This is called a line level. What a level tells you is if it's level. Level means parallel to the ground. Parallel means running in the same direction as something else." It is the familiar for which he reserves his questions.

"I notice that several people have mentioned going back and rereading what they've written," he observed during another discussion of the writing process. "Do other people do that? What do you mean when you say you 'reread' as you write? Do you mean you read every sentence of your story as you're writing it? Or do you just go back once in a while to see if it makes sense? What do you reread *for*?"

Lisa: I go back—no matter what. If I write five pages I'll still go back and read it from the beginning. If I'm stuck I'll go back to the paragraph; if I have nothing to write I'll go back to the whole story.

Scott: I don't go all the way back. All I need is just about four words to get me going. Then I go "putt-putt-zzzzz." I fuel back up, as a car would, and then keep going. It's like a car just backs up a little bit, and then gets gas and then goes again. I just go back to the story, fire up, and then I *go*.

Bill: For you it's a way of getting energy? That's an interesting image—the car going back and then forward. . . .

"Interesting" is a word Bill uses often. He sounds, looks, *is* interested in words, in ideas, in the connections between them. "That's interesting" can lead to a summary—or a new question—or to the start of a whole new inquiry. And discussions that start with the writing process can lead almost anywhere.

Putting the Pieces Together

When I first came to Bill's classroom, I was looking for "writing" lessons. I seldom found them. Although Bill's students often wrote and talked about writing, it was hard for me to predict exactly when they would be doing it and, since I visited only occasionally, hard to arrange to be there when they did.

Often I would arrive at "writing" time only to find that the schedule had been changed that day, and everyone was planning a class trip or involved in a school project. I found myself sitting in on discussions of pizza sales instead of stories, watching Magic Circle instead of taking notes on writing conferences.

Was I wasting my time? I wondered. At first I thought so; later I changed my mind. I had been seeing "writing" as a separate subject, to be studied by itself; that wasn't how Bill saw it at all. To Bill, the fourth/fifth grade curriculum he had put together was all of a piece, his writing program merely one expression of a philosophy of education that shaped the whole. If I could learn about Bill's teaching of writing by listening to discussions of the writing process, I could learn about it, too, by observing science experiments, math lessons, and Magic Circle.

Often, after a visit to Bill's classroom, as I tried to make sense of what I had seen, I turned to Bill himself to help me make connections between seemingly unrelated events. Eventually, we created together a model of partnership different from any other in the project but suited, as it turned out, to our peculiar circumstances. My visits to Bill's classroom were supplemented by long conversations and short notes: "Help!" I would write, "I need more information about ..." or "I don't understand why. ...." And Bill would respond, patiently, often explaining to me at length what he had already explained to Jamie, helping me relate the daily events of his classroom to the governing concerns of his teaching. Bill's wife and seven-year-old son made me welcome in their house, and Bill himself claimed that our conversations, like those he had had with Jamie and other members of the study group, were interesting to him. "Being asked, 'Why did you ... ?' all the time tends to clarify one's thinking," he wrote in his journal.

Bill's journal, which I read again and again as I began to identify, in class and in conversation, the concerns and interests that underlay his teaching, helped me in another way to put together the pieces of this particular puzzle. In it I found a thoughtful person, one who probes beneath the surface of what he sees, one whose answers raise further questions for him. Bill's journal is full of the tongue-in-cheek humor he holds in check in the classroom but allows to glint wickedly through his writing: a sober list of questions to investigate, for instance, interrupted by #8: "There is no #8"; a note to himself in the margin of one journal, in which he both teases himself and spoofs the notes we researchers wrote to him: "Bill—Rereading your journal was interesting, and you touch on many points. Perhaps this is something you should do more often." After reading two years' worth of Bill's journals all at once, I felt better able to follow the ins and outs of his reasoning; after rereading them, I began to feel I knew at least a little of how his mind worked.

I stopped looking for "writing" lessons in Bill's classroom. I was pleased when students were writing when I visited but less disappointed than I had been when they weren't. I began looking, as Bill himself was looking, at the ways students were listening to one another in discussion, at the questions they asked, and at the growing confidence they showed in themselves as writers and as thinkers. I began to look at Bill as a teacher of thinking as well as of writing, and I started to write about his classroom from a new perspective.

Bill was pleased when I finally caught on. When I wrote about his interest in inquiry, he congratulated me. "This is a nice section," he wrote. "You found a pattern and used it to explain a variety of things—nice going!" And, looking back to an old argument, he added a teasing comment: "I guess that inductive stuff works once in a while."

The pieces were falling into place. Where I had once seen chaos, I now saw nine- and ten-year-olds learning to listen to and reason with one another, to make choices, to ask questions. And whether his students were writing stories, measuring sand hills, or planning pizza sales, I saw Bill listening, waiting, ready to turn any event into a focus for inquiry.

Chapter 7

Diane Burkhardt
Eighth Grade

To many students, Diane Burkhardt's classroom is home base, a place to return to again and again during the school day. They come in early, hang around late, even ride their bikes up to the windows on weekends to peer inside and see if Diane or any of their classmates are there, talking, working, or writing. The year I spent with them, the students in Diane's advisory called it home. One lunchtime they hung signs: the area by the windows where Diane keeps a toaster oven and a hot plate became "the kitchen"; the window behind it from which we often threw cold coffee onto the dirt below was labeled "the sink"; the middle of the room where movable desk chairs are casually arranged in a circle was the "living room"; a corner area where Diane keeps paperback books, current magazines, and anthologies of her previous students' writing became known as "the library."

It felt homey to me, too. I was comfortable pulling my chair into the ever-present circle for class discussions, sliding it away whenever writing began, pulling it up to Diane's table by the window to listen as she and a student worked their way through a writing conference. And Diane, too, has come to see her classroom in this way. She writes:

> I used to think teaching was performing and the teacher the main actor in the performance. But I don't view it that way anymore. ... I've stopped thinking of myself as a performer and the classroom as my stage. Now I think of it as my home into which 40–50 students are invited to spend a year with me

and we will get to know each other and I will learn as much as or more than they do.

This is the environment forty to fifty thirteen- and fourteen-year-olds enter each September. With Diane, in groups of twenty to twenty-five, they study both English and social studies. They read and write, speak and listen, think and perform. But Diane's eyes focus on more than the curriculum. She studies the kids themselves, what they need, what makes sense to them, how she can support their growth. For Diane believes that each year she and her students forge a curriculum together, and the better she knows them, the more deeply they can delve into their shared work.

The year I lived in Shoreham, in Diane's home as well as her classroom, I too became involved in the teaching and learning that spilled over into prep periods, after school time, and weekends. Diane worked long hours, beginning early in the morning and often ending late at night; frequently, I kept the same hours, studying her teaching as searchingly as she studied her students.

I was drawn to Diane's classroom, observed three of her four classes each day, and headed for her room on my "off hours" as well. I had lunch there with Diane and the students in her advisory, returned there after school to chat with Diane and whatever students were there, too; eventually, as the year wore on, I began to leave it when they did to join Diane and her students as they attended volleyball games, softball games, and hockey meets or went out for ice cream or pizza.

Before I became a researcher in Diane's classroom, I had had little contact with thirteen- and fourteen-year-olds. I hadn't spent any sustained time with students this age since I had been one myself, hadn't been in school with them since I had attended junior high. But if my memory served me well, I knew that at best I'd be in for a challenging year. I remembered adolescence, particularly the junior high years, as a difficult time, full of turmoil and doubts, sudden upheavals, and changes of identity. At thirteen, I certainly would not have welcomed a researcher looking over my shoulder.

The colleagues I spoke to before the study began confirmed my worst suspicions. Whenever I mentioned that I was about to spend a year studying writing in a middle school, they responded with incredulous looks. "You're *choosing* to spend a year in eighth grade?" they asked, voices rising. "You must be crazy. Kids that age are impossible to teach!"

Were they? I wondered. I didn't know, but as I entered Diane's classroom, I realized that my plan to study the teaching of writing was about to immerse me in a world I had almost forgotten, the world of adolescence.

As I began this study, then, I had several questions: What shape would the teaching of writing take when, in Diane's hands, it met the stormy world of thirteen- and fourteen-year-olds? Would it, in any important ways, differ from teaching as I knew it—when I taught writing to adults, either college students or teachers? Would my assumptions about what mattered in a writing classroom be challenged or forced to undergo some revision due to this change in grade and age level? In the story that follows, I will attempt to answer these questions as I follow Diane and her students through a controversy that plagued them all year, a controversy we called "the process journal issue."

Beginning—or Trying to Begin—with "Process"

Diane had been looking forward to the 1981–82 school year. She had taken the 1979 summer institute with Dan, a seventh-grade teacher, and had been working with him ever since on ways to implement what they had both learned. Since she would be teaching the same group of students he had taught, she planned to begin the year where he had left off—with process journals and writing groups. But, much to her surprise, she discovered on the first day of school that her students were entering eighth grade with, as Matt put it, "a grudge against writing."

At the mention of process journals, there were groans. Diane's announcement that this year the class would start off "with a big push on writing and aim to do a class publication by the middle of November, in time for parent conferences" was greeted with silence. And the letters the students wrote for homework after the first day of classes describing their writing program the previous year and their expectations for this year were tangible proof that the attitudes they brought with them to eighth grade were overwhelmingly negative.

Margaret wrote that, while she liked "the idea of writing groups," most of the kids last year didn't "ask decent questions or give detailed answers." They were, in her words, "deadheads." Jeff said, "I don't like to say this, but there weren't too many positive things about last year's writing program. . . . Hopefully, you have a different system." Brian summed up his attitude by saying, "The subject of writing is really known as mud to me," and Chrissy's comment was echoed again and again by the other students: "The process journal was a bore and just a bother."

Diane was startled. Dan had warned her that the students hadn't liked keeping process journals, but she hadn't been aware that their discontent was either so deep or so widespread. She herself could understand students not liking to write, but being so disturbed over writing groups and publications? This was something she hadn't expected, something, in fact, she felt she'd have to tackle head-on if she and her students were to proceed with the year's work. After the first week of school, she jotted down several concerns in her journal:

> how to deal with the negative attitude toward process
> how fast to move into groups
> how much to assume the kids know
> when and how to talk to Dan

Listing the issues in her journal was some comfort, but the amount of "negative retraining" Diane found herself forced to do was unsettling. "I find myself feeling somewhat down," she wrote in her teaching journal. "I feel like I'm proceeding too slowly. I want to be very excited by what the kids say and do. Sondra said yesterday that I'd be better starting the kids off from scratch. That's true. The problem now is that they think they know something but they actually have some bad habits to break."

Diane decided to tread carefully. Students would do some free writing in their idea logs (private journals), draft several pieces, and then each would choose one piece to revise and edit for publication. Throughout the process, they would meet in writing groups, and each group would tape its discussion so she could, from time to time, listen to the tapes and monitor how well each group was working. Talking and writing about the writing process would be reserved for class time where she could uncover and perhaps defuse the students' explosive attitudes.

On the seventh day of school, then, after students had had some time to think and talk about possible ideas for writing but before they had begun drafting their pieces, Diane asked them to take out their process journals. She began, "I'd like you to make some notes on what you are planning to write or at least thinking about writing for the class publication."

Immediately, the comfortable hum of classroom life gave way to silence. Several students shot Diane concerned looks. Matt broke in with a bewildered complaint, "Mrs. B., I just can't. I mean, I don't know what you mean."

Kristen added, "I thought you were supposed to write process after you wrote, you know, you write what stages you went through in order to write."

Diane responded, "I'm aware that that's what you think. What I'm trying to do is help you expand your notion of what process is. It seems that you all think it has to be done one particular way."

The kids burst out almost in unison, reciting what was becoming an all too familiar litany:

"Last year, we always had to write it after we wrote the piece."

"Yeah, he always assigned process writing."

"Last year, it was graded."

"I hated it. It was so boring."

Tim quipped, "You really want us to love process, don't you?"

And Matt, sensing the ease and good nature with which Diane listened to her students, retorted, "No, she wants us to hate her, that's it!"

Diane smiled and joined in with an ironic tone, "Do you hate me yet?" she asked, looking directly at Matt.

Listening to Diane, I was beginning to get an idea of the way she was choosing to handle this issue. Rather than argue with her students or try to convince them that they hadn't understood what Dan was doing, she accepted their hostility, didn't try to deny it, met it with humor instead of anger. Then, I noticed, she changed pace and in speaking more thoughtfully to the class tried to help them see what it was about the study of the writing process that mattered to her.

"You want to know why I think the writing process is so important?" she asked. "I think all of you are unique, and I'm interested in learning how each of you writes. I think of each and every one of you as a writer. And I think the more you know about how you write, the better you'll be able to do it.

"Think about it," she continued, "all the times you write—notes, letters, assignments. You know there is a thinking process going on all the time that makes up the writer part of us, and that's what you put in the process journal."

The class, subdued now, seemed expectant. Diane continued, "Do you have any idea of what happens to me when I know that I have to write something for next week? I immediately turn to my process journal." And Diane began to read from her journal to an almost rapt group of students: "There's a piece due next week. No idea. I envy people who know immediately. ...."

Process journals. Discovering and documenting one's composing process. Listening to and learning from the discoveries of others who offer what they've noticed about themselves as writers. These were crucial experiences for Diane in the 1979 summer institute. Observing her own writing process taught her about herself. Hearing how others composed brought solace, the shared sense of keeping company with fellow writers. Both experiences freed her to write, to take risks in ways she never had before. Her goal ever since has been to create the same climate in her own classroom; her question, to discover whether eighth graders can find the same freedom to explore, to write, once they begin making their own discoveries about the composing process.

It was a shock, then, for Diane to discover that first week of school that her students resented the very techniques she found so valuable. Wondering how to "spread [her] joy in exploring and documenting the composing process" to her students, she turned to her teaching journal and began to ask herself, "What would I need to know in order to do this?" And she found herself answering:

> I need to know more about what they presently think it means to "write process" or as they say "to process it" as in "Shall we process this piece after we write it, Mrs. Burkhardt?"

Writing led her to speculate:

> The phrase "processing it" bothers me. Is it a verb? Is it something you *do* or something that *is* ... it's there all the time. We have to discover it. What good does it do to discover it?

And her speculations led further to the question that was to guide her teaching for the rest of the year:

> Kids, do you see yourselves as writers? Maybe that's the problem—that they don't, I mean.

Students who see themselves as writers, in Diane's view, know fundamentally that they can write, that they have something worthwhile to say, and that the community they are a part of values their writing. Her plan, to make a "direct attack on the students' narrow definitions of what it means to have a composing process," of what, in essence, it means to be a writer, began to take shape.

Talking and Writing About Writing • In October, on the fifteenth day of school, Diane began class, as she often did, with a question. "What's this you tell me that you can't write process?" she asked good-naturedly.

Brian, quick to rise to the challenge, responded, "We hate it."

Diane laughed, "Oh, that's different. It's quite possible to hate it. But what about this idea that you can't write it?"

Seeing a bemused expression on Brian's face, Diane went on to offer an explanation. "We're doing a kind of exploratory research here. You know, we'd be doing this even if Sondra weren't here. I have the feeling you still think all process entries are the same. We're each different people."

Looking at the student next to her, she continued with some advice and then an image. "Do you think Nancy and I write the same way? In your process journals, you write about your writing. You pay attention to what happens. You crawl outside your body, sit on your shoulder, and look at what is going on in your brain. Now, we all wrote something for today. Let's sit, read through what we wrote, and write for five minutes about whatever comes to mind about writing that piece."

The room quieted down. Diane moved to a round table near the windows, her back to the students, her head bent over her process journal. Margaret covered her page with her hand. Brian began, looked up, began again.

After five minutes, Diane rejoined the circle. "OK," she began, "who learned something they didn't know before?"

Margaret described how she added details to the story she was writing about a teenage girl's struggle to find herself. Kristen reported that her rough draft was a "humble jumble on paper." Jeff explained that by rereading he learned that his draft wasn't as bad as he thought. Jennifer chimed in that hers was worse than she thought. Mike wrote that he drafted his piece while the stereo was on, and Tom confessed that he did his writing during the commercial time on TV.

In October, discussions of the writing process became more common. As the students began to understand what Diane was asking them to do, Diane remembered that she still had a piece of unfinished business to attend to— with Dan. Was he aware of how negative the kids had become, or was it that she and Dan in their planning meetings had never managed to discuss what had really gone on last year? Either way, she felt she needed to talk with him, both for their mutual benefit and that of the students they would continue to teach.

Several nights later, over dinner in a nearby restaurant, Diane broached the subject. Although she had several questions in mind, she found that she didn't need to ask them. Dan admitted that the year had been frustrating and that, rather than talk about it, he found himself coming up against dead-ends, never fully able to find, that year, the right mix among the kids, the method, and himself. Recounting the evening in her journal, Diane wrote:

> Dinner with Dan was wonderful. Not only did we talk about writing, but both of us talked about ourselves with trust and caring. . . . We touched on all the specifics I had in mind—most of them he brought up as things he had said he would do but didn't—publications, really putting time into working with kids on what to write, writing with them, etc. One result is that we know we have to stay in closer touch and make sure that the message kids get about writing is similar from both of us.

Pleased with the talk, Diane returned with renewed energy to classroom issues, focusing her attention once again on helping students increase their grasp of what to write in their process journals. And, with time, the students' journal entries were becoming, it seemed, more informative, more complex, at times, even funny. Greg reported that he hadn't written much because he was "almost empty on thoughts for a while." Jimmy noted that in order to write he had to "block out the sound of the crikets" in the yard outside. Matt, involved in his writing one night, described how he couldn't get back into it once his girlfriend interrupted him with a phone call. Kathy noticed "a steady stream of thoughts." Nancy described the exciting experience of having "an ending just pop into [her] head."

Chrissy wrote elaborate descriptions. The idea for her poem on butterflies came, she explained, "from [her] first aid book in health." "In it," she wrote, "they were talking about butterflies, the kind you put on a cut, and immediately, a picture of butterflies, in color and everything flew into my mind." A few days later, she wrote a detailed description of her French class's recent trip to Quebec. At the youth hostel, Chrissy explained, she "took notice of people" so she "would have something to write about when [she] came home." Her description of a girl "licking a knife at breakfast and then putting it back in a jar of strawberry jam" so revolted her that she "actually felt sick and shivered" as she wrote.

As Diane noticed a change in the journals, a corresponding change took place in her. On a Wednesday evening, late in October, she sat watching the World Series, reading her students' papers and commenting in their process journals. By the time she finished, she felt so "up" that she set out to record what she was feeling "live"—before sleep and a new teaching day intervened:

> . . . I feel "into it"—that old sense of energy derived from good satisfying working time returned at least for tonight, but when I pause to think about how happy and satisfied I am with what I am doing, I realize that I've been feeling good about kids and classes. Things have begun to click.

Responding to Writing • What was it that "clicked"? I wondered. What gave Diane the sense that things were working? Most important, I began to see, was that she was getting to know her students. She saw each one as an individual whose questions and problems, once they were revealed to her, offered opportunities for teaching. As she explained it to me: "My teaching is based on taking a sense of each kid into account." "Basic to everything," she continued, "is relationship-building, and that means that I need to establish some personal contact with each kid." One of the reasons, I realized, that process journals were so important to her was that they provided her with a natural and easy way to establish this contact.

Her comments in journals were based on what students said in class as well as on what they had written. Often they were an attempt to expand students' options. To Brian, who continued to insist that he couldn't "write process," she advised:

> Try to be aware of things that happen while you write that you have never been aware of before. This will not always be the same kind of thing. I don't expect all process entries to be the same. In fact, if they were, I'd begin to worry.

To Kathy, who commented in class that writing in her process journal "took forever," Diane wrote:

> I can easily understand the point you were making in class about the annoyance of writing process entries. Your entries are chock-a-block full of information. It seems you have left out no detail of your revision and why you make the changes. From a teacher's point of view, it's very interesting and informative, BUT I can see that it might be a pain to remember all the points.
>
> If you use this journal at natural stopping points, if you begin your work on a piece by jotting down some notes and thoughts in here, and if you jot down a few more things after you finish—then maybe doing a process journal entry won't seem to be such an intrusion or a pain. . . .

When Jennifer wrote that she couldn't choose a piece for publication because she didn't like any of her pieces well enough, Diane turned her complaint into an opportunity to teach her:

> Well, since you have to publish something, the trick is for you to really listen to yourself and find out what *you want to write.*

She then offered Jennifer some suggestions:

> Use your idea log *every day.*
> - Write about the day.
> - Write about what people do and say.
> - Write about things you feel and think.
> - Write all the things that go through your mind in five minutes (set a timer).
>
> The more you write, the better able you will be to find the ideas, topics, etc. that you want to write about.

When Mike wrote that he was sick of revising, Diane heard the voice of a writer, tired from good, hard work:

> I understand your frustration. I think it's common to a lot of writers to reach a point after working on a piece for a while where you have a hard time remembering what you liked about it in the first place.

And when Scott admitted that he never really liked the topic he chose to write about, Diane suggested that he "remember this feeling the next time we begin working on pieces for publication." She had thought all along that Scott had not been committed to his piece. Now she hoped that he would have sufficient reason to try her suggestions:

> I never felt that you were truly interested in the piece and that is un-doubtedly one of the things which made it hard for you to motivate yourself to finish it, revise it, etc.
>
> That brings me to the subject of topics—how do you choose what to write about? What do you *want* to write? How do you know? How *can* you know? This is where I feel the idea log/private journal can be such a help if you write in it frequently. You (and each of us) experience thousands of *thoughts, feelings, observations* each day. If you recorded *some* of those on a daily basis, you would have a rich bank of writing resources.

Reading through the journals, I noticed that some students began to respond to Diane's interest and attention by revealing more personal sides of themselves. Some admitted feelings that are common enough but not easy to acknowledge even for adult writers—feelings of embarrassment or fear. Jimmy, for example, whose insecurities about writing came from being in an "alternative" English class in sixth and seventh grades, described how he felt after his piece was published:

> I walk through the hall waiting for soneone to walk up to me and say that was a stupid story you wrote then Ill say I no—I just didn't have any thing els to write about so I wrote that—it only took me 10 to fifteen minutes boy I realy put myself down don't I

Diane responded to Jimmy by reassuring him that his feelings were not unusual:

> I love all that you wrote about your anticipated embarrassment and how you would handle it. I bet a lot of kids feel that same feeling. I can relate to it because I've felt the same way sometimes. Funny how we protect ourselves, or at least get ready to protect ourselves just in case somebody says something negative.

In journal after journal, I saw that Diane used whatever students mentioned as an opportunity to teach them—either about themselves or about writing or about both. And she viewed whatever they revealed as a way for her to come to know them better.

In fact, I saw that in these written dialogues Diane's goal was to guide her students as much as she could all the way through the writing process. In order to broaden their understanding of what writing entailed, she encouraged them to examine it from the inside out, to reflect on every aspect of the magazine project as it unfolded. In November, for example, after students had written, revised, edited, and proofread their pieces for publication, Diane asked them to speculate about possible reactions to seeing their work in print.

Margaret had written a teenage love story in, as she put it, "the style of Paula Danziger and Judy Blume." Margie's main character, Jo, "the new girl in town," was trying to find her balance between what the "cool" kids did and what she had been taught was "right." In an opening scene, Jo meets Tony, the leader of the gang:

> When she walked into the store, Jo noticed a bunch of leatherjacketed kids all watching one of the bigger kids try to gyp the Asteroid Attack machine out of its quarters. He succeeded once, then tried again and failed. One of the smaller kids named Richie started to chuckle at his defeat. The much larger kid, named Tony, ordered the boy next to him, who looked like his right hand man, to take Richie outside and teach him how to act. Jo shuddered at the thought that such a small kid was about to get beat up by a much larger boy just for acting his age. He couldn't have been more than 9 or 10.
>
> Jo didn't like rough boys. She liked boys to be gentle. Another thing which bothered her was this boy named Tony. He was obviously the leader of the gang. She didn't like the way he could order everyone around. But there was nothing she could do about it. She was just a girl in Elmont, and as far as the boys were concerned she didn't have an opinion. They could order her around, much as they did the smaller kids, but Jo wasn't going to let this happen. Nobody was going to push her around. ...

Margie's handwritten story covered sixteen pages and went through extensive revisions. She hoped readers would understand the twists and turns of her plot. "Did I make myself clear?" she wondered.

Leslie, who had written about a kidnapping, realized that she was "scared about what other people are going to think." Jimmy, "kinda shy about every one reading my story," began to anticipate how he would feel when his parents read his story about peer pressure and smoking:

> I'll start blushing and get real nervos when my mother reads it and my step father and they start to coment on it then my mother takes it into work and every one reads it and when she has a party and they say who's the one who wrote the story and shell say "hes the one."

Dina, too, wrote about her parents, realizing that she wanted more than polite approval from them when they read her story about murder in the woods:

> I want my parents to read it but I don't want to hear, "Oh! It's a good story!" I want to hear more ideas about how they felt when they read it. But I feel too embarrassed to just come right out and say it.

Lisa, a student who had transferred to Diane's class from another wing of the middle school, hoped that "someone—anyone—would read it."

While she couldn't orchestrate the parents' reading and reactions, Diane made sure, once the magazine was finished, that students read and responded to one another's writing. One of the last activities in this three-month sequence of work was writing letters to authors. Here Diane asked each student to select one classmate to write to, commenting on the impact of that person's writing. Then Diane passed a hat around the room and each student randomly picked the name of a second person to write to, insuring that each student would receive at least one letter. The day the letters were due, Matt came into class singing, to the tune of "Harrigan," "D–O–double N–E–L–L–Y spells Donnelly, Donnelly." He then cheerily asked, "Who's got letters for me?"

As students exchanged letters and began to read, many smiled. Some read them to their friends. Everyone noticed that Margie's story got rave reviews.

Kathy wrote to her, "I love your story. I think my favorite part is when Jo says 'I don't feel like hanging around here listening to you feed your macho image.' " Mike wrote that Margie's story was "very down to earth," and that Jo reminded him of Margie herself. He explained, "I sort of got the feeling you were Jo because I know you and you're not the type of person who lets people push you around and it shows in the way Jo stands up to Tony and finally tells him off." Mike added, "That's not an insult."

Becky, a student in Ross Burkhardt's class, saw the magazine and also wrote to Margie. Becky "loved" the story, thought Jo's "conflict between going with the crowd and being herself was very strong," and remarked, "When Jo spoke to Tony at the end about not proving himself, I almost died."

In the final writing task of this project, Diane asked students to reflect on the entire process. Greg, a student who had difficulty writing, reported that now that he had finished a piece "totally," writing was "getting easier, from getting a plot, to getting it finished, to even grammar." April wrote, "My piece in print! Excellent, terrific!" Dina spoke of "a great feeling of accomplishment . . . as if a weight has been lifted."

Diane, too, felt pleased, and relieved, as the magazine project came to an end. All her students but one had managed to complete the entire process, from writing several first drafts to choosing one to work on through revising, editing, proofreading, and publishing; writing groups had gotten off the ground and sustained the students' efforts through several months of work; and the students now had in their hands tangible proof that they were writers—a magazine, which, because of a mechanical breakdown, had returned from the district's duplicating office on November 20, one day after Diane held parent conferences.

The Process Journal Issue

In December, Diane gave the students a month's "break from personal writing." During this time, they studied the work of Edgar Allan Poe, rewriting several of his short stories from different points of view. Then they practiced for and took the New York State Preliminary Competency Tests, for which they had to write business letters, reports, and persuasive essays.

After Christmas vacation, Diane planned to return to writing and a new round of publishing. She decided to abandon the class magazine format and instead to invite her students to create their own individual magazines. Her decision was based on evaluations from former students of a similar project completed the year before.

Reading through the evaluations one night in December, Diane discovered "a lot of wonderful stuff on the value of publishing—especially on the value of publishing their own magazines. When they wrote about [it]," she remarked, "they wrote with such conviction—even the 'less able' writers wrote with pride of doing something that was completely their own. It makes me think of the whole idea of taking responsibility, of establishing ownership. Individual magazines could be a critical move."

Right before Christmas vacation, then, Diane announced the next magazine project. Before students left, she reminded them to use their process journals to record any questions or ideas that came to them while they were away. When they returned to school in January, she picked up where she had left off, asking students to turn to their process journals either to read what they had written over vacation or to begin writing, again hoping that the journals would serve as a tool to help the students think about this next project.

Immediately, the familiar tension returned. Kristen, hostile, announced, "I didn't write in my process journal."

Brian looked dumbfounded.

Shawn, a student who had just moved to the district, asked, "What's a process journal?"

And an ironic smile crept slowly over Diane's face as she heard herself explaining once again, and not only for Shawn, the purpose of the process journal: "It's a place for you to write about your writing, a place where you can reflect, learn more about how you write."

Given the apparent success of the previous magazine project, Diane and I were both shocked to discover that her students still resented the emphasis she placed on writing about the writing process. Had we missed something? Hadn't she explained it well enough? Hadn't they been finding her comments and questions in their journals useful? Diane decided to take a closer look—at the journals themselves.

When she studied the journals carefully, Diane began to question her own conviction. "Reading through process journals this afternoon," she wrote, "I became very discouraged. I asked myself, 'Why do kids keep process journals? Can they even be expected to do it?' It seems like pulling teeth."

She went on, looking first at her own role, then at her fear that the process journal, so important to her, was merely "an assignment" to her students:

> As much as I've tried to "free kids up" from previous notions of what it means to keep track of one's composing process, I'm afraid I've "overcorrected"; the process journals I read this afternoon all sounded the same. Too many kids seem to be using them simply for a sort of pre-writing planning purpose. I realize that I've caused that by emphasizing that in the past several entries. But that means they're trying to write to please me or to satisfy what they think are my expectations. Is it possible to get more than just Margaret and Chrissy to see a value for themselves in keeping a journal about their writing processes?

Writing led her to reflect:

> What is the value of it? Why should they be interested in it? How will it actually help them? It's not enough to tell them that it's interesting for me to know or that they might learn things that will help others. They have to see it as personally useful. Why would they want to know more about themselves as writers? Do they write for any reason other than the fact that it's assigned?

"Personally useful." How could she help to make the journals personally useful? This was the question Diane and I batted around on the way home from work, over dinner, and late into the evening. We knew that several students turned to their journals for help and used them the way teachers in the summer institute had. Were others willing to? Were they able to? Was it a question of maturity? ability? obedience? intelligence? How could we find out?

It occurred to me that an assignment devised by Elaine Avidon, a colleague of mine at Lehman College, might help us find some answers. At the end of a term, Elaine often asked her basic writers to read through their process journals and to write essays on what they had learned from observing and recording their own writing processes. Diane agreed that having her students do similar research on their process journals might help them—and us—discover whether such scrutiny was, in fact, useful for eighth graders.

The next day in class, Diane gave the students an assignment: to reread their process journals from the beginning of the year and to write an answer to the question, "What do I know about myself as a writer, now, halfway through my eighth-grade year?" The journal was to serve as raw material, as data, for the students' essays. At the end of class, Diane spoke about the importance of being honest. "If you're trying to please me," she said, "then what you write will be BS. It won't mean anything."

Many students responded to Diane's request for honesty. Chrissy, who had written such detailed accounts of her writing process, surprised Diane by writing that the process journal "bored [her] to death." She remarked, however, that she knew she "must do it" if she wanted to improve her writing. Peter said, "I do it just to get it over with and mostly so I won't see on my report card, 'Peter failed to complete 11 process entries.' In other words," he wrote, "I'm not doing this for me, but only for you." Mike felt similarly. He commented, "I'll be very honest with you and I'm not trying to 'bust your chops,' but even after reading over all the entries I didn't get anything out of it."

Of course, not all students were so negative. Matt made two surprising discoveries when he reread his journal. He was amazed at how conscious he was of spelling and how concerned he was over readers' reactions. He had not realized that those two aspects of his composing process were occupying so much of his attention. Leslie realized that she was "always worrying whether or not others would understand [her] pieces," and Kristen noticed that often she has "an idea but can't find the right words."

No one produced anything as extensive as Margaret's eight-page analysis. By studying the notes she made to herself before, during, and after she wrote, Margie discovered a great deal about herself as a writer. Part of her analysis included a list of what she had learned:

> I like to do "freewriting" before I start a peice. It helps me to "clean all the junk" out of my mind. It helps me to settle down. . . .
> My favoret way to use my process journal is to plan what's going to happen in my peice. . . .
> I think it's good that I write my frustrations about how a peice is going because if I stop myself from worring about a peice, I won't try hard enough on a peice, and I wont like it and I'll be ashamed.
> I know where I like to be when I write. I know I want to be alone, I don't want to have time and pressure on my mind.
> I've learned my process for getting my peices the way they are so I will like them.
> I never knew the process of writing a peice was so complicated. I know now that the process journal is really helping me.

Toward the end of her paper, Margie reflected:

> All of a sudden this year I've gotten interested in writing. I would like to say that I get many Joys out of writing. Not so much joy, but satisfaction. The satisfaction of knowing I worked hard on my piece, I'm proud of it, and other people like it too.
> There are certain points when I'm stuck and then I get an Idea and the feeling I get is such releif that it is in a way a JOY. The way ideas come to me sometimes gives me JOY, if that's what you would call it. Put it this way, when the knot in my stomach unties, it's JOY.

In class the following day, Diane asked for volunteers to read what they had written the night before. As the discussion moved around the room, opinions were mixed. Brian admitted that he had "lied about [his] process in the beginning of the year. I thought it had to be done a certain way," he explained. He went on, "I don't write the way a perfect writer writes. You see, I have to have noise, sit awkward, and drink hot chocolate."

Brian's honesty encouraged others. Mike read what he had written about "not getting anything out of the journal." Other students revealed their questions and problems. In listening to the different experiences, I felt the class groping, working to arrive at some new understanding together. Jennifer asked a question that captured the students' confusion. "I still don't understand," she said. "Why do we have to do this?"

Matt, having learned that in Diane's classroom students can respond to their peers' questions, jumped in. "I don't know," he said.

Jeff, venturing an answer, commented, "It's for you, Mrs. B., so you'll know."

Diane nodded, accepting Jeff's answer. But it wasn't enough. If students wrote in their process journals only for her, then they'd never discover what was so useful about them. She had larger goals. She wanted them to move from pleasing her to discovering the benefits for themselves, as she knew some already had. What about Margie? Dina? Tim? she wondered. Why weren't they speaking up?

Although she knew that the period was about to end, she hoped one last question might prompt those who had found value in observing and recording their own writing processes to speak. "Did anyone learn anything else from this assignment?" she asked.

But, with only a moment remaining before lunch, all she received was Jennifer's comment, "Well, last year we *had* to do it one way."

And Diane, frustrated, responded, "How can I pound into your head that there's no set way?"

There was no way to end the discussion either, so students continued to explore the issue informally over lunch. Margie, we discovered, hadn't participated in class because she was bewildered. Over a ham sandwich, she asked Diane, "Why do I find a process journal so useful and others don't?"

Matt came in and sat down next to Diane. "Mrs. B.," he said, "don't be upset." The two of them talked quietly, Matt explaining his confusion, Diane recounting her frustration, until she realized that one way to help Matt might be to show him her process journal. He read it slowly through the rest of lunch. April and Tim sought me out to tell me how bad they felt for not contributing to the discussion. Both of them enjoyed writing in their process journals. April, I learned, was even keeping an extra one at home. And Jennifer, who began lunch by saying, "Well, this year I don't hate the process journal as much," seemed to have a sudden insight. After examining Margie's process journal, she exclaimed for all of us to hear, "I've been doing my process journal like I'm walking backwards. I can get where I want to go, but I'm making it very hard for myself." Laughing, she walked backwards for the rest of lunch.

Diane and I were both touched by what the kids said in class, moved by Brian's honesty, Mike's courage, even Jennifer's stubbornness. Diane recognized that the day was important to her in coming to understand the kids. I recognized that it was important to me in coming to understand Diane. She was struck by the kids' honesty. I was struck by how seriously she took them. That night, after explaining that "the stuff from last year hit me like a slap in the face," she wrote about the class, reflecting on the potential impact of the day's discussion:

> Will today be significant in terms of what happens next for some kids? Any kids? One kid? ... This is the "heaviest" class discussion we've had to date. The honesty is the main thing that stays with me.

Planning for the next day, she saw that it all came down to a choice the kids would have to make:

> At the beginning of tomorrow's class I plan to say that they have a choice to make about their process journals. They know now (I think) that their process journal is mainly for *themselves,* not for me. (Do they *know* this? It's more accurate for me to say that they've been *told* this.) The choice they have

right now is to use the process journal in such a way that it is helpful to them *or* to have it be a chore, a bore, a drag, etc.

Assuming they'd like to choose to make it useful and meaningful for themselves, how can I help them? Modeling? Xeroxing several entries from their peers' process journals? I'll ask them what they think would be most useful.

The next day in class, discussion continued. Diane thanked the students for writing and speaking honestly and emphasized that her goal was to help students discover ways to make their process journals valuable for them. She then stayed out of the conversation for fifteen minutes.

As Margie, Scott, Dina, and Tim talked about the ways they had come to use their journals, other students began to sense new possibilities. When the class became quiet, Tim turned to Diane and asked, "What do you have to say?"

Diane told the students that they had a choice to make regarding the way they used their journals. Then she read the passage about choice that she had written in her journal the night before. When they responded to her, most students said that they thought "models" or "samples" of process journal entries would help them know what the options were. Diane summed up the three-day inquiry by stating, "There seem to be three categories of people on the issue of process journals: those who do it for themselves and find it really useful (minority), those who like the journal OK and don't really mind writing in it but don't find it useful, valuable, or necessary, and those who do it merely because it *must* be done, who write only to please me. They find it a drag."

The kids agreed with her assessment, and Jeff concluded the class by saying, "Mrs. Burkhardt, I'm in the second category but I really want to be in the first one, and I would appreciate any help you can give me so I can move there."

Over the weekend, Diane, an ardent football fan, reported that she was so "obsessed" with process journals that she barely watched the Super Bowl. Working with "a passion for the task," she "read and responded thoroughly to all the 'What I Know About Myself as a Writer' pieces and looked for a variety of entries to publish." As she worked, she began to think of herself as "waging war—but with guerrilla tactics rather than heavy artillery."

Diane took particular care to respond to the students who were negative. To Chrissy, she wrote, "It sounds like you approach your process journal the way some people take medicine: take it because it's good for you. My goal is that it would be more than medicine, that it would be something you want to do because it's helpful, valuable, even necessary at times." She then went on to give Chrissy suggestions about ways to make the task less onerous: "Maybe you should stop writing your entries after you finish a piece. Maybe you should try just writing before or little bits here and there (at natural stops or pauses). Free yourself from complete sentences, from neatness. ... What would it be like for you to try these suggestions? ... I'm searching for ways that may help you view writing process as fun, or as a comfort, or as a release or an exciting discovery."

To Peter, she wrote, "If you've been listening in class you know you're not alone with how you feel. . . . I just hope that you and everyone else will keep an open mind."

To Mike, who risked talking openly about the issue in class, she wrote about the important role he played in the discussion: "Your honesty both in writing this and sharing it in class means more to me than you may realize. I think it helped a lot of other kids to hear you (and Jennifer and Matt, etc.) say this to me. And it certainly was more useful to me than a bunch of phony stuff. I need to know what you think in order to plan what we do in class."

Once back in class, Diane hoped her handout entitled "Excerpts from Process Journals" would "help students see that rather than there being only one set way to document one's composing process, there are many different ways." The handout, seven pages long, was divided into five categories: general concerns about the way we write, getting started and planning, talking and thinking to ourselves, describing and reflecting, and revising.

Each category had five or six examples. Under "general concerns" Diane included an excerpt that showed a writer upset about the act of writing:

> I really *hate* the pieces I've written. I hate them!!! They're five minute jobs.
> I come home, eat something and just put words down on a piece of paper. I
> know I could feel really comfortable if I just sat down and gave my mind a
> chance! I feel so lost when I write now. I feel as if my brain is empty. And it
> hasn't filled up yet. I feel so impatient waiting and waiting for the right ideas.

"Getting started" contained excerpts that showed how students search for possible topics:

> I have some ideas for my next piece but they are not too solid. I'm won-
> dering if I could write about a movie I saw. I'm also thinking of doing a story
> I got from that movie. If I did the story, it would venture deep into psychodi-
> lia!! I'd want the story to be adventurous, I'd want it to be wierd, but I'd want
> it to be understandable.

Some of the excerpts under "reflecting" showed students wondering about life:

> I just finished the piece and towards the end of it had a lot of emotional
> feeling. When I was writing I started to think seriously. You only live once.
> I think about life a lot and sometimes I think I'm rushing it. I never stop
> thinking about it. But I kind of like being young.

Absorbed reading the handout, the students became very quiet, the classroom quite still. When they looked up, it was to point things out to one another. Quietly, Jeff and Mike began to talk. Kathy and Dina began to compare notes. Diane, waiting for the students to finish reading, wrote in her journal, "It's been twenty-five minutes of utter silence—not easy to deal with. . . . They are reading things written by each other. Is that what it does?"

Sitting in class watching the students' reactions, it seemed to me that the handout was already beginning to have an impact and that with time its messages would begin to seep slowly into the students' ways of thinking about writing. The careful way they were reading, the grins, the raised eyebrows, the murmurings over some of the selections, all seemed to suggest that Diane's tactics were beginning to work, to make converts of the opposition. But to find out, to track what was happening, Diane gave the students one more opportunity to reflect on the issue. She asked them, for homework, to write their reactions to the handout. The next day in class, many read what they had written.

Dina was amazed at the similarity between her process journal and those of other students: "While I was reading I would say 'Yeah, that happens to me,' or 'I know what you mean.'" Dawn realized that a lot of things other students wrote about "go through [her] mind, but [she] never even thought of writing them down." Chrissy said she discovered "many different techniques to use . . . and that [she was] going to try something different next time. I really would like to use my process journal to help me," she concluded. Mike wrote, "Now I can just kick off my shoes and relax." And Matt predicted, "I think in the future I'm gonna join those people who are depended upon a process journal."

Most of the students' reactions were positive, but Regina still had a question. "Mrs. B.," she asked, "why *should* we have to learn to like our process journals? If it makes it harder, why do it?"

And Diane, hoping that she and her students might have reached a turning point, responded, "I've asked myself that. I think the process journal is an important tool to help you understand your writing and that your writing will be better because of it. If you really gave it a chance and then chose not to use it, I'd accept that. But I still wonder if you've really given it a chance. So many of you came to eighth grade with your minds closed. What I'm asking for now is a little more openness." Having engaged the students in so much writing and reflection, Diane wanted at least a few more months to see what their dialogue would bring.

Teacher and Researcher

The process journal issue was not the only one to come to a head in January. After four months of living in Diane's home and her classroom, I had some questions. Although Diane's students wrote, revised, and published, it seemed to me that many of them were merely going through the motions, producing writing that was perfunctory and done, as the process journals were, primarily to please her. I had begun to wonder, too, whether Diane had similar questions and if, by raising them, I might offer her confirmation or a fresh perspective.

My raising these questions touched a nerve. It wasn't that Diane didn't ask such questions; she did. But she didn't have answers to them yet, and my questions made that painfully clear. I was not expecting answers, only to join her in her search, but Diane, accustomed to solving classroom problems on her own or with her students, did not have an easy time including me in her inquiry.

The first night I raised such questions, Diane spoke, at first slowly and then more vigorously, about her reluctance and resentment. She felt, she said, that she had been "controlling" what she wrote in her journal just as she had "controlled" my role in her classroom, letting me see only what she wanted me to see. Recently, she had begun to experience my presence as an "intrusion." At first she spoke of wanting a "break from being studied." Then, on reflection, she concluded that what she really wanted to avoid were her own doubts and fears. Exposing them was painful, bringing them into the open seemed "to magnify them, to make them larger than they really were." Her eyes, she felt, could always look away. Mine, she feared, would always see.

And yet in looking together we began to see what neither one of us would have seen alone. Possibilities. Challenges. Questions that were worth our time and attention. She saw that I valued her searching. I learned that it was important to risk challenging and encouraging her, as she challenged and encouraged her students, to examine more closely what she was doing and why she did it.

From that night on, we worked together in new ways. Her journal reflected the change. More willing to expose her doubts, Diane explored new depths in her teaching:

> I'm aware now of other issues deeper than the day-to-day classroom descriptions or anecdotal accounts or plans for class. Right now it feels as though these issues go right to the core. What am I really doing? What's it all mean? How does one day's class relate to the next or the last? What am I doing to help kids write better?

I felt the difference in class. Still the ethnographer, taking notes, participating when Diane asked me to or when I thought I had something to offer, I noticed that a subtle shift had taken place in my relation to the issues. Although the central questions remained in the hands of Diane and her students and it was they who would come to grips with them and discover the answers, I now had a greater stake in the outcome. I had come to care about what happened not because I knew the right answer but because I was included in the inquiry.

Working out a partnership enriched what Diane and I each brought to class, but it did not sidetrack Diane from the issue I raised on that cold January evening. She was as disturbed as I about the seeming lack of connection between the topics most students chose to write about and their genuine interests and concerns and wrote of "the need to help kids anchor their writing in some place." She explained, "Kids write 'stories'—they think of preposterous plots, they write with little regard for their own experience: kidnapping stories, murders, car chases, etc. Some kids do these better than others, but that's not saying much."

The dilemma sent her back to her books, to reread Elbow and Moffett,[1] and

---

[1] Peter Elbow, *Writing Without Teachers*. New York: Oxford University Press, 1973; James Moffett and Betty Jane Wagner, *Student-Centered Language Arts and Reading, K–13*. Boston: Houghton Mifflin Co., 1976.

to her journal, to write and to think, looking for ways to help her students discover topics that mattered to them.

> We talked of some ways to help kids find out what it is they want to write about. Freewriting for example. I read a lot of Elbow this weekend and I know how he uses it and how he "teaches" others to use it. I can do what he says.
>
> What other techniques are there? What tools that we know of to give to kids? Moffett's memory chain, your Guidelines for Composing, these things work for adults. I guess I won't know how useful they are for kids if I don't try them. I want to try them, but I think I better not expect 100% results.
>
> Reading Moffett over the weekend also reminded me of how important it is to have kids read lots of different things. I started looking through many different books and quickly became overwhelmed at how much there is and how important it is.

And again, through writing, Diane led herself deeper into the issue she was writing about, in this instance, the issue of "impelled" writing:

> Here's the question any writer ought to ask himself/herself ... what do I *need* to write? How can we get kids to view themselves as writers in such a way that they will have this sense? I personally don't feel that I've touched it at all. We talk of the power of writing; do kids experience that? Have I experienced it? I've felt the power of an impact on others but what about a sense, a power that comes right at the moment of writing, of shaping the meaning, or of writing from the core of one's being? Is this the goal to strive for?

After writing for several hours, Diane decided on one "goal to strive for": to help students discover, for their individual magazines, topics or issues that mattered to them, that they really wanted to write about. Once they had discovered topics or themes, she hoped that their process journals would help them stay committed to their subjects through the often arduous process of writing and revising.

Learning Forms

Several days later, Diane and I stayed up late discussing the various forms of writing, sometimes called the "modes of discourse." We wondered why so many students wrote "stories." Was it that they didn't know the options available to them? Could it be that they had studied poetry but never tried to write poems? That they had read essays but never practiced writing them? And what about narrative techniques? Were they aware that interior monologues would let them get inside characters' heads? Had they ever tried writing dialogues? Perhaps, we speculated, what they needed was some practice exploring the various forms and narrative techniques before they began their magazines. Furthermore, we asked each other, if they weren't aware of the various options available to them, wouldn't they have very limited means of exploring their themes or topics once they had discovered them?

For several weeks, then, Diane introduced her students to a wide range of writing, emphasizing both form and technique. Her approach was usually the same. She brought in several samples written by her previous students as well as by professionals, asked students to read them aloud, and then after a brief discussion to try writing one or two of their own.

In February, for example, she introduced the students to free verse. After reading and discussing several poems in class, Diane told her students to "go home and try to write a poem in free verse. Think of people, moments, moods—it can be humorous if you want. For a source of material, you might look at your free writing. You may find an idea to take off on. Some of it may be free verse already. Try writing one; if it goes well, try another. The length is up to you. Play around with words on the line. Have a good time."

The next day, Diane began class with a question designed to lead her students into a discussion of the writing process: "How was it to write a poem in free verse?" As the students began to report on their experiences, the discussion moved comfortably and leisurely around the room.

Brian: Hard.

Scott: Fun.

Kathy: I knew what to write, but it felt more like a story than a poem.

Seth: I wanted to do something on sports, but I was afraid you'd think I was copying from the examples you showed us yesterday.

Diane: You know, sometimes something we do in class has an impact on my writing, too. Last week I changed my interior monologue, Seth, because you predicted it, and I wanted to do something not so predictable.

Scott: I knew immediately that I wanted to write about racquetball when you gave the assignment. I had no problem. Everything was so vivid.

Margie: Scott said it was easy, but for me it was hard. I got a lot of ideas about people—like my parents—I didn't know how I felt about them so it was hard.

Brian: It's easier if you know what you're writing about.

Diane: That's true for me too, Brian. I had something on my mind and it just came out. Then I played with form—trying to decide what to put on each line. [*Looking at me*] What about yours?

Sondra: I haven't written a poem in a long time, but I figured that, since you were all writing, I would too. I really enjoyed myself. I wrote a poem about the research project yesterday afternoon during our study group.

Tom: I liked that you just could take one moment like Sondra said yesterday. You didn't have to worry about before and after.

April: When I thought of it as writing, it was easy. When I thought of it as writing a poem, it was hard.

Lisa: I think poems are dramatic.

Jeff: Mine was more like observation and feelings.

John: My father wanted to read mine. After he did, he said, "It doesn't rhyme."

Diane: And you said ...?

John: Poems don't have to rhyme.

[*We all smiled, reminded of our discussion the day before when Brian argued that rhyming poems were "classier," while Diane maintained that she had a prejudice in favor of nonrhyming poems.*]

Matt [*having heard some of the poems Ross, Diane's husband, creates for and about the eighth-grade class*]: Mr. B's poems rhyme, don't they?

Diane: Sometimes he forces rhymes for amusement, but his serious poems rarely rhyme.

At this point, Diane asked for volunteers to read their poems. Tim read first:

My Brother and I

ERIC . . .
You bug me when I'm busy
You steal my socks
You still think I like playing match box cars
You follow me and my friend around

BUT I REMEMBER WHEN I . . .
Tell you to shut up
Yell at you for stealing my socks
Tease you when you play with your cats
Tell you to get lost

ERIC DO YOU STILL . . .
Think of me as a friend,
Someone to talk to,
Someone to look up to,
Someone to help you when you need it
DO YOU STILL THINK THESE THINGS ABOUT ME?

Then Chrissy read:

Tears

Tears will forever be a mystery to me.
They come unexpectedly when I don't want them to.
I try to fight them.
Hoping they will go away.
But it is no use.
My eyes begin to get watery and red.
I wipe them but they just get redder.
A tear rolls down my cheek.
And soon many others follow.

Peter read next:

A man is trying to be funny
He tells a joke

At the end
He looks at all the blank faces
He waits
He starts to get nervos
He stairs
He looks at all the people
Bowing for a smile
He stops at a kid
The kid is smurking
The man smurks back
The kid laughs
Everone copies
The relived man
Walks away

We continued reading, the poems drawing spontaneous applause and murmurs of appreciation. Lisa wrote about music and what the sound of loud drums does to her:

The music seems louder;
The words fade away.
Only the drums are left.
They get louder and faster,
like thunder pounding on the ground.
My heart starts beating harder.
It feels as if it is sitting beside me,
Instead of inside me.
Then it stops.
These's no noise
no drums,
no heartbeat.
Nothing
Just silence.

Leslie wrote about the process of thinking:

What's going through your head?
A penny for your thoughts.
Do you think in sentences?
or just a bunch of words?

Is there really a way to tell?
If you think about your thinking,
You won't get very far.

Margie wrote about her friend, Colleen:

Friends Forever

When we met,
I looked you over,
Short,
Blonde,
With cute freckels,
And mildly self concious.
Then I looked myself over,
Tall,
Brunette,
With freckels fading away year by year and
Not concious about what you thought of me.
Why were we even being introduced?
We could never be friends,
We're so different.

I love volleyball
You hate it
You love basketball
I hate basketball
You like green
I like blue

Could two people so different
Ever become friends?
"Impossible" I thought
But then I made you chuckel
And you made me go hysterical.
You told me your problems and
Shared your secrets with me
When I was there to listen.
This made me realize that,
Your the pitcher,
Im the catcher.
Your the performer,
Im the audience.
Your the melody,
Im the harmony

Although sometimes off key,
We're always back on beat
Within a few measures.
All under the direction of
The always dependalbe conductor,
Understanding.

So please, Col, be my
Friend forever.

By the end of class, a spell had been cast. All of us, teacher, students, and researcher, were touched by words.

Establishing Trust

After several weeks of working with students on the exploration of various forms and techniques, Diane introduced the magazine project in earnest. "Your magazine will focus on a theme," she said one day in the beginning of March. "The theme may be something you've already written about in your idea log or your free writing, or it may be something you will discover in class as we talk and write. But the most important thing to remember about your theme is that it is yours— it is a topic or an idea you choose, that you want to write about."

Diane explained that all of the pieces the students wrote for their magazines would be related in some way to their themes. Discovering themes, then, and looking for ways to shape them became the focus of class discussions. One evening I asked Diane whether she thought the "Guidelines for Composing," which worked for adults, might help her students discover potential themes. Thinking it was worth a try, Diane asked the kids the next day in class to sit quietly and write while she asked them the same questions I asked teachers in summer institutes.

The students were delighted. Nancy called the "Guidelines" a "mind-cleansing operation." Mike said, "It was good to think on paper." Regina commented, "It brought things out you would never think about to write—little things that mean something." But as soon as Diane asked her students to take one of the issues or topics they discovered during the "Guidelines" and to shape it into a piece that could be used in writing groups, an uproar ensued.

"We can't!" the kids protested. "What we wrote is too personal."

Faced with another dilemma, Diane quickly turned the issue back to her students. Reassuring them that they would not have to share writing they considered too personal, she asked them instead to consider what it would take for them to share the type of writing that really mattered to them.

Over the next week, the students explored the issue of trust, as they had the issue of process journals, first in writing, then by talking. After several days of discussion, they began to form a consensus: to share writing that mattered to them, they needed to be able to trust one another; they needed to know that listeners would take their writing seriously; they needed to know that their peers wouldn't make fun of something they had written.

Toward the end of one class, Jeff said, "With people I trust, I could write anything."

Jennifer responded, "I could build up the trust."

But Matt disagreed: "Sometimes you just don't *want* to share things."

Diane used Matt's comment to make a distinction between any writer's right to privacy and the commitment serious writers make when they write what they care about. "I understand the need for writing things that are never shared," she said. "That's the purpose of your idea log. Now we're talking about the writing you will do for your magazines. Ask yourselves, what kind of writing do you want in it? Stuff that is important to you? Or stuff that doesn't matter?

I hope you'll be able to write about things that are real, that are important to you."

Mike commented, "I guess it just means taking a risk."

Diane agreed, "That sounds right to me. If one person takes the risk one week, that has an impact on the group. The first time is the hardest. Sometimes, you know, we wait forever."

The discussion continued:

April: I feel like Jennifer does. If I could be in a trusting group, I would start writing more personal things.

Jennifer: I'd want that—to keep the group together.

Diane: You're saying, "Here's what I want. Now, how do I make it happen?" I've always wondered if writing groups in classes could be as important to kids as they are to teachers. Teachers often wonder if kids can experience the same level of trust that adults can.

Dina: I think we could trust each other.

Tom: I don't. I couldn't trust everyone.

Diane: I'm glad you said that, Tom. I understand that and know that it's something you will all need to work out for yourselves. What excites me now is that it sounds like some of you are willing to set aside past judgments. I think that means you have a chance to create a new level of trust and sharing in your writing groups.

Before the class dispersed, Diane gave students five minutes to write about where they stood in relation to the issues discussed all week. Many had been amazed at what their peers said. Jimmy wrote:

Alot of peopel have the same feelings I do about writing groups.

Bob commented:

I'm sure I could keep my mouth shut and not go telling the story to other people. I could do this because I would definitely demand this for my own story.

Chrissy said:

I don't think anyone should be laughed at when they read their piece because I know how much it hurts when your piece is rejected.

Jeff requested that he be placed in a group with "good friends," because, he wrote:

if I dont care about the people I might be tempted to tell their inner thoughts to someone if I heard them.

Margie wrote:

I will defenatly respect other peoples writing. I would feel good if someone respected and trusted me enough to share too.

Nancy commented:

> I was so involved listening to people in class that I forgot I was there. Every-
> one seemed so serious and mature. I changed my opinions of some classmates
> for the better.

Over the weekend, Diane read and responded to what her students had written and, as she had with the process journal issue, made a handout for her students of lines and phrases taken anonymously from their journals. Entitled "Our Thoughts on Trusting Others Enough to Share Our Writing," the handout showed how similarly the students regarded the issues of trust and sharing.

Diane was excited by this series of classes. She felt as if she and her students had faced another difficult issue, one that could once again have a deep and lasting impact on their understanding of writing and their growth as writers. And she was excited at the thought of what could happen now that the subject of trust had been raised:

> The thought that occurs to me is what an opportunity the kids have *now*
> to make writing groups very special, very different from what they have been
> previously. Since January, this is the second time where I've spoken seriously
> about *choices* that they have to make. The first serious talk of choice and
> opportunity came over the issue of how useful to allow one's process journal
> to be. The second is now. . . . These are the issues and shared experiences that
> are irrevocably woven into the class fabric. They're there always to be part of
> us and the special quality of our "groupness." I have been very *excited* by
> both of these opportunities. I think kids sense their importance just as much
> as I.

It is these kinds of issues, these moments, these kinds of experiences and discussions that, Diane wrote, "renew" her as a teacher:

> These [moments] are unrepeatable. No way does the same thing happen
> next year because I am changed/affected/effected in such a way that the
> circumstances leading up to the critical moments are never going to repeat
> themselves. Am I making this clear? Next year I'll approach process journals in
> a way from September 1st that will reflect the events of this year. Or the
> issue of trust and writing personally will arise in a different way at a different
> time because of what I'm learning now. Similar discussions may take place but
> its overall impact on me/the class will not be the same.
>   I realize now that one of the reasons I do not go stale in the same teach-
> ing assignment from year to year is that these moments and experiences *re-
> new* me each year. I *know* that each year will have these experiences. I never
> know exactly what the specifics will be, because I can never go back to how I
> was before. But always I gain a real sense of my own growth as a
> teacher/person each year—identified with a particular group of kids.

The Process Journal Issue Revisited

As students became involved in the magazine project, many of them began to fill their process journals with reports of their drafting and revising. Many had chosen themes that were personal, that they had discovered by doing the "Guidelines." Kathy had decided to write about "nervousness"—the knot she noticed in her stomach whenever she pushed herself to succeed. Brian planned to write about "competition" as he knew it from the jogging track. Tim had chosen "personal goals"; Mike, "peer pressure"; Leslie, "friends"; Chrissy, "the whole range of emotions people feel"; Margie, "relationships."

Writing about themes and speculating about possible pieces and the composing problems and decisions associated with them became the focus of process journals. In fact, students became so involved in writing and talking about themes that Diane found it difficult to collect their journals. "The students said they needed them to work on their pieces," she reported. Diane even started a trend. When a student had filled an entire notebook, she supplied another. Slowly, students began to notice that Leslie and Dawn had received new process journals, that Margie was up to journal number three, that Kathy and Dina were also expecting new notebooks. Delighted by the ways students were both awed and amazed, Diane reported, "Process journals are becoming the 'in' thing."

Many students used their process journals to talk to Diane. And she continued to use them as a way to teach. Sometimes her comments helped students clarify what they were writing about. For example, in trying to find her theme, Nancy wrote:

> I want to do communication. Not really talking *communication*. It's like can a baby understand its mother without her saying anything? Do they get a calmed feeling from their mother when their upset? Can an animal sense what another animal is thinking? *Can you get a feeling of tensness and anger when you walk into a room of angry people?* That is the kind of communication I want to do. Sensing things I guess.

Diane put a name to Nancy's theme, "nonverbal communication," and remarked, "I like it, especially if you like it!"

With Scott, Diane maintained a rather lengthy conversation on the nature of his theme and how he might refer to it. For example, when Scott wrote:

> I have decided on a theme. I have written racquetball stories in many forms so I want to include that. But I also want to include some other sports. So I want to call it something like: a lot of racquetball and a little bit of everything in sports. Well, something like that—

Diane responded by letting him know that even though she didn't have the answer, she was with him on his search for the right word:

> We need to come up with a word that expresses the basic theme that we were talking about today. It's not coming to me right now though. I'll keep thinking. The important thing is that you have a way of using several pieces and additional ideas.

After reading Diane's comment, Scott wrote back, trying hard to pin down what it was about racquetball that touched him:

> I don't know *why I get such a great feeling from playing racquetball.* I
> also don't know if anything else but racquetball gives me that same feeling of
> joy. Maybe the surroundings of a racquetball court? Because of being totally
> enclosed with four walls? I really don't know. *I wish I did.* Then maybe I could
> discover this same joy in other things. I would love it! *But what is this joy?*
> *Where does this joy come from?* These are some questions I would like to
> know.

And Diane, touched by what Scott had written, let him know that she understood
precisely what he was talking about. In addition, she saw not only a theme·in
his search but also the beginning of an essay. She wrote back:

> This is a wonderful entry. It occurs to me that the questions you raise are
> really your theme. Everyone would like to have something which brings them
> the joy you express and everyone who experiences it wonders what it is and
> where it comes from. I get the feeling you get from racquetball when I teach
> sometimes, or often when I read and respond to journals. So I know what
> you mean. Each of us finds our own answers to those *two key questions.*
> What you wrote here seems to me to be the basis of an essay. ... do you
> know what I mean? We can talk about it at the next opportunity we have.

Bob wrote about the experience of being "stuck." Initially, he blamed it on
not having a "form" to write in:

> I need help! I can't think of anything to write. *It's painful.* I think I can't
> think of an idea because I don't have a form to write. I tried writing a poem
> but it wasn't any good. I mean it really stunk. I need a good form to write in.
> Otherwise I can't think.

Then he had an insight. Form wasn't the problem. The question came down
to what he wanted to write about. But here he encountered another dilemma.
Writing about what he knew sounded corny. Where did he turn? To Diane.

> But maybe form's not the problem. I can't even think of what I'm going to
> write about. All my pieces so far have been about sports. The main reason is
> that I can relate to it easier. I can't relate to competition on Wall Street or
> something like that because I'm not there. I've been trying to write something
> about everyday life. But it's so incredibly corny. It's pretty bad. I think I need
> help from you.

Diane wrote back suggesting that perhaps Bob was "thinking too hard about
[his] theme," reassuring him that they would have a chance to talk the next day.
And when she began to think about it, Diane realized that the dialogue she
maintained with each student was really a "form of conference." "In nearly every
case," she wrote, "the writing back and forth in process journals eventually leads
to an in-person conversation about something that has been written."

In fact, as a window onto the composing process, the process journals seemed
to be helping both Diane and her students. The students' reflections alerted
Diane to problems she might otherwise have been unaware of. They showed
her not only what students were thinking but also where she needed to direct

her teaching. And many students began to notice that their process journals were an aid to writing.

In letters the students wrote to Diane in April reporting on their progress ("Why," Diane asked, "do we teachers think we are the only ones who know the kids' progress?"), they commented on the ways in which they were using their journals. Many students were both pleased and proud of the way they were working. Chrissy commented, "Using my process journal is working well for me now. I used to have to always remind myself to write in it and now I never do. I turn to it for help." Kathy wrote, "Now that I understand it better, it really helps me. I guess you could say I love to fill it up!" Dina reported, "If I didn't have a process journal, I'd probably kill myself. Whenever I have a problem, I turn to it. I realize I'm really the one solving my problems, but my journal helps me out." And Jeff explained, "I've been writing in my process journal alot. I'm using it as a way to talk to you."

Other students still did not find value in their journals but wrote about why they thought this was so. Mike commented, "Now that I think about it, I haven't been using my process journal that much. I just forget to do it sometimes." Brian reported that his "process journal was going slow," but that he thought he could "catch up." Seth joked that his was going "allright, but it sure wasn't like Margie's." "I just don't understand," he commented, "how she could possibly write 5 pages on just one piece. I have trouble with one page." And Bob explained that, while he didn't "mean to sound argumentative," one of the reasons he didn't write a lot in his journal was that it was supposed to be for him and he didn't "need to write a lot in it."

Leslie, who, unlike Bob, did rely on her process journal, felt that her work was "dragging" because for some reason she just wasn't using it. As she put it, "[This] really messes me up." Then she questioned Diane, "How does everybody stay so involved? It drives me crazy."

The majority of the students in Diane's class did "stay involved" in the magazine project for several months. Once they had chosen their themes and had begun drafting possible pieces for publication, Diane's class took on the atmosphere of a writers' workshop. Mondays were reserved for whole class meetings so that students could check in with one another, learn through process discussions what their peers were working on, receive feedback from Diane on her perception of the writing groups, and generally stay in touch with the progress that the class as a whole was making. Class time on Tuesdays through Fridays was used for writing, writing group meetings, revising, editing, or having conferences.

Knowing that there was no way she could mandate when students would "need" a writing group meeting and recognizing that students all worked at different paces, Diane entrusted the students with the responsibility of scheduling their own time. It was up to them to decide when their writing groups would meet and for how long. They needed to determine when to start new pieces or continue revising old ones. They were given the responsibility of deciding when they wanted or needed to have conferences with either Diane or me. Diane kept track of what was going on by initiating class discussions, by asking the students to write her reports on their progress, and by reading what they had written in their process journals. In addition, she posted a wall chart on which each writing group listed its plans for the week.

From the beginning of March, then, students took on a large measure of control over what they wrote, how they wrote it, and when and how they would receive feedback on it. The work seemed to generate its own momentum, and Diane and I noticed that everyone seemed to be working productively. We had reached the time of year Diane likes best, when her relationships with students are strong, and the trust she is able to place in them is a further demonstration of her care and respect.

It was, therefore, a bit surprising for us to watch the panic that ensued when, after returning from spring vacation, Diane mentioned the series of deadlines she was setting in order to have work ready for typing and duplicating. Many students were in no way ready to finish. Nancy and Kathy still had essays to write. Chrissy had just had a new idea for a poem. Bob still had "three 1st person stories and three interior monologues" to take to his writing group. And Diane noticed that even mentioning deadlines had created "a totally different atmosphere." "Kids," she wrote, "were into their own pieces, not so interested in others' work, fighting over whose piece got edited first. Not at all the way they had been during the previous weeks of writing, revising, discussing, etc."

Recognizing that her announcement had "contributed" to what she called "the anxiety over the deadline," Diane called a class meeting. Intending to "relax things a bit," she explained that deadlines, which she was now inviting the students to refer to as "livelines," are useful and important because "they help us see what the limits are, and if we don't have limits, we can go on and on. But," she said, "we can't skip stages just to meet the deadline."

"I've looked at the calendar," she continued. "I think most people can be finished by May 14. That gives you three weeks. Now, you will need to be responsible and keep checking your progress. You have to ask yourself, 'Am I doing every day what I have to in order to make this magazine what I want?' Remember, in many ways this magazine is a commitment to yourself."

When she finished talking, Diane asked if there were any questions. Jennifer repeated the one piece of information she wanted to be sure of. "So," she asked, "there's no deadline this Friday?"

Diane responded, "Right, there won't be a deadline or a liveline right now if it means skimping on the process."

And Matt, speaking as if he could read Diane's mind, asked, "Would it be a good idea to do our planning in our process journals?"

"Of course," Diane said, and, of course, process journals continued to be the vehicle Diane used to write to her students about their own learning and writing.

Having observed her students closely, Diane was well aware of the different ways they worked. As a result, she was often able to remind them of what she knew about them when they seemed to have forgotten it. In responding to Leslie's complaint that her work was "dragging," Diane was able to make an important distinction. "I don't really think of you as working slowly," she wrote, "I think of you as working carefully." Knowing that Leslie was a serious, if not always a prolific, writer, she continued, "I have patience, confidence, and trust that *you* are writing as much as/as fast as it is possible for you to do. You should relax and put some of *your trust* in *my* trust in you!"

Matt was in a state of panic at how slowly his work was progressing. He wrote first about the dilemma he found himself in:

> Last week I got my first piece finalized. I also got another piece in for writing group. I did it again, I didn't make the deadline. I won't make any deadlines because I'm about two writing groups behind everybody. Now theres another piece due friday. By friday I'll only have my second piece finalized when everybody will have three. I'll be a week behind (two writing groups.)

Then he explained why:

> I spend more time on my pieces. I just don't crank out pieces like most people, when you crank out pieces they don't have that much feeling.

Diane recognized Matt's distress, knew from her relationship with him that his panic was real. As a result, she knew she had both to reassure him and to support him in, as he put it, "stepping up the pace." "Please don't put yourself in such agony and pain," she wrote. "You and I will make sure that things work out for you. But," she continued, "the truth of the matter is (as you said earlier today) you need to get your butt moving a bit."

Margaret had a different dilemma. She had spent several weeks composing a fictionalized account of a teenage girl's reaction to her grandfather's death. Although Margie's own grandfather was still alive, the events and emotions she was attempting to portray threatened to overwhelm her. Having spent several weeks on various sections of the piece, she was as upset at the idea of abandoning it as she was at the idea of finishing it:

> While I was reading this [piece] over, I noticed two things—one is, that I wrote this peice sooooo long ago. UGGG. And another thing is that—I don't even like this piece that much. Theres something about it that irks me. What it is—I don't know—
> What kept me from writing? Not liking the peice that much?
> What is my problem?
> I'm mad at myself. How long was it going to take before I realized I didn't really like this peice?
> Is it just because I'm frustrated now, that I'm saying that? I don't think so.
> Maybe I want to get to a peice about my mom—maybe I want to write "light" things, maybe Im just tired. Maybe I need to find out where and when I write best. Certainly its not at 10:00 PM.

There are certain phrases and sentences in the piece I dont like. I like the begining—But the whole things seems like a boring story. Theres no plot.

What is the point of this story?

I think its to write something to tell my Grandpa how much I respect and think of him. Maybe this isnt the mode to use. To me a story should have a beginning to build things up, a middle where it happens and an ending that ties it up. Maybe thats why the little continuation I wrote on Tuesday fourth period was sort of exiting—giving it a twist. Making more of a plot. Do I want it to go that way? I cant get a sincere reaction down with out it sounding corny.

Why do I seem to be resisting so much?

Que Pasa?

Im really unsettled these days. Maybe its got to do with spring fever and not enough sleep, anxiety attacks, friends, etc. Im such a baby. Everythings got to be perfect or else I cant write. I dont really mean that but its been that way lately. I should stick to writing light stuff. Maybe if I could get the magazine done with light stuff, it would be easier I dont want junky stuff that I dont care about but I just cant seem to get into something big lately like a story. To me poems are easier and monologues seem easier. Stories are allways heavy for me.

Diane and I were concerned. We had both read the various drafts, liked the piece immensely, thought, in fact, that it was the best work Margie had produced all year. Hoping that Margie would choose to continue writing, Diane responded first to the piece itself, using what she knew of Margie to guide her. "I KNOW," she wrote, and continued:

Some day when you decide to work on this again . . . the ending where you run out to the beach seems very real. That seems like something that you might do now—go off to be alone and have all those thoughts of outrage and the injustice of it all, your sorrow, etc., then eventually go back home when you felt able to be who you are at home, when you felt that you could "control" your feelings.

Then, both wanting to encourage Margie to continue but knowing that she had to leave the choice in Margie's hands, Diane wrote:

I'm attached to this piece. Still want you to finish it, but respect your decision not to, of course.

In these and many other instances, I saw that Diane was not only building her relationships with her students but was also using her relationships with them to deepen both her understanding and their learning. In fact, several students were also aware of just how much they revealed of themselves to Diane through their writing. One afternoon sitting in the bleachers at an eighth-grade baseball game, Jeff teased Diane about how well she'd come to know them. "Do you want a meaningful relationship?" he asked in the voice of a circus barker. "Just come to Diane's Computer Dating Service. Bring your process journal, your writing group tape, and two or three pieces of writing. Diane will match you up. 100 percent certain to be successful."

While Jeff's proposed plan for a computer dating service might have been successful, Diane's plan for a magazine completion date was not. On May 14, students still had work to do. But with an eighth-grade bike trip to be planned, a new districtwide writing evaluation to be administered, a social studies show on adolescents to be rehearsed and performed, Diane had to restrict the amount of class time devoted to magazines. Those students who were not finished would have to come in after school, work on an occasional free period or when they had completed other assignments, or bring their drafts to lunch or early morning conferences. And "in the rush of everything," Diane noted, "I've let down on process journals. The requirement is still there but I haven't actually sought the kids whose journals I haven't seen in a while."

Diane was torn, thinking on the one hand that "by this time of the year, either the students find a use for it or they don't" and on the other that she "should stay right on top of it, keep working with kids . . . put together another handout." Yet, with all she had to do, trying to reach those students who for whatever reasons did not see the value of keeping process journals was no longer a high priority.

The issue was one of those events in the life of a class that could neither be predicted nor controlled. Diane devoted herself to it, worked long hours, tested, experimented, looked to see in what ways she might open her students' minds and provide them with a tool she believed would ultimately be of use to them. She knew, in the end, it was something she could not force. And so she wrote in her journal, on an afternoon at the end of May, "I will just feel a little guilty about the kids who aren't keeping process journals anymore and continue to enjoy Chrissy's and Dina's and Jeff's and Leslie's and Margaret's, etc."

Beyond Process

If Diane were to view the process journal issue as a fight, then she would probably conclude that she had lost the battle but won the war. Not all of her students experienced, as Dina put it, "the power of the process journal," but many experienced the "power" of writing. They learned what it meant to write about issues that really mattered to them, to choose themes and to stick with them through many drafts of many different pieces. They came to see what it meant to be responsible not only for their own writing but also for the work of members of their writing groups. They had a large measure of autonomy given to them, and, in general, they used it well.

The end of May found students sitting outdoors designing covers or working on titles, doing some final editing or getting last opinions from friends. One morning after students had spread out and begun work, Diane noted that they seemed "very intent. They accept the notion that what they are writing is important—valued." As she looked around, she wrote, "The space of the room makes me wide awake. I see various individuals and feel overwhelming love for each."

Several days later, when not even a fraction of class time could be given over to the finishing of magazines, Diane called the class together as a group. "Now that we're near the end of the magazines," she said, "I want to thank you for being so good and really putting so much of yourselves into this project. You know, in all the time that you've been working and meeting in hallways and other classrooms, not one teacher has come up to me and said, 'What are those kids of yours doing during English?' You've all been really great."

And in her journal she wrote:

> How lucky I am to have students who are so trustworthy and so committed to what they have set out to do.

"Trustworthy." "Committed." I was struck by the words. Would Diane have described her students in these terms at the beginning of eighth grade? Looking back, I remembered a bunch of students who were hostile and angry, who said they didn't like writing and didn't want to write. I remembered groans at Diane's mention of journals, disbelief at her mention of publishing. What accounted for such a dramatic change? I asked myself. How did Diane's students turn from complaining eighth graders to thoughtful, committed writers? Did their trust and commitment just appear? Or was it that Diane saw the potential for trustworthiness in them and worked to bring it out? Did her constant reaching for what was honest in them help make it visible? Or was it just that she was honest with them herself? These were the questions that ran through my mind as I read the students' evaluations of the year. Visible in them, if I had any doubts, was tangible evidence that Diane's students had changed.

Many students thought that their eighth-grade year was the best school year they had ever had. Nancy wrote, "I think I've learned the most in your class since I learned the ABC's. I'm serious. I've also learned that I'm very selfish about what I write. I don't always want everyone to read it because it's a part of me."

Jimmy also felt that eighth grade had been a turning point. "I feel that this year was the best year of my life as far as school goes," he wrote. Then he went on to talk about his perception of writing: "I feel good about my writing. Now I not as nervous about people reading my stories and saying he can't write good or spell for his life." He ended with rave reviews: "I think the writing program here is the best anywhere I think every kid in the world should try writing groups."

Dina, too, noticed an extraordinary change in herself. "I can't believe how my thoughts have changed about writing," she wrote. "In one word I want to say 'I love it' (well maybe more than one word)."

Chrissy explained that six months ago she thought all her writing should be "long," but after completing her magazine, she had learned that "length doesn't really matter." She also commented on the freedom Diane gave the students to manage their own writing group work. "It made me feel like I wasn't pressed for time; if we didn't finish going through a person's pieces, we could do them the next day," she wrote.

Many students who reflected on the year ended up by comparing it to seventh grade. Jeff wrote, "Compared to last year, this class is very close." Leslie, too, saw changes in herself, her writing, and her understanding of writing since seventh grade. She wrote, "Last year, I didn't even know what a process journal was used for! My pieces were short and unmeaningful. None of me was in my pieces. Now, they are fairly long and I care about them, I feel the quality of my pieces has gone up a great deal! It used to be hard for me to write a piece. It was like a chore, I *had* to do. This year, I write on my free time, and I get alot more done." She went on, "Writing groups were also something I was totally lost about last year. It was crazy. I needed a *sheet* to tell me what to do. I love to do writing groups because of the second opinion. They would tell me how to improve it and what wasn't clear enough. They helped me make the piece better . . . I guess the best part of my writing this year is I understand it and I *like* it."

Jennifer was also amazed at the change from seventh grade. She commented, "The 2 magazines we all did this year were great. I remember last year we were *suppost* to do a magazine with 1 piece from each kid and never got it done. When you said magazine I said sure dream on. Now that I did my own magazine I must admit it feels good." What else did Jennifer learn? In her own words, "I got to admit as much as I don't want to that I did learn to use my P.J. [process journal] this year. I did learn alot about my writing too especially how much better a piece comes out when I write about something real to me."

Mike, although currently "sick of his pieces," was "glad about the year" and all the writing the students did. He remarked, "I'm also glad that we don't work out of a textbook and have freedom to write what we want. It was a good year," he said.

Matt and Margie both wrestled with how much of themselves they should put in their pieces. They thought seriously about their writing, worked hard to make it convey the meaning they wanted it to have, but they came down on opposite sides when evaluating their process journals. Matt used his evaluation to wrestle once more with the whole issue. He wrote, "I thought P.J.'s were a *royal* waste at the begining of the year. Now I think a little differently. But sometimes I forget to bring it home and a piece turns out just as good or better. Then I say why is the p.j. needed? I think I got a point. . . . " Then he went on to comment on the prospect of seeing his pieces in print. "I think my magazine is gonna be intense, I can't wait to see it. I love the feeling when you get it finalized."

Margie had no doubts about the value of her process journal. "The best part about all my writing pieces and journals is my P.J.," she explained. "It helped me alot. I remember using it constantly during the fall and the time this spring when I thought I couldn't write real pieces. Mostly during that time I just rambled on. It really was my place to plan and make decisions." And although she chose to abandon her "grandfather" piece, she published several poems, monologues, and stories that mattered to her. Recognizing the importance she placed on her magazine, she wrote, "The part of all my eighth grade writing that I like the most is my magazine. Maybe because my Mom and Dad liked it or I liked their reaction. Plus I'm glad I got down to writing real. This was my biggest success."

Finally, Brian, who viewed the "subject of writing" as "mud" and who initially could be counted on to dislike whatever Diane proposed, had possibly without realizing it been drawn into the excitement of writing. He admitted, "The improvement is much better and the hatred is lesser. I am totally satisfied."

Diane, too, wrote an evaluation of the magazine project, but for her the task was tricky. As much as she thought she should "step back" and separate the products from the students who produced them, she knew she couldn't. As she put it, "I know too much." She explained:

> I know that Karen and Matt and Jennifer and April and Diane and Brian and Jeff really grappled with the concept of a theme, a real issue that means something to them.
>
> I know that maybe Matt and Karin and Jeff (and many others) could have constructed better "stories" if they had not been so personally wrapped up in what they were writing.
>
> I know that Tom and John never wrote so much before, in fact they barely wrote at all before. And maybe he's taking an easy way out and not thinking up a new idea, but John did stick to three different points of view, didn't he?
>
> I know that Jimmy had no confidence in himself as a writer at all because of being in the alternative English class in 6th and 7th grade.
>
> I know that a lot of the kids have put themselves right out there in print for "all the world" to know and I'm touched by that.

As Diane wrote, she was reminded of those students who, for all the work, still seemed to have little or no interest in the class or its accomplishments.

> I also know that Keith left his magazine in his locker and Regina never got hers, and Christian left his "bound" volume in the library.

But when she looked at the project as a whole, she was impressed. It took longer than she planned and, as a result, other areas received less attention than she liked, but, in the end, the magazine project embodied those aspects of classroom life that mattered to her. "Mainly," she wrote, "I know that the kids worked a long time and revised their pieces several times (most of them) and trusted each other and took each other seriously. And all these things that I know are an integral part of any 'evaluation' I do of this project. I can't separate/distinguish the magazine from the kid."

Teacher and Researcher Revisited

The month of June was difficult for Diane. Having come to know and care for her students, she experienced "the end of school" as a "drastic cut off." She began missing the students even before school was over, felt sad knowing that she would rarely see them again except for "a hello at the high school play or the King Kullen Supermarket." She could not be excited about next year's students—to her, they were just names on a roster—or even summer vacation. That would all come in time. In June, all she could see were these students, these relationships, and wonder if any other group could ever be as great.

The year I lived in Shoreham, I too was part of the "cut off." Like Diane's eighth graders, I had become part of the relationships that formed the basis of everything that went on in class. At the end of June, I too was leaving the middle school, never to be in her classroom in the way I was that year.

Separation, distance, and time gave both of us the opportunity to reflect. For Diane, the story of our partnership was the story of a teacher coming to grips with opening her classroom and herself. For me, it was the story of a researcher learning to care more than she ever had about the people she was studying.

When Diane thought about the year, she saw January as a turning point, both in terms of curriculum and collaboration. "Up until that time," she wrote, "I 'controlled' your role in my classroom. Whatever was shared was completely shared on my terms. I invited you to take half the class for a process discussion. Or I asked you to meet with this writing group or that one. Your role went from observer to participant but on my terms."

She continued, "In January you raised some questions I didn't want you to raise. Not that they weren't good questions. Of course they were. They were the issues I was thinking about myself. I resented it because I hadn't worked out the answers. I didn't want to talk about them, but we did. Eventually I was glad we talked of all those things. In fact, that night sticks in my memory as crucial in what we built together from that point. As painful as it was at the time, I look back on it with real joy now. With joy and with thanks to you for taking the risk."

After those talks in January, Diane never again felt as though she were "under the microscope." Once she let me in on her thinking, included me in her doubts and fears, stopped assuming she had to have all the answers, she no longer felt "studied or scrutinized." As she explained it, "I wasn't trying to hide from you anymore, and, as a result, we began collaborating in a way I never anticipated. You either, I bet."

Diane was right. I had no way of anticipating in September, when school began, how involved I would become in her classroom, how important she and her students would become to me. Initially an outsider to eighth graders, slowly I became an advocate, a friend. Reading their drafts and their process journals, I became absorbed in their writing. Visiting their writing groups, I wanted to return, to hear more. And the longer I worked with them, the more I realized that I was coming to understand them.

Eighth graders, I saw, wanted to be taken seriously. When they were, they responded, revealing more and more of what mattered to them. Eighth graders also liked to be silly and to laugh, and I saw that when Diane laughed with them they began to laugh or at least smile at themselves. Eighth graders, like my own adolescent peers, had doubts and fears, were constantly wrestling with who they were and what they wanted to become. But, I realized, the doubts and fears that made them vulnerable also made them accessible. I saw, too, that when adults they trusted reached out to them, they were glad more often than not for a shoulder to lean on, a person to confide in. Learning about the students, I noticed, not surprisingly, that I was becoming as absorbed in their lives and the life of the classroom as Diane was.

How had this happened? I wondered. What in her classroom had been so compelling? What was it that I responded to so deeply? At first I thought it had to do with Diane's personality, with the way she included me, for example, in class discussions. Then I thought it had to do with me, with my own desire to be involved in what was going on. Finally, I saw that no one answer would ever completely explain my involvement.

I did respond to Diane and to the way she drew me into classroom issues. I did feel "at home," knowing what she planned to discuss and how she planned to discuss it. I did like being, as she put it, "a partner" in her thinking. And so I saw that my involvement was, in part, a result of my own preferences, but I knew that it was also a result of the way Diane set up the environment that drew everyone in—her students as well as me—and that part of what drew us in was that we had a hand in shaping whatever went on. One reason, I knew, was inextricably linked with another, just as my understanding of eighth graders and their writing was tightly interwoven with my understanding of Diane and her teaching.

Diane, I saw, used every available tool to reach her students. Writing, one of the subjects she taught, was also a vehicle for her teaching. Writing to reach her students, she also encouraged them to use writing to reach into and help discover themselves. And when something related to writing mattered to her, like the process journal issue, the discussions on trust, or the choosing of themes, I saw that she didn't let go; she worked and thought and reworked and rethought until something valuable had taken place for her and her students. She did not always convince every student to go along with her, but she showed them repeatedly what it meant to be committed to an idea or a project.

I saw that Diane's students learned from her example. Being honest with them gave her the right to ask for honesty in return. Speaking straight to them about what mattered to her encouraged them to speak straight, too. And as I listened to them, I often heard the insights of adults expressed freshly in the language of kids.

This was Diane's secret, I thought. She knows how to reach thirteen- and fourteen-year-olds—and, by reaching them, she helps them catch sight, underneath their questioning and confusion, of the fine human beings they are. Diane, I realized, treated her students as adults, people whose points of view merited respect, knowing full well that they were kids who were learning, all the time, about life. Seeing her job, in part, as helping them come to grips with growing up, she wrote: "The kids I teach are in the midst of adolescent turmoil. If I can be who I am in class that may be the most important thing I ever teach them."

And so Diane was herself in class and out of it. She did not draw neat boundaries around her life as a teacher. She let classroom issues spill over into her world outside of school and brought her friends, her visitors, her outside interests and concerns into her classroom.

Similarly, I drew no neat boundaries around my role as researcher. I allowed myself to be drawn into the life of her classroom because I sensed that there was something valuable to be learned that way. Occasionally, though, a doubt would cross my mind. Was I too involved? I asked myself. Was my attachment to the kids clouding my vision? Had I, in ethnographic terms, "gone native"?

Looking back, I have fresh conviction rather than doubt. I *was* deeply involved in Diane's classroom, but what tempered my attachment was time—and the reflection that accompanied it. Several years later, I see that immersing myself in Diane's class taught me what remaining aloof and distant could not. For one of the lessons brought home to me that year is that real learning, learning that matters and has an impact on the learner, occurs—in Diane's classroom at least—through immersion in the issues at stake. Through involving myself so fully in Diane's teaching, I gained a deeper understanding of the people I was studying, the task I had taken on, and a sense, as Diane put it, of "my own growth, connected to a particular bunch of kids." By living in her classroom, I found my own convictions about the teaching of writing strengthened.

Diane loves teaching writing, she says, because it allows her to deal with "real issues." The year I studied her teaching, the issues had to do with understanding process journals, with choosing themes, with thinking about and making a commitment to writing. But always there in the background were other issues as well: issues of growth and trust and honesty. And it was these more fundamental issues that, when they came to light, brought me to see the limitation of thinking that the teaching of writing was merely instruction in "the writing process." For accompanying Diane's interest in what her students wrote and how they wrote it was her commitment to the students themselves. This dimension of her teaching, which we came to call "the hidden curriculum," held in our eyes a simple but seldom appreciated truth: that writing only develops through the development of the writer. If this were the goal teachers aimed for, I realized, the teaching of writing would always present similar challenges— whether the students were fourteen or forty.

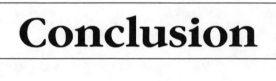

Conclusion

Chapter 8

The Art of Teaching

hat have we learned by looking at teaching through teachers' eyes? In what ways did our immersion in six teachers' classrooms affect our perception of what it means to write and to teach? How do these individual portraits come together and offer us larger views of what it means to teach writing?

When we embarked on this research, we thought that after four years of study we would be able to describe the procedures and principles that enabled the teachers we observed to teach writing effectively. The more we studied our data, however, the less we were able to disentangle procedures from the classrooms in which they were used or principles from the teachers who acted on them. What we saw most clearly, in fact, were the unique ways these teachers and their students shaped and reshaped the work that went on among them. And as we watched and talked to and wrote about six teachers, we came to appreciate the art of teaching itself—an art which, although it consists in part of various techniques, can no more be reduced to a formula or prescription than the artistry of dancing, painting, or playing the violin.

As the study progressed, we realized that just as there is no one way to write so there is no one way to teach writing. Rather, how teachers teach writing, or probably anything else for that matter, is a function of who they are, what matters to them, what they bring with them into the classroom, and whom they meet there. How they go about their work can be affected in certain important ways by conditions in the school, in the community, in the culture at large, but what affects teaching most deeply and dramatically are the themes, the interests, and the deeply felt concerns that affect and give shape to teachers' lives.

This recognition led us away from traditional analytic procedures to look for an approach more suited to our intent: to portray these teachers and their classrooms in their fullness and uniqueness. We found what we were looking for in the realm of narrative. As a result, we changed our view of the data we had collected. Our fieldnotes and memos no longer appeared to us as records of behavior to be distilled and dissected but rather as outlines of stories to be refined and reworked: the challenge of our task to sift through our data to discover tales that tell of teaching in its own terms. In one sense, then, our conclusions are the stories we have already told.

In another sense, though, our conclusions grow out of these stories and extend beyond them. For each story raises questions and points to broader issues. What kinds of settings, for example, support teaching as we have described it here? And when such settings exist, what precisely do they allow for? In this chapter, we first present a description of the Shoreham-Wading River Central School District, a setting that supports inquiry and change. Then we discuss what we have learned through studying six teachers teaching: our enlarged understanding of what it means to write, to learn, and to teach writing.

The Setting in Shoreham-Wading River

If our goal in the research project was to understand how teachers, after taking the Writing Project summer institute, made changes in their teaching, we also knew we had to look beyond the teachers, outside their particular classrooms, to study the settings and school environments where such changes occurred. For we knew that change—particularly in classrooms—rarely occurred in isolation. In Shoreham, we discovered a climate conducive to innovation.

We noticed, first of all, that teachers in Shoreham-Wading River were not required to teach writing according to a prescribed curriculum. Even the Writing Project summer institute, although backed by administrators and supported by the Board of Education, was not a mandated program. Those teachers who were interested were welcome to take it. Those who took it and found value in it were encouraged to use as much or as little of it as they wanted—or to take what they had learned and rework it to suit their own needs and the needs of their students. And the Project was invited back for second and third summers only after the teachers said they wanted a second and then a third institute. Eventually, Sondra and Richard met directly with the teachers to plan the summer work, to design courses that would meet the needs of both returning and new teachers and that would address the teachers' increasing understanding and sophistication in the area of writing instruction. One administrator aptly described the evolution of the Writing Project in Shoreham. "This project really took shape according to what the teachers wanted," he said. "They know that it belongs to them."

In addition to shaping the direction of their writing project, teachers in Shoreham-Wading River help to shape many of the curricular and administrative decisions that affect them. In the early days of the district, teachers and administrators took part in designing the environments they now work in: the branching wings of the middle school and high school, the lofts and study corners and colorful carpeting of the elementary schools. In 1971–72, when the middle school opened, teachers and administrators worked collaboratively to draft a "Statement of Philosophy"; ten years later, they revised it and hung the new version in the main office. Today teachers work together to design new courses and revise old ones— to experiment, for example, with a new journalism course or a writing course using computers. They meet regularly with administrators to decide what courses will be taught and who will teach them, they are expected to submit their own budgets requesting supplies, and they spend a great deal of after-school time discussing with their administrators and one another the philosophy, pedagogy, and practical day-to-day running of their schools.

Of course, support for budgetary items is easy to come by when a district receives tax revenues from a nearby nuclear power plant, and this kind of support is enormously important. Because of it, elementary school teachers in Shoreham-Wading River seldom have more than twenty students in their classes (and often fewer), middle school teachers seldom more than twenty-three, and high school teachers seldom more than twenty-five. Because of it, teachers in Shoreham-Wading River order the books and films they want, have access to duplicating machines, tape recorders, typewriters, media equipment, and computers, take students on field trips, and travel with one another to conferences and professional meetings.

Yet money and the benefits it brings are not the only factors operating in Shoreham. Many school districts in the country have budgets based on substantial tax revenues, yet the school boards that control them all too often choose not to put their resources so directly in the hands of teachers. The budget offers welcome support to the teachers in Shoreham, but it is by no means the only source of support. In addition to using their substantial budget wisely, the Shoreham-Wading River school board and its administrators offer their teachers what districts with less money might surely try: colleagueship and respect, coupled with the right to control how they will spend their time and the directions their professional lives will take.

A setting so supportive of teachers and their work, so imbued with a spirit of respect for innovation and change, proved fertile ground for our inquiry into the teaching of writing. Curious about the inner workings of the school system, we found ourselves welcome not only in the classrooms but also in the administrators' offices and invited often to attend parent conferences or school board meetings. Just as the teachers were encouraged and supported to study and learn, to ask questions, to reflect on what they had discovered, so were we. We present now the fruits of our learning by examining first our involvement in the classrooms and then what that involvement revealed to us about writing and teaching.

The Impact of Immersion

We chose from the start of this study to immerse ourselves in the lives of the teachers we were studying. We observed them and talked with them at work and at home, in department meetings and on hall duty. We thought, in fact, that the more genuinely we could live as members of their communities—within their classrooms and within their school district—the better we would come to understand them and the deeper our understanding would be. And so we let ourselves become caught up in classroom projects, school issues, and community controversies to gain what ethnographers call "an insider's perspective."

In our view, such a perspective was invaluable. Living in the district and participating in the daily life of the classrooms allowed us to construct a view of the teachers we were studying that was grounded in the lives we had each lived. And since we felt that it would have been misguided—if not dishonest— to assume that we, as observers, could ever separate ourselves from our own acts of observation, we never tried to become impartial or disinterested onlookers; rather we tried, as much as possible, to keep track of the ways we entered into, affected, and interpreted classroom life. In the end, we came to appreciate that immersion, far from limiting the value of what we had learned, enhanced it. For only by immersing ourselves in these classrooms could we have learned to see them as the teachers themselves did.

Our being so deeply involved would, we knew, have an impact on the teachers and their teaching. We were aware, of course, that we could never know whether the teachers would have taught differently or seen themselves differently had we not been in their classrooms. Such a vantage point was impossible. We were there, and our being there was part of the story.

Interestingly, the effect teachers noted most often was that our presence offered them fresh ways of seeing. Len put it this way:

> Having a researcher in my classroom inspired me to look deeply into my own teaching, to reflect upon it and really examine it in a way that I was unused to. I had taught on my feet a lot and always done a good job but the extra pair of eyes made me much more aware of what was happening.

Diane, too, felt that our eyes highlighted aspects of classroom life—aspects the teachers might sometimes have preferred to leave in darkness:

> Did you ever think that all your presence did in our classrooms was to magnify what goes on anyway? The presence of another pair of eyes and ears means that it seems bigger or more apparent than it would if there weren't an observer other than ourselves. By ourselves (alone) we can ignore what we see or close our eyes or look away to other things. With you here we are always in some ways seeing things through your eyes.

Our presence, as Diane implied, was intrusive. It made the teachers confront aspects of their teaching lives they had previously chosen to ignore, had been aware of only on the periphery, or had perhaps nodded at with only fleeting or passing attention. It brought them, in other words, a kind of visibility that, although at times reaffirming, was also unsettling. For, by making their teaching visible, they made themselves visible and exposed themselves to a risk: that by scrutinizing what they did closely, they might discover that the ground they stood on was not as firm as they had thought, the assumptions they cherished more open to question than they had realized.

Yet scrutiny, risky as it was, also brought rewards. Looking deeply at their own teaching, the teachers gained the kinds of insights into what they did and why they did it that led to reassessment, reevaluation, experiment, and change. Frequently, their insights confirmed our view of their teaching as well. Living as closely as we did with the teachers, examining almost every aspect of their teaching lives with them, we had trained our eyes to see in ways that complemented theirs. Together we developed a vocabulary, a common way of seeing, a shared sense of what mattered in writing classrooms. Steeped in the details, the particulars of classroom life, the jokes, the successes, the dilemmas and crises, we came to see, by being so fully a part of them, the ways these writing classrooms evolved.

Writing Communities

Viewed up close, what struck us most often about the classrooms we studied was that they were communities that often had lives of their own. First graders and fourth graders paired off in corners, talking, writing, collaborating. Eighth graders headed out of their classrooms with tape recorders under their arms to find quiet places to work and record their writing group discussions. High school students sprawled in hallways and stairwells, intent on their writing. Sometimes it was hard to find the teachers. They, too, had merged into the various communities; like their students, they were writing, pairing off for conferences, or meeting with writing groups.

These observations flew in the face of what observers normally expect to see in well-run public school classrooms: teachers up front, talking, explaining, assigning work; students at their desks, listening, speaking only when called on, working quietly. But what we observed was not merely a change in format. Writing, traditionally seen as a solitary task, had become in these classrooms a communal endeavor.

Traditional assumptions about how writing happened, of who could learn from whom, or of who owned or had access to knowledge, had, for the most part, vanished. No longer were teachers the sole sources of knowledge in their classrooms. Instead, they created settings in which students wrote for and learned from one another. And when they were no longer constrained by the need to write merely to please their teachers, some students, some of the time, discovered a freedom and depth of expression they had rarely known before.

The teachers, however, did not relinquish their authority. At their best, they used it creatively, to enable students to discover their own. They set up situations in which students could work alone or in pairs, in trios, in groups of four, and so on. And, out of their interaction with their classmates, the students began to experience new roles: as readers, helpmates, listeners, advisors, co-inquirers, seekers of aid for their own work, and authors whose writing could, at times, have an impact on others.

Each role was, in itself, instructive. Writers often learned that their peers could see something in what they had written that they hadn't seen themselves. Readers often learned that to respond usefully they had to respond genuinely, to probe their own personal reactions. Together readers and writers taught one another what it meant to serve another's writing, to aid in another's growth. Each interaction—reading, responding, talking, collaborating, advising, revising— enriched what readers and writers brought to the next interaction and the next; as the year wore on, readers and writers accumulated complex sets of skills and experiences to draw on again and again as they continued to read and to write together.

In these classroom communities, then, we read an underlying message in the flexible structure and altered use of authority: the teachers were teaching their students to value and rely on their own capacities to create, to express themselves, to exercise their own authority as they became increasingly independent readers and writers.

Teaching Communities

Looking back, we see that the writing communities in these classrooms did not come about by accident. The shift in authority structure and the proliferation of roles in the classroom had been implicit in our work with the teachers since 1979, from the time of the first summer institute. What we came to see, however, by studying their classrooms closely, was that the teachers did not merely apply a model that was shown to them in summer institutes. We saw, rather, that teachers were successful in creating communities in which students engaged in an honest struggle to find their own voices when the teachers, too, were struggling to find theirs.

The Act of Reflection • The six teachers we studied taught writing most effectively, we thought, when they brought an attitude of openness to their work, an attitude that enabled them to see, by stepping back regularly to reflect, both the impact and the limitation of what they were doing. Reflection, as they practiced it, then, entailed a willingness to look openly and repeatedly at what they were doing with the knowledge that they had always more to learn. Reflection, as they practiced it, seemed to lie at the heart of their teaching.

We became aware of the importance of reflection as we read through teaching journals. Although the journal was originally a requirement for the study group, for most of the teachers it became more than a way to help us collect data. At the beginning of the study, Diane wrote, "I want this journal to be for me—I can't do it if it's just an assignment for a course." Diane was stating what most of the other teachers felt as well: to make their journals worth keeping, they would have to find ways to make them fit their own needs as teachers. The journals would need to be part of an authentic inquiry.

As Diane and the other teachers discovered meaningful ways to use their journals, they found themselves raising doubts, questioning themselves, speculating about students or about what they themselves were doing in class. As they wrote at home at night or at school early in the morning, on school trips, or in hotel rooms at conferences, they found themselves standing back and examining their teaching as it unfolded.

Sometimes the teachers saw, as if for the first time, the learning taking place right before their eyes. "Writing about my teaching has already changed me," wrote Audre, early in the first year of the study. "I'm listening harder, hearing more, and therefore finding delight more often and sometimes in the smallest comment which at another time would have gone unnoticed."

At other times, the teachers found themselves perplexed. Diane, like others, often recorded doubts and questions:

> I sometimes wonder if I confuse kids by accepting a great deal about them and their writing. Do they think I don't care? Do they understand that I trust them to be doing the best job they can and if they aren't, it is in some way a violation of mutual trust? ... I wonder what they expect from me in terms of response to a piece. Can they put my comments (oral or written) in perspective? Do they think whatever I say should carry more weight? How anxious are they to please me rather than themselves?

Ross raised a question which proved to be a recurring theme for him all year:

> Is it me, Ross Burkhardt as a person, to whom or for whom they are writing, or is it the process approach itself that is clear to them and that provides them with an audience and a sense of power?

As we observed the teachers at work, we asked ourselves what the habit of reflection contributed to teaching. In the journals we thought we could see the connection: teachers who inquired into the nature of their teaching taught writing in the same spirit of inquiry. Realizing that there was always more to see than they had originally suspected, these teachers demonstrated with their teaching what they also believed to be true about writing: that there was always more to learn, that teaching, like writing, was subject to revision. In fact, we realized that insight in teaching and writing often sprang from the same source: the questioning that required one to pause, to look closely, to think for oneself, to engage what was yet unknown.

Collaboration: Reflection in Concert with Others • Initially, reflection for these teachers occurred as a solitary quest. But as the year wore on and the teachers became accustomed to bringing their teaching journals to the study group and reading from them to one another, their solitary acts of inquiry were shared.

Soon one teacher's questions sparked another's. Something Len said or wrote made Bill reconsider what he was doing; Bill's comment affected how Diane or Audre saw something; what they said in response had an impact on the whole group—week after week, for years. Our original question, "How do teachers use the writing process approach to teach writing?" broke open, flew apart, fell in pieces around us. What is the writing process approach anyway? we were soon asking. What does it mean when we say we want our kids to write? What is teaching? Or writing for that matter?

Through writing and talking about such questions, we entered into a dialogue, one that cut across traditional school boundaries. Elementary school teachers pursued questions with secondary school teachers; we, as university researchers, looked for answers in the schools. Together we became a community of inquirers: teachers and researchers writing and thinking together, trying to understand, to formulate knowledge we all felt was worth knowing, to shed light on the act of teaching.

We worked well together. The seeds of our collaboration had been sown in the summer institutes; they grew to maturity in the study group. Over the years, we had come to hold similar values and to act in similar ways. The teachers in each of their classrooms and all of us together in the study group acted on the premise that everyone's contribution mattered, everyone's questions and reflections would be granted their own authority, everyone's differences enriched what we brought to the class, our different perspectives augmented what we each drew upon once we left.

Our constant questioning and continuing weekly dialogues were refreshing. Initially tired after a day's work of teaching or of taking fieldnotes, we often left study group awake. Those few hours together were a constant reminder that each individual's search for meaning—at whatever level, for whatever purpose— was enriched and strengthened when it was shared with and appreciated by the community whose existence fostered it in the first place.

The Act of Writing

The six teachers we studied all established writing communities in their classrooms. All encouraged students to engage in acts of inquiry and reflection. All guided their students through acts of meaning-making that entitled the students to think of themselves as writers. Because of this, at first, the classrooms looked alike to us. But, on closer examination, we saw that similar activities and similar events had different meanings for different teachers. Slowly, as we unraveled their stories, we caught nuances, shadings, hues.

In examining the act of writing, for example, we saw that all the teachers, except Reba, often wrote in class. Was "teacher as writer," then, the most basic feature of all of these classrooms? Certainly, we had expected to see something of the sort. That teachers ought to write along with their students was one of the unspoken messages of the summer institute. But when we examined the teachers' behavior closely, in context, we saw that the mere fact of writing in class was not in itself as illuminating as how each teacher used writing to express his or her own temperament, tone, and personal concerns.

Ross, for example, had often won applause for writing and then performing poems that celebrated events in his life and the lives of those around him. After the summer institute, Ross not only wrote but also recited and performed his poems in class, bringing this aspect of his nonteaching life into the classroom, using it to teach and, he hoped, to inspire his students. Audre, on the other hand, was self-conscious when she read her writing in public and had rarely discussed her writing process with anyone. But, having come in the summer institute to accept the messiness and even what she called the "madness" of her writing process, she began to reveal to her students this previously hidden aspect of her writing life—encouraging, she hoped, those who were embarrassed by the messy sides of their writing processes to accept them more readily.

When Bill wrote with his students, we saw that he often used discussion of the writing process as a base for inquiry into thinking patterns and problem-solving strategies. When Len wrote with his students, he was more likely to see and discuss the writing process in psychological terms, frequently taking note of barriers to writing and looking for ways to break through them.

Diane used writing, in class and out, as a means to know her students. Writing back and forth in process journals, in letters and notes, she and her students developed the relationships that underpin her approach to learning and sustain her as a teacher. And Reba, as we know, rarely wrote but, daring to overcome her reluctance, found her own unique way to impart to her students the confidence she herself had never learned in school.

These differences were, at first, unsettling for us. It seemed that no matter where we looked or which aspect of teaching we tried to get hold of, nothing would fit together smoothly. Most of the teachers wrote, but at different times, in different ways, for different purposes. All were, in one way or another, writers in their own classrooms, but the writing they did seemed always to be colored by who they were outside the classroom—by what mattered to them as people.

We thought for a time that a teacher's uniqueness might be our ultimate finding, a conclusion that made sense to us, given that writing—and teaching as we were coming to understand it—were such personal acts. Yet, left to stand on its own, such a conclusion seemed inadequate, even incomplete. It implied that the teaching of writing could occur in any old fashion, according to one teacher's whim on one day, another's fancy the next. We suspected, though, that an even more fundamental understanding guided the teachers as they worked.

The more closely we examined their teaching, in fact, the more we became convinced that however different they were in temperament, tone, and personal inclination, the teachers all shared a common goal: that the students, like their teachers, pursue or discover expressions of their own genuine voices and that, like their teachers, they construct from their reading and writing a deeper knowledge of the world. Beneath their differences, we realized, lay a common view of what the act of writing makes possible.

Writing, in the hands of these teachers, became not a search for right answers but rather a search for genuine expression—the quest to say something in one's own voice, in a voice that rings true to the writer as well as to the reader. Rather than ask students to recapitulate what someone else had said or thought, the teachers invited their students to say and think what they had never said or thought before. And as students in these classrooms gained courage in picking up their pens, their writing began to reflect the underlying commitments of their teachers—commitments to voice, honest insights, fresh perceptions, all grounded in the students' own developing senses of themselves.

Such writing, we saw, is not merely a function of certain kinds of assignments. It is fostered and nurtured and actively promoted by teachers who create settings that allow it to flourish. The question, then, is how teachers create such settings.

Teaching as Enabling

The six teachers we studied all entered their classrooms steeped in the conviction that the students they encountered there were already writers. As a result, they saw their jobs not as instructing nonwriters in the methods and procedures of writers but rather as enabling developing writers to become more fully the writers they already were. Seeing students as writers gave them a different view of what it meant to teach. In fact, the teachers often thought they needed "not to teach." At times, they felt that what was most needed was for them to stand aside and let their students find their own way.

In study-group discussions, we began to think that this kind of nonteaching, this need to "get out of the way," was crucial for the kind of teaching we called "enabling." Yet such teaching was difficult to define—and even more difficult to enact—for each teacher had to find his or her own balance between imposing judgment and allowing for students' spontaneity, between controlling students' actions and offering free rein. The teachers all wrestled with this dilemma as they examined what it meant to use their expertise in the service of their students' growth.

Bill, for instance, wrote eloquently of the pain he often felt as a teacher who tried to "get out of the way":

> Can I convey the overwhelming difficulty of giving up control, of having patience, of "knowing" in my heart of hearts that probably the less I do, the more and better kids will write? Getting out of the way is a hard thing for an activist teacher. It's the feeling of not being needed or wanted. It's the pain of setting up a circumstance that makes me superfluous in so many ways.

Diane questioned the phrase we had been using:

> I don't know about "getting out of the way." Yes, get out of the way in terms of thwarting or limiting kids, don't be the reason they can't grow, but I don't want to be *out* of the way. I want to be with them on the way. I like the image of partnership better than the image of the teacher collecting dust in the corner while the students merrily do their thing.

And Audre defined "getting out of the way" as having the students go on ahead of her and then, if they chose, to invite her to join them. She put it this way: "It's your party. I'll try to provide something nourishing—the place and the fixin's—but you get the party together, then call me up."

Ross, a natural performer, probably wrestled the longest and hardest with the notion of "getting out of the way." The first year of the study was difficult for him. The give-and-take he was accustomed to with his students never materialized, and the failure of several important projects led him to ask whether he was, after all, an enabler. He, and we with him, wondered whether his role as performer was too overpowering. In taking center stage, was he leaving too little room for students to grow? Was he, in other words, too much *in* the way?

In 1982–83, a year the study continued but not in his classroom, Ross experimented. He tried to "get out of the way." He deliberately read his work last—or not at all. He deliberately let his students choose the theme for the next multimedia show rather than supply it himself. Yet as the year went on and Ross talked about his teaching at our study group, we saw that trying *not* to perform forced Ross to work against his own grain. Trying to stay in the background, he cut himself off from one of his strengths and felt, understandably, not quite comfortable in his classroom.

Ross's struggle brought several questions to light: Was performing at odds with enabling? Are teachers who perform too focused on themselves to be of help to students? Was the writing process approach better suited to teachers who had less difficulty "getting out of the way"? We decided it wasn't so simple. All the teachers in the study knew that they, too, at times, took center stage; they, too, performed and controlled students' attention and students' actions. Audre and Len, for example, were often the first in class to read their writing, especially when students seemed hesitant or shy. Diane spoke of herself as a "benevolent dictator": controlling, orchestrating, in charge of what was going on even when it looked as though she wasn't. Bill, Reba—each imposed limits and set deadlines.

Performing or not, "getting out of the way" or not—again, we could not reduce the art of teaching to a formula. And we saw, once again, that whatever aspect of teaching we chose to examine, there was no one way to do it. We could not describe a set of classroom techniques which would work for everyone or even predict which ones would *not* work for anyone.

We saw that, for Ross, performing was a way of expressing confidence in himself and his students, of reaching out to the eighth graders in front of him. In 1981–82, when his year turned sour and hostility pervaded his room, Ross turned inward. His performances became fewer and those he did became increasingly self-involved and hollow. In subsequent years, however, when he used himself and his poems to reach out, once again, to his students, his teaching and his performances were, once again, enabling.

Ross, in fact, discovered that enabling did not exclude performing but that he could, at times, share the stage more readily with his students. Visiting his class briefly during the third year of the study, we noticed a small but visible sign of the change. Two years before, we had become accustomed to seeing Ross's many drafts of a piece displayed on a wall in his classroom, showing the revisions he made as he moved from draft to draft. This day, as we entered his classroom, we saw displayed on the wall several drafts of a student's piece of writing. Above the display was the sign "Writer of the Week." Ross's reply, when we asked him about it, was "Oh, this is just a way I thought of to let kids see I'm not the only one who revises a poem six times." Ross was working, we realized, to show students that their writing—not only his—was central to the class.

We focus here on Ross because his teaching forced us to consider some particularly difficult—and initially disturbing—questions. Through his example, we came face to face with the unsettling idea that it is not what a teacher does every day—reading first or last, organizing assignments or encouraging students to organize them—that makes the greatest difference in class. What is most important, we realized, seems to lie beyond content or method.

Yes, we thought, the writing process approach the teachers had learned was useful. Implicit in this approach are notions that, in our view, would help any teacher support students' growth as writers: begin with real writing, not with skills or exercises; work from strength; listen for and help students discover their emerging meanings; respect individual differences; establish an atmosphere of trust; risk making mistakes oneself by being a writer and learner in the classroom, too. But, we saw, the specific techniques, the approach, even the powerful notions we advocated, were not in themselves sufficient.

The Art of Teaching

More and more, as the study progressed, we found ourselves looking beneath or beyond the methods teachers used to the ways they saw themselves, their classrooms, and their students—in short, to the realm of seeing. We became interested in the ways teachers construe and communicate their views of their students' competence to their students. And we began to think that how teachers interpret what they see in front of them determines how they act and how they teach.

If, for example, teachers see in their students competent, capable human beings, they seem to act in ways that naturally enable their students to explore, to grow, to stretch themselves beyond their own limitations. If they do not, if, as a result of classroom problems or their own assumptions, students appear to them as incompetent or incapable, no technique or approach they use appears to be particularly effective. For teachers, in subtle and often unintended ways, communicate their unspoken views to their students. And when they view their students as capable and competent, when respect for each learner is fundamental to their way of seeing, they naturally create with their students powerful contexts for learning—contexts in which the techniques they have learned can be of real benefit.

In our view, what effective writing teachers do, first and foremost and then over and over again, is to offer invitations to their students to become writers. There is no specific technique or form of knowledge required to accomplish this feat. What seems essential, rather, is that teachers embody the belief that students, in their eyes, are already writers. Once students are willing to see themselves as enabling teachers see them, they can, with help from these teachers, fashion for themselves new skills, new roles, and new identities: as members of a community of inquirers, as thinkers who shape and reshape what they know, and as writers who discover how to communicate, often movingly and effectively, their own views of the subjects they are studying, the concepts they are learning, the many worlds they are inhabiting.

If teaching writing, then, ultimately derives from how we see our students and how they come to see themselves, we suggest that no matter how well we impart content or transmit information, no matter how many effective techniques we know, we must also discover within ourselves ways to convey to our students our belief in their capacity to write and to learn. And we can only impart such a view when we enter our classrooms knowing and acting as if every student there is and always will be, with or without our help, a learner, a person able to make and discover meaning out of his or her existence—a person, in other words, who is and always will be, with or without our help, a writer.

Teachers who act in ways that are consistent with this view experience with their students the excitement that accompanies the possibility of creation. Together as readers and writers, together as learners, they weave stories, read writing, make meaning. Individually and in concert, they enact the age-old calling to express what most matters. Learning from one another, they turn their classrooms into what many educators have, for centuries, hoped classooms could be: communities where each individual contributes to the act of bringing forth, of creating, not only writing but also the culture of the classroom itself. Such communities are a joy for researchers to study in, for students to learn in, for teachers to teach in. Such communities, in our eyes, are created through teachers' eyes.

Epilogue

In 1982, 1983, and 1984, as we sat in our office at Lehman College, poring over teachers' journals and students' drafts, sifting through our piles of data to look again and again, from different angles, at the same set of events, we sometimes felt we were living in a time warp. In New York, we were reading and writing about the past; in Shoreham-Wading River, the present was unfolding.

As we wrote, first graders became second graders, then third, then fourth graders; eighth graders moved to high school; high school students graduated and went to college. And teachers, too, moved on.

In the second year of the study, Audre introduced reading logs at the beginning instead of toward the end of eleventh grade. Diane renamed process journals "writing diaries" and found new ways of explaining them to her students. Len returned to teaching social studies and experimented with ways to help his students produce "academic" writing without losing their voices. Bill and some of his students became interested in word processors and started an investigation of the ways fourth and fifth graders use them. Reba and her students agreed to forgo conferencing for one period a week so that Reba could write in class. Ross had a good year and then a better one.

"If only you could be here *this* year," the teachers would say to us when we visited Shoreham. "It's so much better. . . " "You wouldn't believe. . . " "You'd love what I'm doing now!" And we knew they were right. We *would* have loved the new work built on work we had seen, would have loved to follow the teachers and students we knew as they broke new ground. But we couldn't stay; we had unfinished business with the past.

And so we returned to our office to write about teachers and students—who are changing even as we write. As our pages pile up, they are filling new ones. As we end our story, theirs continues.

Appendixes

Appendix A

Guidelines for Composing

Introduction

Traditionally, teachers help students with their writing after they produce first drafts. Sometimes we offer our students help before they begin writing by working with them on strategies for planning and organization. Only recently have we known how to help our students *while* they are in the process of writing.

The guidelines for composing are designed to guide writers through the composing process, from finding a topic worth writing about to discovering what to say about it. They consist of a series of questions that ask writers to look back in order to move forward, to question themselves, to search for the right word—to do what many skilled writers do naturally.

The guidelines also direct writers to look for a "felt sense." This term, coined by Eugene Gendlin, refers to the physical sensation that often accompanies barely formed impressions. To Gendlin, a felt sense is always rather murky and puzzling. But as we name this felt sense, as we put words to it, what was formerly inchoate and diffuse comes into focus. At this moment, we experience a "felt shift," the sense of relief that accompanies new understanding.

To explain felt sense, Gendlin gives the example of knowing you have forgotten something but not knowing what it is. For example, you are on your way to work, but something keeps nagging at you. What is it? you ask. What did you forget? Notice that you don't know what it is, but you have a physical felt sense. You feel your pockets. Is it your keys? No. You search your mind. The papers you meant to copy? You've forgotten the papers, but that's not it. The idea doesn't satisfy the physical sensation. You still have that wordless discomfort. All of a sudden, it comes to the surface: the book you promised to return. That's it. It's still sitting on your desk. You feel a sudden physical relief, an easing inside. You have just experienced what Gendlin calls a "shift" in your felt sense.

A similar process operates when writers write. If we pay close attention, we can notice that the meanings we construct while writing often come to us first in the vague, puzzling way Gendlin describes. We have a sense of what we want to say, but we're not quite sure how to say it. As we write, we begin to make discoveries about our subjects and to clarify what we mean. At such times, we often say that we are "on the right track." At other times, we hit dead ends, uncomfortably aware that something is missing but not sure what it is. In these instances, it is our felt sense that often serves as our internal guide, the criterion that helps us judge whether or not our words capture our intended meaning. When they do, we can experience the shift Gendlin describes. When they do not, we need to pause, consult this complex bodily feeling once again, and continue writing.

The guidelines for composing aid writers in the act of meaning-making described above. Based on the questions, writers normally produce a set of notes, which can later be shaped into a draft.

Procedure

If you choose to use these instructions with a class, in a writing workshop, or in a one-to-one tutoring situation, it is useful to inform people ahead of time that you will be inviting them to ask themselves a series of questions and that they will have time to write after each one. Advise them that the questions are meant to be guides; they may not fit everyone's experience. Some questions may be distracting for a particular writer and should be ignored. The writer can tune in again when he or she is ready to listen. Before you begin the guidelines, ask people not to interrupt you and to hold questions. Afterward, give them time to continue writing, and then invite them to express in writing their reactions to the exercise. Remember, however, that what people write during the guidelines may be personal or private. The notes they produce are not meant to be shared in a group unless the writers themselves choose to share them.

The sentences in brackets are meant for teachers. They are not to be read aloud as part of the exercise.

1. Find a way to get comfortable. Shake out your hands, take a deep breath, settle into your chair, close your eyes if you're willing to, relax. [In this first step, you are helping people become aware of their inner states. Being able to do this will make it easier for them to locate a felt sense. As people sit quietly for several minutes, ask them

to notice if they feel any tension in their arms and necks. Ask them to pay attention to their breathing as they inhale and exhale. If there is some laughter in the room or some noise outside, ask them to notice it and then to come back quietly to themselves and their breathing. When people seem quiet and relaxed, go directly to the question in point 3. If they seem to be out of sorts, unruly, or disruptive, begin with the question in point 2. With practice, you will know which opening question will work best for a particular group.]

2. Ask yourself, "What's going on with me right now? [short pause] Is there anything in the way of my writing today?" [short pause] When you hear yourself answering, begin to make a list. [Leave time for people to write—about 1 or 2 minutes.] Now that you've noted all the distractions, I'd like you to take that piece of paper and set it aside. Perhaps, now that they are down on paper, those distractions won't intrude so much. If you'll relax and get comfortable again, I'll continue. [Go to point 4.]

3. Ask yourself, "How am I right now? [short pause] What's on my mind?" [short pause] When you hear yourself answering, begin to make a list. [Leave time for people to write—about 1 or 2 minutes.]

4. Now ask yourself, "What else is on my mind? Is there anything I'm interested in that I might write about today? Does a particular person, place, or image come to mind?" Jot these down. If you came here today with a specific topic in mind, put that on your list too. If you can't think of anything, write the word "nothing." [Again, leave a few minutes for people to write.]

5. Ask yourself, "Now that I have a list—long or short—is there anything else I've left out, any other piece I'm overlooking, maybe even a word I like, something else I might at some time want to write about that I can add to this list?" Jot down whatever comes to mind. [The purpose of points 3 to 5 is to make an inventory of possible topics for writing.]

6. Now you may have one definite idea or a whole list of things. Look over your list and ask, "Which one of these items draws my attention right now? Which one seems to stand out? Which one could I begin to write on even if I'm not certain where it will lead?" Take the idea or word or issue and put it at the top of a new page. Save your list for another time. If nothing seems to jump out at you, choose something for the sake of the exercise.

7. Now take a deep breath, relax as we did earlier, and settle comfortably into your chair. Realize that you already know a lot about your particular topic. Without delving into any one part, see if you can jot down all your associations to or thoughts on this topic. For instance, ask yourself, "What are all the parts I know about this topic? What can I say about it now?" Spend as long as you need writing down

these responses but remember not to stay on any one response too long. Perhaps you will write a list, a bunch of phrases, notes to yourself, or stream-of-consciousness writing. [This can take about 5 minutes.]

8. Now I'm going to interrupt you and ask you to set aside all the pieces you already know. I want you to take a fresh look at this topic or issue, to grab hold of the *whole* topic—not the bits and pieces—and ask yourself, "What makes this topic interesting to me? What's *important* about this that I haven't said yet? What's the *heart* of this issue?" Wait quietly and see if a word, an image, or a phrase comes to you from your felt sense of the topic. Write whatever comes. [You may need to repeat point 8 slowly.]

9. Take this word or image and explore it. Ask yourself, "What's this all about?" Describe the image or word. As you write, let your felt sense deepen. Continue to ask yourself, "Is this right? Am I getting closer? Am I saying it?" See if you can feel when you're on the right track. Notice when you write if you can experience the shift of, "Oh yeah, that says it." [Allow at least 5 to 10 minutes here for people who are writing. If someone is not writing, continue with point 10.]

10. If you're at a dead end, you can ask yourself, "What makes this topic so hard for me?" or "What's so difficult about this?" Again, pause and see if a word or image or phrase comes to you that captures this difficulty in a fresh way.

11. You can continue along now, writing what comes to you. When you stop you can ask, "What's missing? What hasn't yet gotten down on paper?" And again, look to your felt sense for a word or an image.

12. After a while, ask yourself, "Where is this leading? What's the point I'm trying to make?" Again, write down whatever comes to mind.

13. Once you feel you're near or at the end, ask yourself, "Does this feel complete?" Look to your body for the answer. Again, write down whatever answer comes to you. If the answer is no, pause and ask yourself, "What's missing?" Then continue writing.

14. Now you may have anywhere from one to several pages of notes that can form the basis of a piece of writing. Ask yourself, "What form would work best for what I'm trying to say? Is this a story? A poem? An essay? Something else? Who's talking? Whose point of view is this? Is there another point of view I can use?" Make some notes about the shape your piece will take.

15. When you feel you have a shape for your piece, begin writing it. [If some time remains in the session, encourage people to continue writing. If there is no time left for writing, proceed to point 16.]

16. Now, for the next _____ minutes, review your notes from the beginning of the exercise and write about what happened. What was this

experience like for you? This last piece of writing will be shared with the group.

During the discussion that follows, people may reveal that they have had strong responses to the guidelines. It is important to allow people time to express their reactions. The guidelines may work differently for each person each time you do them.

Sources

Gendlin, Eugene. *Focusing.* New York: Bantam Books, 1981.

Perl, Sondra. "Understanding Composing." *College Composition and Communication,* Vol. 31, No. 4, December 1980.

Appendix B

Responding in a Writing Group

Tips for Writers

1. Read your piece, twice if necessary, and allow at least 30 seconds of silence after each reading for impressions to become clearer in the minds of your responders.
2. Don't rush your reading of the piece.
3. Don't quarrel with your group's reactions. Maybe what you see is truly there, and they're blind. But maybe what they see is there too—even if it contradicts what you see. Just listen and take it all in as though it were all true. Don't be tyrannized by what they say. It is your job to decide what to do next. The cardinal rule is: listen; don't defend!

Tips for Responders

1. Use active listening. Tell what you think the writer is trying to communicate by restating what has been written, either by paraphrasing, summarizing the gist of what has been read, or using some of the author's own words.
2. As the piece is being read, underline words or phrases that catch your attention. What about those words makes them stand out? What parts of the piece do you like best? How do those parts affect you? Be sure to respond to specific sections of the writing. A general response, such as, "I like it," or "That was good," is not very helpful.
3. Let the writer know if there is anything in the writing that seems con-

fusing, out of place, unclear. Explain why you are bothered by that particular item.
4. Ask the writer:
   (a) Where do *you* feel you had a problem?
   (b) Where do *you* feel you were successful?
   (c) How else can the group help you?

Note: Some people find it easier to respond than others. The group can easily develop a dynamic in which the same people respond and others remain silent. Agree ahead of time that everyone will respond *once* to the entire piece before more specific responses are developed.

Sources

Elbow, Peter. *Writing Without Teachers.* New York: Oxford University Press, 1973.

Perl, Sondra. "Developing a Vocabulary of Response." NYC Writing Project, 1979.